I0473458

Cumulative Effect

For years, cyber security was the 'poor relation' in many boardrooms: treated as inferior to other priorities, seen as an irritating cost centre and assumed to be money that could be spent 'better' elsewhere. That mindset is rarely the result of a single bad decision. It is inertia, the cumulative effect of multiple factors and, above all, a lack of understanding of how dramatically the landscape has changed over the past 25 years.

This book is written as a practical wake-up call for Board Members and CEOs. It reframes cyber security as a leadership issue rooted in the inherent insecurities of the internet on which modern organisations are built, encouraging leaders to think as if they operate in a high-crime area. It then shows how to translate that mindset into board-level oversight: strengthening domain and subdomain controls and certificate management, expanding organisational KPIs to include correctly chosen cyber measures (such as year-on-year reduction in IT ecosystem complexity) and making explicit decisions about unmanaged devices such as BYOD and home computers.

The book also introduces a 'cyber security risk-reward' lens for business cases, reshaping how leaders assess digital transformation, agile delivery, SaaS sprawl and shadow IT. It clarifies shared security responsibility and how to implement and manage it properly, then broadens the conversation to supply chain cyber risks and dependencies across all vendors and service providers, not just IT. It highlights the strategic importance of DNS ownership and management, examines the cyber implications of reliance on 'digital monopolies' such as Microsoft or CrowdStrike and makes clear that compliance does not equal security: standards and frameworks may help, but they do not guarantee real security. Finally, it tackles modern boardroom pressure points, including avoiding FOMO-driven decisions, assessing AI adoption through a cyber risk lens and planning for post-quantum cryptography.

Dr Vladas Leonas is a subject matter expert and specialises in ICT Strategies, their implementation and ICT Operations, gateway reviews and internal audits, enterprise risk management, cyber security, governance, procurement, and compliance. Over the last 25 years, he has held eight CIO and CTO positions.

Security, Audit and Leadership Series

Series Editor: Dan Swanson, Dan Swanson and Associates, Ltd., Winnipeg, Manitoba, Canada.

The scope and mandate for internal audit continues to evolve each year, as does the complexity of the business environment and speed of the changing risk landscape in which it must operate. The fundamental goal of this exciting series is to produce leading-edge books on critical subjects facing security and audit executives and practitioners. Key topics addressed include Leadership, Cybersecurity, Security Leadership, Privacy, Strategic Risk Management, Auditing IT, Audit Management and Leadership, and Operational Auditing.

Cumulative Effect
Cyber Security Guide for Directors and CEOs

Dr Vladas Leonas

CRC Press
Taylor & Francis Group
Boca Raton London New York

CRC Press is an imprint of the
Taylor & Francis Group, an **informa** business

Designed cover image: Shutterstock ID: 77894635

First edition published 2026
by CRC Press
2385 NW Executive Center Drive, Suite 320, Boca Raton FL 33431

and by CRC Press
4 Park Square, Milton Park, Abingdon, Oxon, OX14 4RN

CRC Press is an imprint of Taylor & Francis Group, LLC

© 2026 Dr Vladas Leonas

ISBN: 978-1-041-22073-2 (hbk)
ISBN: 978-1-041-22074-9 (pbk)
ISBN: 978-1-003-73051-4 (ebk)

DOI: 10.1201/9781003730514

Typeset in Sabon
by SPi Technologies India Pvt Ltd (Straive)

To my family

Contents

Foreword

It is hard to imagine today's world without the Internet. People get news from the Internet, and do banking using the Internet, businesses interact with each other using the Internet, and the list goes on and on.

The Internet was born a revolution, but built with blind spots. Like the Enigma breakthroughs that ended wars, its promise was historic. Yet, unlike Bletchley Park's relentless focus on security, the Internet grew with function prioritised over protection. This is a foundational flaw that persists more than 40 years later.

The core of the web, including websites, Domain Name System (DNS), Internet Protocols (IPs), and Content Delivery Networks (CDNs), is the digital equivalent of a city without locks. Teenagers, like the Scattered Spider group, exploit obvious, preventable vulnerabilities. No nation-state sophistication is required, just unnecessary gaps and lazy oversight.

Despite the billions spent on public relations, cyber insurance, and expert consultants, many organisations fail to address the basics of cybersecurity. The term "social engineering" has become a convenient excuse for security lapses, deflecting from the real issue: incompetence. Until digital infrastructure is treated with the same respect as physical security, breaches will continue unabated.

This book, among other very relevant topics, delves into the critical yet often overlooked role of DNS in cybersecurity. It highlights the institutional failures of organisations like the Internet Engineering Task Force (IETF), the Internet Corporation for Assigned Names and Numbers (ICANN), and the SANS Institute, which have all fallen short in protecting users and infrastructures from systemic risks.

Consider a typical organisation, a mid-sized enterprise headquartered in Australia with offices across multiple countries and a staff of thousands. In pursuit of efficiency and cost savings, the company has adopted a fully cloud-based infrastructure. They utilise well-known operating systems, cloud services, and productivity tools supplied by the usual tech behemoths.

Despite having a seasoned Chief Information Security Officer (CISO) and a substantial security budget, our typical company's reliance on cloud-based infrastructure and third-party providers exposes it to significant risks. The company's lack of DNS-specific expertise and oversight is symptomatic of a broader industry trend. This is not a rare oversight; it is the norm.

Big tech providers, too, bear immense responsibility. Their products are often shipped with default configurations that prioritise convenience and performance over security. Telemetry, pre-installed monitoring agents, and auto-updating cloud features introduce unseen vulnerabilities.

Our typical company's reliance on its providers' reputation rather than actual vetting is symptomatic of a larger problem. In no other industry would this be acceptable. Imagine a food manufacturer outsourcing ingredients without quality checks or an airline using engines from a vendor without inspection. Yet in tech, the shiny brands and polished marketing obfuscate real risks.

The narrative underscores the urgent need for visibility into multiple activities (including DNS), regular audits, and comprehensive training for security personnel. It calls for a paradigm shift in how security certifications, government policies, and technology providers address cyber security.

W. Edwards Deming once transformed the world by resetting the quality of engineering. He showed that excellence is not an afterthought but must be built into the system itself. Today, we face a crisis of equal scale in cyber security.

Entire nations and industries are left exposed by elementary failures: insecure domains, subdomains, DNS records, servers, and broken PKI. These are not sophisticated exploits – they are open doors, left unguarded through negligence, ignorance, or complacency. The result: $32 billion lost every single day.

We cannot patch our way out of this. We cannot audit our way to safety. Like Deming's revolution in quality, we need a total reset - where security is systemic, continuous, and non-negotiable.

This is the call: abandon hollow platitudes. Accept accountability. Design security into every process, every system, every decision. Anything less is national self-sabotage.

The race to the bottom will only accelerate if our institutional leaders, corporate executives, and security professionals continue to delegate their understanding of foundational technologies and the **cumulative effect** that is a result of these technologies not being fully understood. Examples of the incidents in the book are a good illustration of how the **cumulative effect** works, as all of them are a result of the **cumulative effect**.

Ignorance is no longer an excuse. It is a choice. And with that choice comes accountability. This book is a clarion call for accountability and a roadmap for evolving our approach to cyber security in an increasingly interconnected world.

Andrew J. Jenkinson, *CEO of Cybersec Innovation Partners*

SPECIAL NOTE ABOUT THE AUTHOR

Dr. Vladas Leonas stands at the intersection of academic insight and practitioner expertise. A cybersecurity expert with decades of hands-on experience, Vladas is one of the rare few who not only understand the theoretical underpinnings of the digital world but also engage daily with its operational realities. His work spans deep technical domains, national policy, and enterprise security strategy, making him one of the most relevant voices in today's fragmented and misunderstood cybersecurity landscape.

I've had the privilege of knowing Dr. Leonas for over 5 years and consider him both a friend and one of a small circle of genuine experts in this field. While we may hold differing political views on some matters - something we both regard as healthy and intellectually honest - our alignment on one foundational truth is unwavering: basic security is not optional; it is existential. In an era when personal data is commodified, privacy is undermined by design, and security tools often double as surveillance mechanisms, Vladas has remained focused on what truly matters.

Writing books like this one is not a commercial endeavour - it is a form of advocacy. It's a laborious, thankless task unless you are driven by a deep desire to share knowledge, provoke thought, and challenge institutions that have gone too long unchallenged. My heartfelt thanks go to Vladas for his dedication, resilience, and commitment to lifting the veil on the systemic failures that put us all at risk.

In an era where global interconnectivity defines every facet of modern life, the notion that the average individual, organisation, or enterprise can operate outside the reach of surveillance or exploitation is a dangerous illusion...

Andrew J. Jenkinson, *CEO of Cybersec Innovation Partners*

Preface
Why you should read this book

"Everything's got a moral, if only you can find it."

Alice's Adventures in Wonderland by Lewis Carroll

The Internet has become the lifeblood of today's society. It fuels B2B, B2C, G2C, delivery of the latest news and movies, and communication between people via social networks and messengers. Our dependence on the Internet has become critical, and Internet failure has become a potential single point of failure for a lot of organisations, both in the private sector and governments.

Over the last 20–25 years, cyber security shifted from being a back-office matter to the forefront and suddenly turned into a matter of survivability and business continuity. Think of the financial and reputational damage an organisation may suffer from a cyberattack.

According to IBM,[1] the average cost of a cyber security breach reached US$4.9 million in 2024. However, "the average temperature across the ward" may not be a very meaningful parameter to look at, so think of this number ranging from several hundred thousand dollars for a small organisation to almost one and a half billion dollars for a large organisation.

Microsoft estimates that in 2025, the world will experience 600 million cyberattacks per day,[2] and according to a 2024 Sophos study, 59% of organisations were hit by ransomware in the last 12 months. The rapidly growing number of cyberattacks results in the rapid escalation of the cost of cyber security. According to Gartner, global cybersecurity spending is projected to reach US$212 billion in 2025, with a 15% year-over-year increase. IDC states that the global cyber security spending will grow 12.2% in 2025 and cross US$377 billion by 2028, which will eclipse the GDP of Portugal, which in 2024 was US$308.7 billion. The US and Western Europe will lead, accounting for over 70% of global security spending.

In New South Wales, cyber fraud surged by 95% over a 3-year period, according to the Bureau of Crime Statistics and Research.[3]

These are mindboggling numbers!

Let me ask you, what is this money being spent on? It is mainly spent on treating the symptoms and monitoring. It is not being spent on treating root causes, which can pile up and result in a **cumulative effect**, or on the prevention of emerging threats.

Think of a patient who is being given a medicine that treats symptoms only but does not treat the root cause. Of course, this medicine alleviates the pain, but it may result in more problems in the future. If a patient continues to eat unhealthy food (read - organisation continues to increase the complexity of the organisation's IT ecosystem) and neglects exercising (read - organisation continues to utilise an agile approach), we know in advance what the consequences will be. But somehow, this logic is not being applied to the cyber security world.

It is important to understand that every dollar pumped into digital transformations increases the complexity of the organisation's IT ecosystem and thus - its cyber security exposure; that continued use of the agile approach increases the organisation's cyber security exposure; that the absence of the right metrics (e.g., a year-on-year decrease in the complexity of the organisation's IT ecosystem) results in the continuation of the "treat the symptoms" approach; that failure to understand the insecurities of DNS, as well as neglecting the proper management of domains, subdomains, and certificates, is likely to result in a cyber security incident, and so it goes on and on.

This book identifies numerous areas that need to be understood and addressed as a matter of urgency before it is too late.

Most of the readers heard the sentiment that "generals always prepare to fight the last war," which is widely attributed to Georges Clemenceau, French Prime Minister during the later years of World War 1. The idea is that military leaders tend to rely on **past** successes and **familiar** tactics rather than anticipating new threats or adopting innovative approaches.

But the world has changed, and it is unwise not to change organisations' approach to cybersecurity. Generals don't send cavalry against tanks anymore, but Boards keep doing an equivalent of this.

I remember vividly how 30 years ago, my CEO was not able to send an email or compose a simple MS Word document and used her Executive Assistant to help with this. Can you imagine today's CEO who can't handle email and MS Word?

The same is happening with cyber security. What happened to enterprises over the last 20–25 years (because of the Internet and digital revolution) mandates that every Board member and CEO have a holistic understanding of cyber security and each of the underlying aspects. The proposed book is aspiring to give them this understanding and to prompt a thinking process that, hopefully, will result in actions improving organisations' cyber security posture.

So, it is the right time not only to shift the focus on cyber security but also to start looking at it holistically, rather than seeing it simply as timely patching and malware detection. And this shift has already started.[4]

Although today, Boards and CEOs have some understanding of cyber security, it is typically fragmented and does not allow them to see the full (and big) picture. A narrow vision of only some aspects of cybersecurity does not allow them to consciously and intently drive improvements in organisations' cyber security posture.

Why is it holistically important? Cyber security is a complex and multi-faceted area that includes many aspects.

The introduction explains the **cumulative effect** using as a well-known Log4j incident as an example, explains the consequences of this incident, and dissects the root cause down to the components leading to this **cumulative effect**. The following chapters discuss these and other components that can result in **cumulative effects**. In addition to this, the book covers the topics of emerging threats (quantum computing and AI), directors' personal liability, and limitations of cyber insurance.

Some of these components and aspects are not under our control (like the insecurity of von Neumann computer architecture and the inherent insecurity of the Internet due to the inherent insecurity of Internet protocols like TCP/IP, DNS, and BGP). And it is very important to understand that we can't do anything about it, unless we want to go back to manual processes and the use of pen and paper.

Other aspects can and should be influenced by the Boards and CEOs who should consciously drive step-by-step organisations' cyber security posture improvements and make balanced decisions based on, firstly, understanding and, secondly, performing explicit "cyber security risk-reward" ratio analysis.

This book was also partially prompted by the growing number of CIOs coming from a non-IT background and thus lacking typical IT "scars and burnt fingers" that come with significant practical experience in IT, which used to be a typical feature of CIOs 20 or more years ago.

The book's title reflects the fact that the organisation's overall cyber security posture is a result of a **cumulative effect** of multiple factors discussed in it. The book starts with an example of a **cumulative effect** in cyber security on the back of the actual large cyber security incident. This example clearly shows that this incident (and, more importantly, its consequences) is a result of a **cumulative effect** of several factors that are discussed in the following chapters. As such, one of the intents of the book is to identify areas causing **cumulative effect**, highlight them for Boards and CEOs and assist them in conscious minimisation of likely **cumulative effects**.

Although this book uses some examples from my "Cyber Insecurity: Examining the Past, Defining the Future", it is a different book with a focus on the **cumulative effect**. It is structured differently. This is not a recipe book; it is more of a menu book. Each chapter is split into three sections: an appetiser with key points, a main course with key points explained, and a dessert (for those who are still hungry) with more technical and other related details.

At the end of each main course section, there are several questions for the reader. These questions position the book not only as an explanation of the problem but also as something readers can actively engage with to reflect on and improve their organisation's cyber security posture.

Readers are expected to write down their initial answers to each of the questions after they have finished the chapter and then, again, after they have finished reading the book to answer these questions again. Then, readers are expected to review these questions and their initial and later answers. This will most likely give the readers a different perspective on the state of cybersecurity of the organisation and will give them guidance about what they, in their role, can do to improve the organisation's cyber security posture.

This structure enables Board members and CEOs to get a holistic understanding of multiple facets of cyber security and focus on the organisation's cyber security improvements that can decrease the probability and hopefully impact of **cumulative effects**.

The sequence of the chapters is deliberate, as, for example, it is more logical to discuss the agile approach (Chapter 5) after a discussion about the digital revolution (Chapter 4) that caused its massive proliferation and to discuss insecurities of Internet foundational protocols like TCP/IP, DNS, and BGP (Chapter 9) after a discussion about the heavy dependency of organisations on the Internet – as a result of the digital revolution (Chapter 4), the proliferation of Cloud services (Chapter 6), SaaS (Chapter 7), and supply chain dependencies (Chapter 8).

NOTES

1 https://www.ibm.com/reports/data-breach.
2 https://explodingtopics.com/blog/cybersecurity-stats.
3 https://publicsectornetwork.com/insight/whats-shaping-investigations-and-integrity-in-government-australia-2025?psncampaign=anznewsletteraug25&utm_campaign=ANZ%20Primary%20-%20Monthly%20Newsletters&utm_medium=email&_hsenc=p2ANqtz-_mowqr1Z8uFG2040CIkAGzRCCc2YXUEiTr2f4Hy6NA3FDe8_KctPv6SifaUsWSCnLd7MepYu6JjY9VhnFPL-ILMMOnFXn9_UZuH8xXQvpNXcunbSkAl7QR4x-8whViygse9kiy&_hsmi=377552409&utm_content=377552409&utm_source=hs_automation.
4 https://www.mckinsey.com/capabilities/risk-and-resilience/our-insights/competitive-advantage-through-cybersecurity-a-board-level-perspective.

About the author

Dr Vladas Leonas entered ICT during the mainframe and punched card era and witnessed first-hand the emergence and proliferation of mini-, micro-, and personal computers and networks. Throughout his career, he has worked in multiple public and private sector industries and tertiary education organisations.

He is a Fellow of ACS, a Fellow of IEAust and a formally trained auditor (ISO/IEC 27001). He is also an Adjunct Professor at the Australian Graduate School of Leadership.

Dr Vladas Leonas is a subject matter expert and specialises in ICT Strategies, their implementation and ICT Operations, gateway reviews and internal audits, enterprise risk management, cyber security, governance, procurement, and compliance. Over the last 25 years, he has held eight CIO and CTO positions.

Acknowledgments

I am grateful for the encouragement, support, comments, and invaluable suggestions provided by Professor Mike Gruntman, Jim Hegarty, Andrew J. Jenkinson, Kim Loane, Matthias Muhlert, Rachel V. Rose, Adam Summons, Dan Swanson, Sorin Toma, and my wife Karina.

Introduction
Personal liability and cyber insurance

"Off with her head!"

Alice's Adventures in Wonderland by Lewis Carroll

APPETISER

- In Australia, directors and officers of companies have fiduciary duties, which include duties of care, skill, and diligence under the Corporations Act 2001. These duties extend to managing and mitigating risks, including those related to cyber security.
- Personal liability for cyber security lapses is a significant risk, underscoring the importance of diligent oversight and proactive measures.
- As cyber threats continue to evolve, the personal responsibility of directors and officers in managing cyber security has never been more critical.
- Dilemma: the cost of adequate cyber security may result in uneconomic or unaffordable technology products.
- The history of cyber security and the law reflects a continuous struggle to keep pace with technological advancements and the evolving nature of cyber threats.
- The implication is that the law is always in a catch-up mode.
- This makes legislation less useful and less effective in the fight against cyber security threats or attacks. Cyber security legislation is almost always reactive due to several inherent challenges and dynamics of the digital realm.
- The complexity and unpredictability of cyber threats, as threat actors tend to innovate much faster.
- The legislative process involves multiple stages of review, debate, and amendment, which is usually time-consuming.

DOI: 10.1201/9781003730514-1

- Lawmakers often need to balance competing interests, such as privacy rights, business interests, and national security concerns.
- Cyber security is a global issue, and cyber incidents can cross national boundaries, making it challenging for individual countries to address issues unilaterally.
- The Internet transformed crime in the form of cybercrime into a global business.
- Legislation can assist in addressing cyber security issues, albeit slowly, but unfortunately, legislation often lacks the foresight needed to pre-emptively tackle emerging threats. As cyber security continues to evolve very fast, the law will continue to struggle to keep up.
- For many organisations, cyber insurance has become an essential part of their risk management strategy.
- Cyber insurance is often seen either as a *"silver bullet"* or as an *"out of jail ticket."*
- While cyber insurance provides some financial relief, *it does not magically evaporate the consequences of a security breach*.
- The biggest negative of cyber insurance is that it creates a false sense of security.
- Every cyber insurance provider will likely conduct a risk assessment to determine if the organisation qualifies for cyber insurance. An organisation may fail to meet the cyber insurance provider's requirements.

MAIN COURSE

Looking 15 years back, CEOs never used to get fired for cyber security breaches. It was invariably the CIO or other technology executive who took the fall for a technology or process mishap so serious that it actually damaged the organisation and its reputation. Today, however, the blame goes increasingly straight to the top, considering the massive financial, reputational, and legal damage organisations experience today.[1]

These are just some of the examples:

- May 2014, Target Chairman and CEO Greg Steinhafel (Target breached in November-December 2013)
- February 2015, Co-Chairman of Sony Pictures Amy Pascal (Sony Pictures was breached in December 2014)
- September 2017, Equifax CEO Richard Smith (Equifax was breached in May-July 2017)
- March 2019, the CEO of LandMark White, Chris Coonan (LandMark White was breached in February 2019)

- November 2023, Optus CEO Kelly Bayer Rosmarin (Optus was breached in September 2022).

In the era where cyber threats are as prevalent as ever, the responsibilities of directors and officers in managing cyber security are coming under increased scrutiny. Increasingly, Boards, regulators, and investors are turning up the heat; corporate leaders, not just CISOs, are facing financial and legal consequences for data breaches.

In early September 2025, the Board of Qantas Airways voted to penalise CEO Vanessa Hudson and other top executives for a June 30 cyber incident that exposed the personally identifiable information of nearly 6 million passengers, deducting A$800,000 (US$522,000) from their bonuses.[2] If the Quantas Board ruling foretells a new era of holding CEOs financially accountable for cyber security, it will represent a welcome shift for CISOs, experts say.

The last time it became publicly known that a Board withheld compensation from a CEO for a cyber security breach was in 2017, when Yahoo's Board denied CEO Marissa Mayer her $2 million bonus over the mishandling of multiple breaches that exposed the personal information of more than 1 billion users.

In Australia, **personal liability for directors and officers concerning cyber security is a growing area of concern**, as the legal arena evolves to address the complexities of cyber threats and data breaches.

As reported in the 2025 NACD Public Company Survey,[3] in a time of rapid technological advancement, significant regulatory shifts, and mounting stakeholder expectations, there are a few trends that reveal notable realignment in Board priorities and areas requiring attention:

- There's a **significant discrepancy between Board recognition of cyber-security risk and action**, for example, **gaps remain** in reporting, **metrics**, and access to expertise.
- **CEOs are under the microscope, with their performance subject to increased scrutiny.**
- **Supply chain governance has spiked as a Board priority.**
- **Cyber risk, AI disruption, and economic volatility have converged, demanding a new level of Board foresight and fluency.**

In Australia, directors and officers of companies have fiduciary duties, which include duties of care, skill, and diligence under the Corporations Act 2001. These duties extend to managing and mitigating risks, including those related to cyber security.

As cyber threats continue to evolve, the **personal responsibility of directors and officers in managing cyber security has never been more critical**. In Australia, personal liability for cyber security lapses is a significant risk, underscoring the importance of diligent oversight and proactive measures.

By understanding their legal obligations and taking appropriate actions to safeguard their organisations, directors, and officers can better protect themselves and their companies from the ever-present risks of the digital age.

The Australian Securities and Investments Commission (ASIC) has warned that directors who ignore cybersecurity obligations could face:

- **Fines** - Small business penalties start at $19,000; large corporations can be fined over $50 million for non-compliance.
- **Legal Action** - Directors can be personally sued for failing to prevent cybersecurity breaches; shareholders and customers can take legal action if inadequate security measures result in data breaches.
- **Regulatory Investigations** - ASIC has increased scrutiny on businesses that fail to implement proper cybersecurity governance.

According to Australian Prudential Regulation Authority (APRA) Executive Board Member Geoff Summerhayes: "In light of evidence that **Boards frequently don't understand, or are not adequately informed about cyber risks,** we're no longer prepared to simply take their words for it – we want compliance independently verified… If Boards are unwilling or unable to make the required changes in a timely manner, we will consider using formal enforcement action."

Some large legal firms published guides for Boards and senior management, for example:

- Allens (jointly with the UK firm Linklaters),[4] among other recommendations, highlighted the **importance of defining the organisations' risk appetite** (see Chapter 2) and the **importance of having cyber security expertise on the Board.**
- MinterEllisonRuddWatts,[5] among other recommendations, stressed the importance of long-term cyber risk management.

It appears that Boards do not understand cyber security and relevant contract clauses.[6] So, the simple question is: "How can Boards manage an organisation's cyber security posture without understanding it?"

Proofpoint found that 30% of companies that were successfully attacked experienced a direct monetary loss. That's an increase of 76% year over year. Concerns about costs and risks mean that more companies than ever are buying cyber insurance. A World Economic Forum survey found that **71% of organisations have cyber insurance.** And Allied Market Research projects that the global cyber insurance market, which is currently valued at $12.5 billion, will reach $116.7 billion by 2032.

At a time when digital technology permeates every aspect of our lives, the intersection of cyber security and law has become increasingly important. The evolution of cyber security and its legal framework reflects the broader changes in technology, society, and global politics. In the early days of computing, the primary focus was on developing and harnessing the potential of new technologies. The concept of cyber security as we understand it today was virtually non-existent.

The 1970s marked the advent of networked computing with the development of ARPANET, the precursor to the modern Internet. This period saw the emergence of basic security concerns as researchers and early users of ARPANET began to recognise the risks associated with networked systems. The first known computer virus, the Creeper virus, appeared in 1971, highlighting the need for mechanisms to protect against malicious software.

During this time, legal frameworks were also beginning to evolve. In 1986, the US enacted the Computer Fraud and Abuse Act (CFAA), which criminalised unauthorised access to computer systems and was one of the first legal measures to address cybercrime.

The 1990s witnessed the explosion of the Internet, which revolutionised how people interacted with technology. With this growth came an increase in cyber security threats, including hacking, identity theft, and the spread of malware. Notable incidents such as the 1999 Melissa virus and the 2000 ILOVEYOU virus underscored the need for more robust cyber security measures.

In response to these threats, laws, and regulations began to evolve rapidly. The European Union introduced the Data Protection Directive in 1995, which was a pioneering effort to protect personal data and privacy. In the US, the Cybersecurity Act of 2000 aimed to enhance the nation's cyber security efforts, and the USA PATRIOT Act of 2001 included provisions related to electronic surveillance and cyber security.

The early 2000s saw a growing awareness of the need for comprehensive cyber security policies. The establishment of the Department of Homeland Security in the US in 2003 included a focus on cyber security, highlighting its importance at a national level. Internationally, agreements such as the Convention on Cybercrime, adopted by the Council of Europe in 2001, sought to address cybercrime through enhanced cooperation and legal frameworks across borders.

The 2010s and beyond have been marked by sophisticated cyber threats, including advanced persistent threats (APTs) and state-sponsored cyber-attacks. High-profile incidents such as the 2017 Equifax data breach and the 2020 SolarWinds attack have demonstrated the rapidly evolving nature of cyber threats and the need for robust defences.

In response, legal frameworks have continued to evolve. The General Data Protection Regulation (GDPR), enacted by the European Union in 2018, represents a significant advancement in data protection law, imposing strict requirements on how organisations handle personal data. In the US, the California Consumer Privacy Act (CCPA) and subsequent state-level privacy laws have mirrored some of the GDPR's provisions, emphasising consumer rights and data protection.

Canada enacted the Personal Information Protection and Electronic Documents Act (PIPEDA), which governs the collection and use of personal data, and developed the Canadian Cyber Security Strategy, aimed at enhancing the nation's resilience to cyber incidents. Canadian law also emphasises the importance of compliance, risk management, and collaboration among public and private sectors to mitigate threats.

The global nature of cyber threats has led to increased international cooperation. Initiatives such as the Paris Call for Trust and Security in Cyberspace, launched in 2018, aim to promote norms and principles for responsible behaviour in cyberspace.

The history of cyber security and the law reflects a continuous struggle to keep pace with technological advancements and the evolving nature of cyber threats. As technology continues to evolve, the interplay between cyber security and the law will remain a critical area of focus, requiring ongoing innovation and international collaboration to protect individuals, organisations, and nations from emerging cyber threats.

The implication is that **the law is always in a catch-up mode.** This makes legislation less useful and less effective in the fight against cyber security threats or cyber-attacks. Cyber security legislation is almost always reactive due to several inherent challenges and dynamics of the digital realm. Here are the main reasons why this tends to be the case.

The first reason is rapid technological advancement. The pace of technological development has increased significantly, especially in the last two decades, and keeps increasing. We have continuous change where technological advancement outstrips the speed at which laws can be developed and implemented.

New technologies can introduce new vulnerabilities and attack vectors that legislation cannot anticipate because they are typically either unintended consequences or simply the result of flawed software development, such as insufficient testing. Vulnerabilities may also be the result of rising complexity, hyperconnectivity, the rush to bring new products to market, poor usability, incorrect, or inappropriate usage or deployment or other factors.

Moreover, technological evolution can result in new types of cyber threats emerging. Legislators can only address these issues after they have become evident and, sadly, may have already caused significant damage or disruption.

The second reason is the complexity and unpredictability of cyber threats, as threat actors tend to innovate much faster. Cyber threats are diverse and continually evolving, ranging from simple phishing attacks to sophisticated state-sponsored cyber espionage. This unpredictability makes it difficult for lawmakers to anticipate and create comprehensive, forward-looking legislation. Many cyber threats are unprecedented, and there may be no historical precedent to guide legislative action. As a result, laws often respond to specific incidents or trends that have already been observed.

The third reason is that the legislative process involves multiple stages of review, debate, and amendment, which is usually time-consuming. By the time a law is passed, the cyber threat landscape may have shifted, necessitating additional amendments or new legislation. Legislators are fighting back with one hand tied behind their backs, whereas threat actors are free to innovate at will without any governing process, standards, or codes of practice.

Legislative bodies almost always encounter delays due to political disagreements, competing priorities, and the need for extensive consultation with stakeholders. This can slow down the development of timely and effective cyber security laws.

The fourth reason is linked to complex economic and political considerations. Lawmakers often need to balance competing interests, such as privacy rights, business interests, and national security concerns. This balancing act can lead to compromises that may not fully address emerging threats or may delay the introduction of new laws. As much as these compromises attempt to achieve some form of consensus and to keep all stakeholders happy, these compromises more often than not leave all stakeholders unhappy. Remember this saying, "A camel is a horse designed by a committee," attributed to Sir Alec Issigonis, the designer of the iconic Mini car?

The influence of powerful technology and cyber security industries can affect the legislative process. Organisations may lobby against strict regulations or advocate for specific provisions that may not align with the views of cyber security professionals and best practices for cyber security.

The fifth reason is the cost of cyber security. Technology can be made more secure. Sadly, this comes at a cost, often a significant cost. Longer product development cycles, additional testing, compliance, and greater complexity are just some of the contributing cost factors. **The cost of adequate cyber security may result in uneconomic or unaffordable technology products.**

Also, one must not forget the complex relationship between security and usability, which presents a challenging paradox, as enhancements in one area frequently compromise the other. Stricter security measures, such as complex password requirements, multifactor authentication, and frequent software updates, can frustrate users and lead to decreased engagement or outright avoidance of secure practices. Conversely, prioritising usability may create vulnerabilities, as simpler systems might lack the necessary safeguards to protect sensitive information. This contradiction highlights the need for a balanced approach that promotes both security and user experience, encouraging the development of intuitive security solutions that do not sacrifice protection for ease of use. Achieving this balance is crucial in fostering a culture of security without alienating users.

The sixth reason is the reactive nature of cyber incidents. Significant cyber security incidents, such as data breaches, ransomware attacks, or large-scale cyber espionage campaigns, often prompt immediate legislative responses.

These incidents can highlight vulnerabilities and drive lawmakers to address specific issues revealed by the attacks. Media coverage and public outcry following major cyber incidents can spur legislative action. Lawmakers may be motivated to enact laws in response to public demand or media attention, rather than as part of a proactive strategy.

Lastly, it is about global and jurisdictional challenges. Cyber security is a global issue, and effective legislation often requires international cooperation. The need to coordinate with other nations and align with international standards can complicate and delay the legislative process. Cyber incidents can cross national boundaries, making it challenging for individual countries to address issues unilaterally. Legislation may need to respond to cross-border challenges and collaborate with international partners, which can slow down the process.

Another challenge with the law (or better to say with the lack of its applicability) is associated with its jurisdiction. **The Internet transformed crime in the form of cybercrime into a global business.** It is all well to have international laws and agreements between the "Five Eyes" countries and the EU. But if cyber criminals reside in Russia or one of the African or South-East Asian countries, it is practically impossible to rely on the law to prosecute them.

Although legislation can assist in addressing cyber security issues, albeit slowly, unfortunately, legislation often lacks the foresight needed to pre-emptively tackle emerging threats. As cyber security continues to evolve very fast, the law will continue to struggle to keep up. There is a growing recognition of the need for more proactive approaches, including adaptive regulatory frameworks and enhanced collaboration between stakeholders to anticipate and mitigate risks before they manifest.

For many organisations, **cyber insurance has become an essential part of their risk management strategy.**

Let's talk about cyber insurance that is often seen either as a "silver bullet" or as an "out of jail ticket." But is this really true?

Surely, cyber insurance may help with several things, like protection against financial losses, legal protection, mitigation of reputational damage, and compliance with certain industry standards. But it comes with **high direct and indirect costs.** And **don't forget about coverage exclusions and limitations.**

Because security breaches are so costly and cybercrime is so common, many insurers have become more stringent in their underwriting processes. Some have lowered caps for payouts and narrowed their coverage offerings as well. This means that the requirements the organisation may be expected to meet will be fairly complex.

Every cyber insurance provider will likely **conduct a risk assessment to determine if the organisation qualifies for cyber insurance.** The process will help them to determine how much coverage they can offer and what organisation will need to pay for it. The risk assessment might be as quick and simple as a questionnaire or as complex and time-consuming as a third-party audit. Qualifying for the underwriting process is a journey. Excessive claims against cyber insurance policies have forced cyber insurance providers to ask too many "invasive and intrusive" questions of prospective policyholders in an effort to keep their exposure to a minimum.

Failure to meet the insurer's requirement may result in refusal to offer the organisation cyber insurance. Meeting these requirements may be costly (and these are the "indirect costs" mentioned earlier).

While cyber insurance does provide some financial relief, it does not magically evaporate the consequences of a security breach.

Probably the **biggest negative of cyber insurance is that it creates a false sense of security.** While cyber liability insurance can help protect organisations from financial losses and reputational damage resulting from cyber-attacks, **it's not a substitute for strong cybersecurity practices.**

For those interested in this topic, it is important to read this 3-year-old article by John Davidson published in the Australian Financial Review (AFR) and titled "Cyber insurance's dirty little secret: It's useless."[7] Despite the article's age, the conclusions are still valid.

QUESTIONS

These questions are important, as they prompt thinking and allow the target audience to understand the organisation's potential exposure and what they personally can do to improve the organisation's cyber security posture. To get answers to some of these questions, the target audience may need to go to their CIOs and CISOs:

1. Do directors and officers of the organisation understand their legal duties, obligations, and liability regarding cyber security under Corporations Law, privacy law, and cyber security regulations such as ASIC, APRA, GDPR, and critical infrastructure laws in a global multi-jurisdictional context?
2. Do directors and officers of the organisation understand the limitations of legal protection offered by current laws in the area of cyber security? Do directors understand they can be held personally liable if governance is inadequate?
3. Has the Board clearly assigned cyber risk oversight responsibilities, and do the assigned or designated accountable and responsible staff have the appropriate expertise and resources to discharge their obligations?
4. Does the organisation have documented evidence that all possible measures to prevent cyber security incidents have been taken? Will this document withstand cross-examination in the court of law? Will it offer enough protection to directors and officers of the organisation?

5. Did the organisation attempt to study recent high-profile cyber security incidents? Can it happen here? What are the consequences?
6. Does the organisation have appropriate cyber insurance cover? What events or types of incidents are included in that coverage? Is a potential cyber security incident linked to Board negligence by a regulator included or excluded from coverage?
7. What are the limits, exclusions, and carve-outs of the organisation's cyber insurance coverage? How does the cyber insurance coverage map relate to the organisation's cyber security exposure? Does the organisation have an accurate and timely understanding of its cyber exposure? How frequently does the organisation review its cyber security exposure mapping against its cyber insurance?
8. Does the organisation's cyber insurance policy cover regulatory investigations, fines, penalties, and legal costs directors may face personally? Are there any limits placed on these costs?
9. How are notification obligations handled? Is there an agreed and documented notifications process? Could a late or incorrect response void cyber insurance coverage? Do you understand when the Board will be notified about a potential or actual cyber incident?
10. How quickly must the insurer be notified in the event of a breach to preserve coverage? Are the organisation's key officers aware of this responsibility?
11. Who in the organisation is responsible for liaising with the insurer, legal counsel, and regulators during a cyber incident? Is there a designated accountable person?
12. Does the organisation's cyber insurance policy include access to forensic experts, PR and/or crisis management experts, legal specialists, and cybersecurity experts?

DESSERT

As technology continues to advance, the legal landscape will need to adapt. Emerging technologies such as AI (see Chapter 13), blockchain and quantum computing (see Chapter 13) present new challenges for cyber security and require innovative legal solutions. Issues related to digital sovereignty, cross-border data flows, and the regulation of emerging technologies will be central to future legal and policy developments.

AI (see Chapter 13) opens a plethora of new risks and challenges related to cyber security, especially when the majority of users and senior executives do not understand how AI works and what risks are associated with its use.

Quantum computing (see Chapter 13), on the other hand, poses a significant threat to traditional encryption methods, which rely on the difficulty of factoring large numbers or solving discrete logarithm problems. Quantum computers, leveraging principles of quantum mechanics, could potentially solve these problems exponentially faster than classical computers, rendering current encryption schemes vulnerable to breaches. In response, the development of quantum-resistant or quantum-strong encryption algorithms is underway, designed to withstand attacks from quantum computers. These new algorithms aim to secure data against future quantum threats, ensuring the integrity and confidentiality of information in a post-quantum world, as the race to both advance quantum computing and secure digital communications intensifies.

Interestingly, blockchain is often described as a solution in search of a problem, highlighting the technology's potential that sometimes outpaces its practical applications. While blockchain offers notable capabilities such as decentralisation, transparency, and immutability, many proposed use cases struggle to demonstrate tangible benefits over existing systems. Industries ranging from finance to supply chain management have explored blockchain for its promise of enhanced security and efficiency, but the challenge lies in finding scenarios where its unique attributes provide clear advantages. As stakeholders seek to integrate blockchain, the focus is increasingly on identifying specific problems it can effectively address rather than merely implementing the technology for its own sake.

Achieving global cooperation for consistent cyber security laws remains a formidable challenge, primarily due to differing national interests, legal frameworks, and varying levels of technological advancement. Even if first-world countries can agree on international standards and regulations, enforcement becomes problematic, especially when cybercrimes originate from jurisdictions with lax laws or where law enforcement is limited, such as in Russia or Nigeria. This disparity hampers effective prosecution, as countries may be reluctant to extradite offenders or cooperate in investigations that cross borders. Consequently, the lack of a cohesive global framework undermines efforts to combat cybercrime effectively, leaving many nations vulnerable and highlighting the need for more robust international collaboration and consensus.

Key Laws Governing Cybersecurity for Directors in Australia include[8]:

- Corporations Act 2001 - Directors must act with care and diligence. Negligence in cybersecurity preparedness can be considered a breach of duty, leading to legal consequences.
- Privacy Act 1988 - Businesses must protect customer data under the Australian Privacy Principles (APPs). Cyber breaches due to poor security can result in substantial fines.
- Security of Critical Infrastructure Act 2018 - Critical sectors must report cyber incidents and implement mandatory security controls.

Insurance experts will thoroughly evaluate a company's cyber risk profile and set appropriate policy pricing and policy limits or deductibles (in Australia, deductibles are called "excess") that align with the assessed risk level. It is likely that this assessment will consider the following elements of the organisation's cyber security posture:

- Does the organisation have strong cyber security controls?
- Does the organisation use Multifactor Authentication (MFA)?
- Does the organisation have a solid incident response plan?
- Does the organisation have strong network security?
- Does the organisation use encryption of data at rest and in transit?
- Does the organisation have an operating security training and awareness program?

NOTES

1 https://assured.co.uk/2023/post-breach-red-faced-ceos-youre-fired/.
2 https://www.csoonline.com/article/4062724/qantas-cutting-ceo-pay-signals-new-era-of-cyber-accountability.html.
3 https://www.nacdonline.org/all-governance/governance-resources/governance-surveys/surveys-benchmarking/2025-public-company-board-practices--oversight-survey/.
4 https://www.allens.com.au/globalassets/pdfs/sectors-services/data-privacy-cyber/cyber-and-data-governance_apr22.pdf.
5 https://www.minterellison.co.nz/insights/cyber-risk-and-litigation-some-guidelines-for-directors-and-boards.
6 https://www.itnews.com.au/feature/cyber-contracts-not-meeting-boards-needs-kaine-mathrick-tech-ceo-619722?eid=1&edate=20250825&utm_source=20250825_AM&utm_medium=newsletter&utm_campaign=daily_newsletter.
7 https://www.afr.com/technology/cyber-insurance-s-dirty-little-secret-it-s-useless-20220504-p5aig0.
8 https://chillit.com.au/the-high-cost-of-cybersecurity-negligence-what-directors-must-know/#:~:text=Directors%20can%20be%20personally%20sued,to%20implement%20proper%20cybersecurity%20governance.

Chapter 1

Cumulative effect

"And what is the use of a book," thought Alice, "without pictures or conversations?"

Alice's Adventures in Wonderland by Lewis Carroll

APPETISER

- In IT, the "cumulative effect" refers to the combined impact of multiple changes, events, or actions over time, where each individual contribution may seem small, but the overall result becomes significant.
- Just one example of a cumulative effect:
  - Over 35,000 Java programs impacted.
  - Almost half of all corporate networks globally have been actively probed.
  - Over 60 variants of the exploit have been produced within 24 hours.
  - One Australian Federal Government Department devoted 33,000 hours to dealing with this vulnerability.
  - Full remediation is very difficult to achieve for a vulnerability that is so pervasive and is not a "one and done" process.
  - While an organisation may have been fully remediated at some point, as they've added new assets to their environments, they are likely to encounter this vulnerability again and again.

MAIN COURSE

In IT, the "**cumulative effect**" refers to the combined impact of multiple changes, events, or actions over time, where each individual contribution may seem small, but the overall result becomes significant. This concept

DOI: 10.1201/9781003730514-2

is relevant in various IT contexts, such as performance, security, and user experience.

In security, the "**cumulative effect**" refers to the gradual weakening of a system's defences due to a series of small, seemingly insignificant changes or events over time. These changes, individually minor, can combine to create significant vulnerabilities that attackers can exploit.

So, what happens if these changes are not insignificant or minor? Intuitively, **in this case the cumulative effect is amplified even further**.

Let's have a look at some significant developments in IT:

1. Rapid growth of the number of components in IT ecosystems (see Chapters 4 and 5).
2. Exponential growth of complexity of IT ecosystems because of the item above (see Chapters 4 and 5).
3. Supply chain challenges because of both items above (see Chapter 9).

Do they have a **cumulative effect?** The short answer to this question is "Yes." Let's have a look at the following example.

Some of the readers may have heard and remember the Log4J vulnerability and associated panic?

The Log4j vulnerability, also known as Log4Shell, is a critical vulnerability discovered in the Apache Log4j logging library in November 2021. Log4Shell essentially grants hackers total control of devices running unpatched versions of Log4j. Researchers consider Log4Shell a "**catastrophic**" **security vulnerability** because it is so widespread, as Log4j is **one of the most widely deployed open-source programs** in the world and is so easy to use. Jen Easterly, director of the US Cybersecurity and Infrastructure Security Agency (CISA), called it "**one of the most serious I've seen in my entire career, if not the most serious.**"[1]

Log4j is a widely used open-source logging library for Java applications. It allows developers to log information, such as error messages and user inputs, within their applications. Due to its ubiquity, vulnerabilities in Log4j, particularly the Log4Shell vulnerability (CVE-2021-44228), have posed significant security risks. This was a **zero-day vulnerability** (a vulnerability in a system or device that has been disclosed but is not yet patched).

Let's have a look at the consequences of the Log4j vulnerability.

Over 35,000 Java programs were impacted by Log4j vulnerabilities. As of 14 December 2021, **almost half of all corporate networks globally have been actively probed**, with **over 60 variants of the exploit** having been **produced within 24 hours**. On December 1, 2022, Tenable® announced the results of a telemetry study examining the scope and impact of the critical Log4j vulnerability in the months following its initial disclosure.[2] According to the data collected from over 500 million tests, 72% of organisations remain vulnerable to the Log4j vulnerability as of October 1, 2022. The **data**

highlights legacy vulnerability remediation challenges, which are the root cause of the majority of data breaches.

When Log4Shell was discovered in November 2021, organisations around the world scrambled to determine their risk. In the weeks following its disclosure, organisations significantly reallocated resources and invested tens of thousands of hours of effort to identify and remediate this vulnerability. One Australian Federal Government Department reported that its security team devoted 33,000 hours to Log4j vulnerability response alone.

Tenable® found that as of December 2021, one in ten assets was vulnerable to Log4j, including a wide range of servers, web applications, containers, and Internet of Things (IoT) devices. October 2022 data showed improvements, with 2.5% of assets still vulnerable. Yet nearly one-third (29%) of these assets had recurrences of Log4j after full remediation was achieved.

"Full remediation is very difficult to achieve for a vulnerability that is so pervasive and it's important to keep in mind that vulnerability remediation is not a 'one and done' process," said Bob Huber, chief security officer, Tenable. "While an organisation may have been fully remediated at some point, as they've added new assets to their environments, they are likely to encounter Log4j again and again. Eradicating Log4j is an ongoing battle that calls for organisations to continually assess their environments for the flaw, as well as other known vulnerabilities."

Another interesting comment was made by senior threat researcher Sean Gallagher from Sophos, who said, "Honestly, the biggest threat here is that people have already gotten access and are just sitting on it, and even if you remediate the problem somebody's already in the network … It's going to be around as long as the Internet."

And this is just one vulnerability! Now, ask yourself, "How many other zero-day vulnerabilities are lurking in an organisation's IT ecosystem?"

In the above example, we have explored the cumulative effect of just three factors. What would be the cumulative effect if we add the von Neumann architecture (see Chapter 3), TCP/IP, DNS and BGP (see Chapter 10), the proliferation of the Agile approach (see Chapter 6) and other factors discussed in this book?

The next 5–10 years will bring more high-profile cyber incidents and outages with significant customer and reputation impact, unless conscious effort is made by Boards and CEOs to address factors described in this book and contributing to the cumulative effect.

Some people may ask: "Where do I start? There are so many contributing factors!" In reality, all of them need to be addressed. But a good start will be to focus on a conscious year-on-year decrease of the size and complexity of IT ecosystems, proper DNS management, understanding of (and managing) the shared responsibility concept for Cloud/SaaS security and use of an agile approach and supply chain security.

This book is focused on the factors that create and can further exacerbate the **cumulative effect** in cyber security and aspires to attract the attention of Board Directors and CEOs to these factors, hoping that they can start making conscious choices and decisions about improving organisations' cyber security posture.

Questions at the end of each chapter and the target audience's answers to these questions are very important, as they prompt thinking and allow the target audience to understand the organisation's potential exposure and what they personally can do to improve the organisation's cyber security posture. To get answers to some of these questions, the target audience may need to go to their CIOs and CISOs.

Another important issue that is a part of the **cumulative effect** is trust. That being one of trust. Or rather, the breakdown of trust. What we are seeing, compounded as each event is reported in the public arena, is the ongoing erosion of the trust that is sought and needed when processes are digitised.

Without trust, a lot of the promised benefits of digitising some public-facing processes are questioned, and some erode completely.

For example, all the talk about the settlement of property reverting to manual payments to avoid the scam of settlement funds being diverted to fake accounts is often used by one of my colleagues. It won't be possible to revert to manual completely with the impending removal of cheques (unless this removal is cancelled), but it will get more cumbersome and less convenient. Extrapolate this out to other areas, and it becomes the norm not to trust anything. Ridiculous. The promise of digital efficiency is lessened because of the lack of trust. So, security is bigger than just organisational reputation or costs; it is society's route to being more convenient, expedient, and efficient.

Before 9/11, we were innocent enough not to have security for air travel; 9/11 put an end to that. We will never go back to those more convenient days. What is IT's 9/11 equivalent? Cyber security is fundamental, and it is still not given the right attention at the Board and C-Suite level.

QUESTIONS

These questions are important, as they prompt thinking and allow the target audience to understand the organisation's potential exposure and what they personally can do to improve the organisation's cyber security posture. To get answers to some of these questions, the target audience may need to go to their CIOs and CISOs.

1. Does the organisation have an accurate, up-to-date, and holistic (reasonably complete) understanding of its cybersecurity risk exposure that is aligned with the organisation's risk appetite statement?

2. Have you or anyone in the organisation considered the **cumulative effect** of any of the above-mentioned factors? Is this **cumulative effect** reflected in the organisation's risk register?
3. Was anything done to mitigate (or at least alleviate) the organisation's risk associated with the **cumulative effect** of the above-mentioned factors?

DESSERT

The adjective **cumulative** describes the total amount of something when it's all added together. For example, eating a single chocolate doughnut may be fine, but the **cumulative effect** of eating them all day is that you'll probably feel sick.

The origin of *cumulative* helps remember the meaning - it comes from the Latin *cumulatus*, for "to heap." If something is cumulative, it is heaped together so it can be counted up to get a total number. The cumulative rainfall for the whole year isn't just the amount of rain that fell in one month, but rather the number of inches that fell every month that year to get the total, cumulative amount.

The term "**cumulative effect**" is more often used in the areas of environmental impact and health and refers to the combined impact of multiple actions or events over a period of time, where the overall effect is greater than the sum of each individual action. Essentially, it's about how repeated exposure or actions can lead to a significant outcome, even if each individual instance seems minor.

If we look retrospectively at cyber security incidents over the last 10 or so years, it is easy to see that 99.9% (if not 100%) of them have been performed by malicious actors like cyber criminals and nation-state threat actors. Cases when people do this to prove that they can do it have become almost non-existent.

Cyber criminals want to steal organisations' data to demand ransom and often to sell this data later on the **dark web** (the dark web is the WWW content that exists on darknets (overlay networks) that use the Internet but require specific software, configurations, or authorisation to access[3]).

Nation-state threat actors either want to steal certain national security-related or sensitive data (including Personally Identifiable Information (PII)) or to cause disruption to various important, often essential, services like the power grid or water supply.

Now that we have established the main purposes of cyber-attacks, we can talk about both the root cause and the distribution mechanisms.

The root cause is always the same: the insecure nature of the von Neumann computer architecture that allows malware. And it is important to understand that there is nothing that organisations can do to get rid of this root cause.

Distribution mechanisms can be different and can be based on various insecurities like unmanaged domains/subdomains, invalid/missing certificates, using insecurities of APIs, TCP/IP, DNS, BGP, phishing, etc. The common thing of all distribution mechanisms is that their main purpose is to plant malware into the organisations' IT ecosystems.

And these distribution mechanisms keep evolving! Today, malware can be hidden in images (any image format like JPEG, PNG, or GIF can be edited to conceal malware)[4] or even in filenames![5] These techniques often can bypass most traditional security defences.

A combination of the root cause and one or more distribution mechanisms creates a **cumulative effect.** Often, there are multiple factors contributing to this **cumulative effect,** as shown earlier.

It is important to understand that certain factors can contribute to and further exacerbate this **cumulative effect** by increasing organisations' cyber security exposure. Among them are the fast-growing size and complexity of organisations' IT ecosystems (that nobody understands end-to-end), the rapid growth of the number of APIs used (as a result of the move from monolithic applications to the microservices approach), the proliferation of the agile approach (that is prone to creating new vulnerabilities), the lack of understanding of insecurities of TCP/IP, DNS, BGP, etc.

NOTES

1 https://en.wikipedia.org/wiki/Log4Shell#:~:text=In%20the%20United%20States%2C%20the,and%20advising%20vendors%20to%20prioritize.
2 https://kbi.media/tenable-research-finds-72-of-organisations-remain-vulnerable-to-nightmare-log4j-vulnerability/.
3 https://en.wikipedia.org/wiki/Dark_web.
4 https://www.baeldung.com/cs/malware-hidden-image-files and https://www.welivesecurity.com/en/malware/malware-hiding-in-pictures-more-likely-than-you-think/ and https://www.opswat.com/blog/how-emerging-image-based-malware-attacks-threaten-enterprise-defenses.
5 https://www.itnews.com.au/news/attackers-weaponise-linux-file-names-as-malware-vectors-619803?eid=1&edate=20250826&utm_source=20250826_AM&utm_medium=newsletter&utm_campaign=daily_newsletter.

Chapter 2

CIA, risk appetite, and risk exposure

"Who in the world am I? Ah, that's the great puzzle."

Alice's Adventures in Wonderland by Lewis Carroll

APPETISER

- What is the organisation's risk appetite?
- What happens if the organisation's actual cyber security exposure is not aligned with the organisation's risk appetite?
- Have you ever thought about the "cyber security risk-reward" ratio.
- Confidentiality, Integrity, and Availability are considered the three most important concepts in cyber security. Each letter in the CIA triad represents a foundational principle in cyber security.
  - *Confidentiality* is about measures to prevent sensitive information from unauthorised access attempts.
  - *Integrity* is about consistency, accuracy, and trustworthiness of data, which must be maintained over its entire lifecycle. Data must not be changed in transit, and steps must be taken to ensure it can't be altered by unauthorised people.
  - *Availability* is about information being consistently and readily accessible to authorised parties.
- In today's environment, one probably should also add *Privacy* to this triad.
- Some also add to this list *Authenticity* and *Non-Repudiation*.
- Privacy is about specific rules and measures for storing and processing Personally Identifiable Information (PII).

DOI: 10.1201/9781003730514-3

MAIN COURSE

Whether you spell it "cybersecurity" or "cyber security," it means the same thing. The UK's National Cyber Security Centre (NCSC) spells it as two separate words, and I will stick to this spelling. Spell checkers generally don't flag either method of spelling as incorrect. The only conclusion is that both spellings, "cybersecurity" and "cyber security," are correct and mean the same thing.

Information security and cyber security technically are related but distinct fields. The focus of cyber security is on protecting devices, systems, and digital information (data) from cyber threats, while information security encompasses broader protection of information in all forms and is sometimes considered an umbrella term that includes cyber security.

Historically, it was considered that cyber security is concerned with protecting electronic and mobile devices against attacks in cyber space, while information security (Info Sec) is concerned with protecting the confidentiality, integrity, and availability of information. Protection of devices against attacks in cyber space is needed to ensure the protection of confidentiality, integrity, and availability of information. As a result of this, in today's world, one can observe the rapid convergence of these two terms.

For the purposes of this book, we will treat both terms as interchangeable and will use the term cyber security.

Cyber security is the practice of protecting systems, networks, and data from cyber-attacks. It involves the application of technologies, practices, policies, processes, and controls to mitigate the impact of cyber threats. Cyber security aims to protect computer systems, applications, devices, data, financial assets, and people against ransomware, malware, phishing scams, data theft, and other cyber threats.

The UK's NCSC uses a very short and simple definition of cyber security: "Cyber security is how individuals and organisations reduce the risk of cyber-attack." It then elaborates:

> "Cyber security's core function is to protect the devices we all use (smartphones, laptops, tablets and computers), and services we access - both online and at work - from theft or damage. It's also about preventing unauthorised access to the vast amounts of personal information we store on these devices, and online."

Every organisation has a certain level of risk appetite. For example, the risk appetite of a state electoral commission is vastly different from the risk appetite of a 2-man start-up. What is the risk appetite of your organisation? Is it documented anywhere? What are the means to ensure that the organisation's **actual cyber security exposure** is aligned with the organisation's risk appetite? What happens if the organisation's actual cyber security exposure is not aligned with the organisation's risk appetite?

I suspect that every reader of this book is very familiar with the concept of "risk-reward" ratio that compares the potential loss of an investment to its potential gain. A good risk/reward ratio typically ranges from 1:2 to 1:3, where potential rewards are at least double or triple the risks. Lower ratios below 1.0, such as 1:3, are preferred as they maximise returns while minimising risks over time.

People usually think about the "risk-reward" ratio in terms of investment. But what about cyber security risks? Have you ever thought about the "cyber security risk-reward" ratio? How is this aligned with the organisation's risk appetite?

We will talk more about this in some of the following chapters that discuss the consequences of the digital revolution and the use of certain project management methodologies (see Chapters 5 and 6).

QUESTIONS

These questions are important, as they prompt thinking and allow the target audience to understand the organisation's potential exposure and what they personally can do to improve the organisation's cyber security posture. To get answers to some of these questions, the target audience may need to go to their CIOs and CISOs.

1. Does the organisation have an explicitly documented statement about its risk appetite?
2. If the answer to the previous question is yes, does the documented organisation's risk appetite properly define it?
3. Is the organisation's risk appetite understood by the top three tiers of leadership and management below the Board?
4. In your opinion, how big is the gap between an organisation's risk appetite and risk exposure? Has the organisation performed an independent review to identify potential gaps (and if any - their size) between the organisation's risk appetite and risk exposure?
5. Have you ever thought about the "cyber security risk-reward" ratio? How does the organisation determine the "cyber security risk-reward" profile of every major project or initiative?
6. Is the organisation's "cyber security risk - reward" ratio aligned with the organisation's risk appetite?

DESSERT

Today, almost everything (and the use of "almost" here is just to avoid somebody raising an obscure example proving that something is not) is dependent on IT, and we can talk about network security, application security, information (or data) security, operational security, etc. However, we can and should talk about three cornerstones underpinning cyber security - Confidentiality, Integrity, and Availability (or in short - CIA).

The importance of this security model speaks for itself: Confidentiality, Integrity, and Availability are considered the three most important concepts in cyber security. Each letter in the CIA triad represents a foundational principle in cyber security.

> **Confidentiality** is about measures to prevent sensitive information from unauthorised access attempts.
>
> **Integrity** is about consistency, accuracy, and trustworthiness of data, which must be maintained over its entire lifecycle. Data must not be changed in transit, and steps must be taken to ensure it can't be altered by unauthorised people.
>
> **Availability** is about information being consistently and readily accessible to authorised parties.

In today's environment, one probably should also add Privacy to this triad.

> **Privacy** is about specific rules and measures for storing and processing Personally Identifiable Information (PII). PII is information that, when **used alone or with other relevant data, can identify an individual.**

Lately, some tend to add to this **Authenticity** (the property that an entity is what it claims to be, or in plain English, authenticity basically means that a person or system is who it says it is and not some impostor) and **Non-Repudiation** (the ability to prove the occurrence of a claimed event or action and its originating entities, or in simpler terms, Non-Repudiation essentially means that someone can't perform an action and then plausibly claim that it wasn't actually them who did it).[1]

When this chapter was finished, Qantas announced a **massive breach** resulting in the **theft of PII of 5.7 million of its customers,** including the PII of the Australian Prime Minister. According to Qantas, the breach occurred at one of the outsourced overseas call centres, which highlights supply chain risks, even if the outsourced service provider provides non-IT services (see Chapter 9) - another example of the **cumulative effect.**

NOTE

1 https://chillit.com.au/the-high-cost-of-cybersecurity-negligence-what-directors-must-know/#:~:text=Directors%20can%20be%20personally%20sued,to%20implement%20proper%20cybersecurity%20governance.

Chapter 3

The fifth column

"Begin at the beginning," the King said gravely, "and go on till you come to the end: then stop."

Alice's Adventures in Wonderland by Lewis Carroll

APPETISER

- At the dawn of the computing era, there were two competing computer architectures: von Neumann (or Princeton) architecture and Harvard architecture.
- The principal difference between the two is that von Neumann architecture uses the same memory both for instructions and for data to be processed, while Harvard architecture uses two separate blocks of memory - one for instructions and one for data to be processed.
- At the time, the decision was made (and rightly so) in favour of a more flexible and cheaper-to-implement von Neumann architecture.
- Devised by John von Neumann around 1945, von Neumann architecture is insecure by design, as it lacks separation of instruction memory from data memory, allowing transfer of control into data space that may contain hidden malicious code.
- When this happened, the Internet was not even on the horizon, and Thomas George Watson, then president of IBM, infamously said, "I think there is a world market for maybe five computers."
- When the Internet took over the world, it brought new, faster, and wider-reaching malware distribution methods.
- Inherent insecurities of von Neumann architecture have been further exacerbated by some of its implementations, as was discovered in 2017 and 2025.
- Have you heard about Meltdown, Spectre, and Shade BIOS?

DOI: 10.1201/9781003730514-4

MAIN COURSE

The term "fifth column" originated in Spain (originally quinta columna) during the early phase of the Spanish Civil War that started in 1936. The term is conventionally credited to Emilio Mola Vidal, a Nationalist general during the Spanish Civil War (1936–39). As four of his army columns moved on Madrid, the general referred to his militant supporters within the capital as his "fifth column," **undermining** the loyalist government **from within.** It gained popularity in the Republican faction media in early October 1936 and immediately started to spread abroad. The term "fifth column" is defined as a clandestine group or faction of subversive agents who attempt to undermine a nation's solidarity by any means at their disposal.

At the dawn of the computing era, there were two competing computer architectures: von Neumann (or Princeton) architecture and Harvard architecture. The principal difference between the two is that von Neumann architecture uses the same memory both for instructions and for data to be processed, while Harvard architecture uses two separate blocks of memory - one for instructions and one for data to be processed.

At the time, the decision was made (and rightly so) in favour of a more flexible and cheaper-to-implement von Neumann architecture. When this happened, the Internet was not even on the horizon, and Thomas George Watson, then president of IBM, infamously said: "I think there is a world market for maybe five computers." No one at this stage could predict either the sheer number of computers today or the creation of the Internet.

Use of von Neumann (Princeton) architecture allows storing both instructions and data in the same memory, which in turn allows lower implementation costs, more flexible memory utilisation, and higher design simplicity and regularity. However, this architecture also brings some unpleasant side effects, like, for example:

> "Devised by John von Neumann around 1945, **von Neumann architecture is insecure by design. Lack of separation of instructions memory from data memory** (unlike in Harvard Architecture) **allows the transfer of control into data space that may contain malicious code.**" [1]

And then the **Internet has taken over the world** and brought with it **new, faster, and wider-reaching malware distribution methods.** However, independently of malware distribution methods, a significant number of types of cyberattacks are conceptually based on the fundamental feature of von Neumann (Princeton) architecture - lack of discrimination between instructions and data, which allows easy substitution/insertion of maliciously behaving components.

What does this mean? It actually means that any computer used by the organisation can become the "fifth column" or a "traitor." Think about this using the following analogy. An organisation is a fortress with multiple gatekeepers. If one or more gatekeepers are compromised, they can let the enemy inside the fortress.

In addition to this, the inherent insecurities of von Neumann architecture have been further exacerbated by some of its implementations, as was discovered in 2017 and 2025.

Ask your CIO how many computers are used by the organisation. If your organisation is using Software-as-a-Service or allows BYOD (Bring Your Own Device) and use of home devices, your CIO will not be able to answer this question, even if asset management in the organisation is 100% accurate. Now, ask your CISO the same question. Did you get the same answer?

Now, ask each of them separately how many unsupported versions of computers/devices, operating systems, and applications are in the organisation's IT ecosystem. This is a very important question (and the answer is even more important), as unsupported components significantly increase cyber risks and exposure.

But whatever answers you may be able to squeeze out of your CIO and your CISO, think about how big your potential "fifth column" is (or how many gatekeepers can be potentially compromised). Do you feel comfortable with the answer?

QUESTIONS

These questions are important, as they prompt thinking and allow the target audience to understand the organisation's potential exposure and what they personally can do to improve the organisation's cyber security posture. To get answers to some of these questions, the target audience may need to go to their CIOs and CISOs:

1. Which business and technology architectural decisions may result in the increase of the organisation's exposure to malware?
2. How big is the attack surface? How many computers are used by the organisation? How many servers? How many firewalls, routers, bridges, switches, and Internet connections? How many Cloud and SaaS solutions? Is the organisation's asset management up to scratch? Are all devices patched to the right level, and do they have the latest version of protection used by the organisation (EDR or XDR)?
3. Does the organisation allow the use of home devices? Are all devices patched to the right level, and do they have the latest version of protection used by the organisation (EDR or XDR)?
4. Does the organisation allow Bring Your Own Device (BYOD), including smartphones that are not managed by the organisation, to be connected to the organisation's network(s) and systems?
5. How many computers and devices (see question 2 above) are used by the organisation but not managed by the organisation?

6. How many unsupported components are in the organisation's IT ecosystem?
7. How many Apple computers are used by the organisation?
8. What happens if one or more of the above-mentioned items (see questions 2 and 5 above) are compromised?
9. Based on how many computers and devices are in the organisation (see questions 2 and 5 above), what is the probability of one or more of them being compromised?
10. What can be done to reduce the number of computers and devices used by the organisation?
11. What is your role in reducing the size of the attack surface, including complexity, shadow IT, and the number of computers and devices used by the organisation?

DESSERT

Creation of malicious software (or malware) and computer viruses was actually predicted by John von Neumann in 1966 in his work, Theory of Self-Reproducing Automata.[2] His prediction became true in 1971 with the creation of a worm called "Creeper." Contrary to what every non-technical person says, "Macs are not susceptible to viruses." The first computer virus found in the wild, dubbed "Elk Cloner," was designed to target Apple II computers. It was written in 1982 by a then-15-year-old, who wrote such programs to play pranks on his friends. The very first PC virus, dubbed "Brain," was born in 1986. It changed the information security world as we know it today. It originated in Pakistan but quickly spread worldwide to Europe and North America.

Inherent insecurities of von Neumann architecture have been further exacerbated by some of its implementations, as was discovered in 2017 and 2025.

The Meltdown and Spectre vulnerabilities[3] were initially discovered in 2017, with hardware vendors notified on June 1, 2017, while the public announcement was delayed and publicly disclosed only in January 2018, to allow for coordinated disclosure and mitigation efforts. Meltdown and Spectre work on personal computers, mobile devices, and in the Cloud.

Meltdown and Spectre exploit critical vulnerabilities in modern processors. These hardware vulnerabilities allow programs to steal data that is currently being processed. While programs are typically not permitted to read data from other programs, a malicious program can exploit Meltdown and Spectre to get hold of secrets stored in the memory of other running programs. This might include passwords stored in a password manager or browser, personal photos, emails, instant messages, and even business-critical documents.

Meltdown breaks the most fundamental isolation between user applications and the operating system. This attack allows a program to access the memory, and thus also the secrets, of other programs and the operating system.

Spectre breaks the isolation between different applications. It allows an attacker to trick error-free programs, which follow best practices, into leaking their secrets. In fact, the safety checks of said best practices actually increase the attack surface and may make applications more susceptible to Spectre. Spectre is harder to exploit than Meltdown, but it is also harder to mitigate.

Both personal computers, mobile devices, and the Cloud (see Chapters 7 and 8) allow Meltdown and Spectre exploitation. Depending on the Cloud service provider's infrastructure, it might be possible to steal data from other customers.

Basic Input/Output System (BIOS) is a firmware program that initialises hardware components and loads the operating system when a computer starts. It acts as a bridge between the hardware and the operating system, providing essential startup instructions and allowing users to configure system settings. Modern computers often use Unified Extensible Firmware Interface (UEFI), which is a more advanced successor to BIOS. As reported at Black Hat 2025 by Kazuki Matsuo, a security researcher from the Japanese Futures Forward Research Institute (FFRI) Security,[4] researchers have developed a method for running malware in a computer's BIOS - a place where no security software can reach.

It was called "Shade BIOS," and, unlike UEFI rootkits and bootkits, Shade BIOS distinguishes itself by requiring essentially zero interaction with an operating system (OS). Thus, it allows an attacker to perform malicious functions from beyond where any antivirus, endpoint or extended detection and response (EDR/XDR), or operating system security tools can see or touch.

While the firmware-stored computer startup code would normally be flushed after the OS starts up and resumes control, Matsuo's Shade BIOS malware prevents this. Instead, Shade BIOS retains BIOS memory regions that would normally be overwritten and keeps UEFI drivers and protocols active, maintaining device access that would normally be under OS control. Effectively, Shade BIOS-style malware becomes an "attacker-exclusive OS" that runs along the legitimate operating system, nearly undetectable.

As a result, attackers can create persistent malware that hides below a computer's operating system, making it effectively invisible to endpoint detection and response tools, new security research suggests. This malware allows attackers to access devices, communicate with command-and-control (C2) servers, and exfiltrate data without ever touching OS application programming interfaces (APIs) that security products monitor for anomalies.

Evidence from leaked intelligence documents such as Vault 7 from the CIA and the NSA, which referenced tools such as DerStarke, DEITYBOUNCE, BANANABALLOT, and the commercial vector-edk BIOS hacking kit sold to governments, suggests nation-state actors are focusing on UEFI/BIOS exploits.

As more researchers begin to explore and refine the BIOS runtime space, Shade BIOS may soon mark the beginning of a new chapter in stealth malware.

NOTES

1 https://cybertheory.io/why-are-we-here-and-what-to-do-about-it/.
2 https://cba.mit.edu/events/03.11.ASE/docs/VonNeumann.pdf.
3 https://meltdownattack.com/.
4 https://www.darkreading.com/endpoint-security/shade-bios-technique-beats-security.

Chapter 4

Complexity tax

"She generally gave herself very good advice (though she very seldom followed it),"

Alice's Adventures in Wonderland by Lewis Carroll

APPETISER

- Richard Branson: "Complexity is your enemy. Any fool can make something complicated. It is hard to make something simple."
- Steve Jobs: "Simple can be harder than complex."
- Tony Robbins, "Complexity is the enemy of execution."
- Bruce Schneier (who is famous for his saying, "If something is free, you're not the customer; you're the product"): "Complexity is the worst enemy of security, and our systems are getting more complex all the time."
- Metcalf Law: a linear increase in the number of team members or components leads to an exponential increase in communication complexity.
- Jeff Bezos' "The Two Pizza Rule": teams should be small enough to be fed with two pizzas.
- The ever-growing complexity of an organisation's IT ecosystems has brought us to a situation where, in any reasonably-sized organisation, nobody has a full and detailed understanding of the ecosystem and its interdependencies.
- Organisations with higher-than-average technology complexity spend 25% more than average companies and 58% more than organisations with low technology complexity.
- The most significant cost factor is the number of applications per end user:
  - Organisations with a large number of applications employ 27% more Full-Time Equivalents (FTEs) than average companies.

DOI: 10.1201/9781003730514-5

- World-class IT functions support 44% fewer applications per end user than typical organisations.
- Zachary Ginsburg: "The two new emerging risks relate to complexities of the IT and political environment made highly visible to executives and Boards by current events."
- One of the challenges is that simplicity is more difficult to achieve than complexity, but if we deal with this difficulty at the start, we will profit from simplicity in the end. If we give in to complexity at the start, then we will be paying for it forever!
- We need to have a simplicity-first mindset; that is the only way we will end up with simplicity.

MAIN COURSE

Let's start this chapter by quoting Richard Branson: "**Complexity is your enemy.** Any fool can make something complicated. **It is hard to make something simple.**"

Humans have a **natural tendency to overcomplicate things**, and it has ever been so; even Confucius knew this, as he said, "Life is really simple, but men insist on making it complicated."

Steve Jobs once said, "**Simple can be harder than complex:** You have to work hard to get your thinking clean to make it simple. But it's worth it in the end because once you get there, you can move mountains."

It is also worth mentioning here another quote, this time from Tony Robbins: "**Complexity is the enemy of execution.**" In fact, one can go further and say that complexity is the enemy of success, because if we cannot execute, then we cannot be successful.

Why did I start with all these quotes? I did it because:

- **Complexity steals our focus;** it's impossible for us to focus on complex things.
- **Complexity steals our confidence,** and without confidence, we seriously impact our ability to be successful.
- **Complexity steals our understanding,** and without understanding, the quality of our solutions and actions is reduced.
- One of the **main reasons technology projects fail** so **often** is their (underestimated) **complexity.**
- The rate of complexity growth is rapidly increasing with the **uncontrolled proliferation of new tools, our interconnectedness and globalisation.**

One may ask, what does this have to do with cyber security? The answer is very simple, according to Bruce Schneier (who is famous for his saying,

"If something is free, you're not the customer; you're the product"), as he has written in his book "Data and Goliath: The Hidden Battles to Collect Your Data and Control Your World": "**Complexity is the worst enemy of security, and our systems are getting more complex all the time.**"

The ever-growing complexity of organisations' IT ecosystems has brought us to the current situation where, in any reasonably-sized organisation, **nobody has a full and detailed understanding of the IT ecosystem and its interdependencies.** This results in an enormous amount of effort going into maintaining these IT ecosystems and often results in unpatched software required to maintain interoperability, as replacement/upgrade is costly and takes a long time. This also exponentially increases the risk of potential supply chain attacks and makes Public Key Infrastructure (PKI) management even more challenging.

This is just one real-life example of growing complexity. Those who used to do this in the "good old days" would treat the task of setting 75 new user accounts and email addresses as a laborious but pretty simple task. Today, setting up a new tenancy for 75 users in MS 365 requires design documents exceeding 300 pages and making decisions about how to set hundreds of parameters!

Brooks' Law (1975) was also formulated by Robert Metcalf in 1980. In software and systems development, the importance of effective communication is often overlooked. It's easy to think that software development is a purely technical matter; however, when working in a team, communication becomes a critical component. A **linear increase in the number of team members leads to an exponential increase in communication complexity,** or as Metcalfe's law states that the **value of the network is proportional to the square of the number of nodes.**

A solution to this challenge was proposed by Amazon CEO Jeff Bezos and is known as "**The Two Pizza Rule**": this concept suggests that teams should be small enough to be fed with two pizzas. This keeps the team size manageable and communication channels to a minimum.

Everything in this world has pros and cons. It is well known that solutions to various problems usually come with various side effects, and medication is one of the best examples of this situation.

So, when multiple organisations got sick and tired of the complexity, inflexibility ("one size fits all"), high cost and long "time to market" (associated with changes) of monolithic systems, a solution called microservices was invented. Microservices are an architectural and organisational approach to software development where software is composed of small independent services that communicate with each other using well-defined Application Programming Interfaces (APIs). This solution enabled organisations to make changes to individual parts of microservices-based solutions faster, cheaper, and easier. The explosion of APIs driven by digital expansion resulted in **41% of organisations managing at least as many APIs as applications.** This directly impacts the organisation's cyber security posture, as APIs create a new attack surface.

At this stage, there is insufficient understanding of risks associated with APIs and our ability to secure APIs, as even properly configured APIs can be exploited. API security is important because organisations use APIs to connect services and to transfer data, so a hacked API can lead to a data breach.

Malicious actors love APIs because they often hold the keys to a lot of valuable information. If not properly secured, APIs can potentially expose sensitive data. By targeting API endpoints in a distributed denial-of-service (DDoS) attack, malicious actors can significantly disrupt an organisation's operations. More importantly, as various components of microservices-based solutions evolve, the same happens to APIs, and they start living their own life.

As was correctly predicted by Gartner, API attacks would become the most common type of cyberattack by 2022 and beyond. This is because applications (and organisations) are getting more APIs, and there are more Cloud-based services that can be used to deploy them. For these reasons, over the next few years, API breaches are likely to become much more common and more sophisticated. This **affects the security of both organisations and their customers, as well as some of their suppliers.**

Some of the recent attributed to APIs major cyber security breaches in Australia include[1]:

- Vinomofo Data Breach - On October 10, 2022, Australian online wine retailer Vinomofo experienced a major data breach that potentially exposed usernames, emails, phone numbers, addresses and encrypted passwords of up to 500,000 of their customers.
- Medibank Data Breach - Medibank, one of Australia's largest health insurers, suffered a massive data breach in October 2022 that exposed customer data, including full names, addresses, phone numbers, email addresses, dates of birth, and bank account details of up to 9.7 million of their customers.
- MyDeal Data Breach - Australian online retailer, MyDeal (a Woolworths Group subsidiary), identified on October 14, 2022, that it suffered a data breach that exposed the private information of about 2.2 million of its customers.

Now, back to the complexity of IT ecosystems. What drives the growth of the complexity of IT ecosystems? As many organisations embark on digital transformations (see Chapter 5) and race to adopt new Cloud computing technologies and systems (see Chapters 7 and 8), they quickly discover that with new systems, applications, and processes come monumentally high levels of complexity.

The current trend of replacing monolithic systems with microservices-based solutions contributes to complexity growth, too. And, as we know, complexity increases exponentially with scale.

Let's have a look at what this means for our ability to grasp, understand, and manage complex IT ecosystems. Let's have a look at a real-life example. Consider an organisation that employs approximately 15,000 staff and contractors with an IT department of slightly over 160 staff and contractors, some of whom have been with the organisation for up to 30 years. The organisation uses more than 4,000 applications.

How many connections (not counting network infrastructure components, domains, subdomains, and websites) are there? If we use on average 4–5 connections per application, this amounts to at least 16,000–20,000 connections. Is there a human being who can understand (and deal with) this complexity? Not surprisingly, nobody in the IT department of this organisation had full end-to-end visibility and understanding of the IT ecosystem. It is important to note that this organisation went through a series of Mergers & Acquisitions (M&As) and divestments. Partially because of this, or partially because of the complexity of the IT ecosystem, the majority of documentation is not up to date, and significant portions of documentation are simply non-existent.

As such, the next very important question is - can this IT ecosystem be secured reliably, and if yes, what is the level of confidence that it is secured at any given point in time? Can any level of Essential 8 maturity (see Chapter 12) be achieved in such an environment? Can ISO/IEC 27001 (see Chapter 12) be meaningfully implemented in such an environment? The answer to these three questions is **"No,"** and the reason for this is very simple - it's complexity.

According to the Senior Director of Research of Gartner Risk & Audit Practice, Zachary Ginsburg, "The two **new emerging risks relate to complexities of the IT** and political environment made highly visible to executives and Boards by current events."

When we are talking about complexity, we should not forget the complexity of DNS (see Chapter 10). One more thing to remember - the bigger the organisation's IT ecosystem, the higher typically is the supply chain risk (see Chapter 9).

The good news is that the complexity problem is starting to be recognised.[2]

To increase our chances of success, we need to increase simplicity and reduce complexity and the clutter that comes with it. It is possible, but to do so, **simplicity should be our starting point**, not our goal. We cannot engineer simplicity into complex situations so easily. **It's much easier to start simple and try to avoid complexity as much as possible.**

One of the challenges is that **simplicity is more difficult to achieve than complexity**, but if we deal with this difficulty at the start, we will profit from simplicity in the end. **If we give in to complexity at the start, then we will be paying for it forever!**

We need to have a **simplicity-first mindset**; that is the only way we will end up with simplicity.

QUESTIONS

These questions are important, as they prompt thinking and allow the target audience to understand the organisation's potential exposure and what they personally can do to improve the organisation's cyber security posture. To get answers to some of these questions, the target audience may need to go to their CIOs and CISOs.

1. Do the organisation's CIO and CISO have an appreciation of the size and complexity of the organisation's IT ecosystem?
2. Does the organisation perform formal impact analysis of IT ecosystem complexity (increase in the number of components, systems, APIs, SaaS solutions, service providers, etc.) for any new project and/or initiative it is undertaking?
3. How many people in the organisation have a full and detailed understanding of the ecosystem and its interdependencies?
4. Does the organisation attempt to decrease the size and complexity of its IT ecosystem, and what has been (is being) done to decrease the size and complexity of the organisation's IT ecosystem?
5. Does the organisation have visibility of TOTAL IT costs? Did anyone benchmark the full IT ecosystem (including outsourced service providers, Cloud, SaaS, software licences/pay per use) cost?
6. How many domains and subdomains are used by the organisation?
7. When was the last time an independent audit of the organisation's domains and subdomains was done? How many unmanaged domains and subdomains were discovered?
8. How many certificates are used by the organisation? Do you see this as a risk? What is the probability of something going wrong?
9. Which certification authorities (trusted entities that issue digital certificates to verify the identity of websites, organisations, and individuals) are used by the organisation? Where are they located, and are they all trusted?
10. Does the organisation use wildcard certificates?
11. How frequently does the organisation renew certificates? Does the organisation use any certificates with expiry over 200 days? Tip: it is proposed to have expiry dates 200 days after September 2025, 100 days after September 2026, and 45 days after April 2027. Domain-verification reuse is reduced, too, of course, and pushed down to 10 days after September 2027.
12. Are certificate renewals automated?

DESSERT

PKI is a set of roles, policies, hardware, software, and procedures needed to create, manage, distribute, use, store, and revoke digital certificates and manage public-key encryption.[3] PKI manages digital certificates and public keys, enabling secure online communication and data protection. The purpose of PKI is to facilitate the **secure electronic transfer of information for a range of network activities** such as e-commerce, Internet banking, and confidential emails. It is required for activities where simple passwords are an inadequate authentication method and more rigorous proof is required to confirm the identity of the parties involved in the communication and to validate the confidentiality and integrity of the information being transferred. PKI involves the creation, management, distribution, use, storage, and revocation of digital certificates, which act as electronic passports or driver's licences for online entities. PKI underpins various security technologies like digital signatures and encryption, ensuring data integrity, authenticity, and confidentiality.

There are two ways one can look at complexity. One is a **micro-level**, or application-level complexity; the other is a **macro-level**, or IT ecosystem-level complexity.

The **Micro-level** has been described by Larry Tesler. The **law of conservation of complexity**, also known as **Tesler's Law** or the **Waterbed Theory**, is an adage in human-computer interaction stating that **every application has an inherent amount of complexity that cannot be removed or hidden.** Instead, it **must be dealt with**, either **in product development** or in the **user interaction.** This poses the question of who should be exposed to the complexity.

For example, should a software developer add complexity to the software code to make the interaction simpler for the user, or should the user deal with a complex interface so that the software code can be simple? Larry Tesler argued that, in most cases, an engineer should spend an extra week reducing the complexity of an application, vis-à-vis making millions of users spend an extra minute using the program because of the extra complexity. However, Bruce Tognazzini proposed that people resist reductions in the amount of complexity in their lives. Thus, when an application is simplified, users begin attempting more complex tasks.

It is a well-known fact, for example, that **software complexity** in aerospace systems **is increasing exponentially. The number of lines of source code** in aerospace systems is **doubling about every 4 years.** That **trend has been in place for at least five decades** and applies to both commercial and military aircraft. A good example of this is the growth of the code size for space missions that shows growth from about **50 lines** of code for the Mariner mission **in the early 1960s** to **about 5,000,000 lines** of code for the Mars Science Lab **in the early 2010s.**

It is now the right point to remember Frederic P. Brooks, Jr and his famous book "The Mythical Man-Month: Essays on Software Engineering," which was first published in 1975. Its central theme is that adding manpower to a software project that is behind schedule delays it even longer. This idea is known as **Brooks' Law.** Brooks's observations are based on his experiences at IBM while managing the development of OS/360. He had added more programmers to a project falling behind schedule, a decision that he would later conclude had, counter-intuitively, delayed the project even further.

As always, everything is not black and white, and microservices-based solutions come with numerous other side effects. One of them is the potential for uncoordinated development of various subcomponents that, in time, may (and likely will) result in messy architecture. But there are two immediate side effects that are worth discussing.

The first of these two side effects is linked to the exponential growth of complexity at the **macro-level.** When, instead of a monolithic solution, an organisation moves to a microservices-based architecture, the number of connections explodes. And this has an impact both on supportability (including, but not limited to, patching and testing) and on cyber security. One may argue that, similar to Brooks' law, moving to microservices architecture does not improve "time to market" if the organisation wants to perform adequate rigorous testing and maintain its desired cyber security posture. The other side effect impacting an organisation's cyber security posture is associated with the introduction of APIs, as APIs present a new attack surface.

Complexity comes with a high cost, too. According to Hackett Group's benchmark study on the **cost of complexity**, it was documented that:

- Organisations with higher-than-average technology complexity spend 25% more than average companies and 58% more than organisations with low technology complexity.
- The most significant cost factor is the number of applications per end user:
  - Organisations with a large number of applications employ 27% more Full-Time Equivalents (FTEs) than average companies.
  - World-class IT functions support 44% fewer applications per end user than typical organisations.

An organisation's IT ecosystem is the network of services, systems, providers, and other organisations connected to the organisation that creates and delivers information technology products and services. This ecosystem includes entities that are connected to but not always controlled directly by the organisation, such as, for example, a third party. Cloud computing resources used by the organisation are also part of its IT ecosystem. All of the assets associated with all of the IT ecosystem entities define the organisation's attack surface, and as such, the size and complexity of the organisation's IT ecosystem matter.

Human memory, as considered by cognitive neuroscience, which is a blend of cognitive psychology and neuroscience, is composed of three parts: sensory, short-term, and long-term. Let's focus for a minute on short-term memory.

Short-term memory (or "primary" or "active memory") is the capacity for holding a small amount of information in an active, readily available state for a short period of time. For example, short-term memory holds a phone number that has just been recited. The duration of short-term memory is estimated to be on the order of seconds. The commonly cited short-term memory capacity of 7 ± 2 items was discovered by a cognitive psychologist, George A. Miller of Harvard University's Department of Psychology. It was published in 1956 in Psychological Review and is occasionally referred to as Miller's law. It is often interpreted that the number of objects an average human can hold in short-term memory is 7 ± 2.

The term "working memory" was coined in the 1960s by Miller, Galanter, and Pribram. Working memory is a cognitive system with a limited capacity that can hold information temporarily. Effectively, working memory is the retention of a small amount of information in a readily accessible form. Working memory is often used synonymously with short-term memory, but some theorists consider the two forms of memory distinct, assuming that working memory allows for the manipulation of stored information, whereas short-term memory only refers to the short-term storage of information. Whether we accept that working memory and short-term memory are the same, the well-accepted fact is that working memory is a small amount of information that can be held in mind and used in the execution of cognitive tasks. Without going too deeply into cognitive neuroscience, we must acknowledge that our attention is limited and that our memory is imperfect.

NOTES

1 https://www.upguard.com/blog/biggest-data-breaches-australia.
2 https://www.itnews.com.au/feature/less-complexity-more-confidence-true-security-requires-real-clarity-620248?eid=1&edate=20250916&utm_source=20250916_AM&utm_medium=newsletter&utm_campaign=daily_newsletter.
3 https://en.wikipedia.org/wiki/Public_key_infrastructure.

Chapter 5

Digital revolution (and its consequences)

"Who are you?" said the Caterpillar.

This was not an encouraging opening for a conversation. Alice replied, rather shyly, "I - I hardly know, Sir, just at present - at least I know who I was when I got up this morning, but I think I must have been changed several times since then."

"What do you mean by that?" said the Caterpillar, sternly. "Explain yourself!"

"I can't explain myself, I'm afraid, Sir," said Alice, "because I am not myself, you see."

Alice's Adventures in Wonderland by Lewis Carroll

APPETISER

- On 19 July 2024, cyber security company CrowdStrike distributed a faulty update to its security software that caused global problems with Microsoft Windows computers running it:
  - Roughly 8.5 million systems crashed and were unable to properly restart.
  - It was called the largest outage in the history of information technology and "historic in scale."
- Conservatively, the cost of this outage is estimated at least $1.5 billion in losses.
- Digital transformation is the integration of digital technology into all areas of the business.
- This approach results in an *ongoing escalation of the organisation's reliance on IT.*
- Matthew Anderson: "We need to *shift our focus from prioritising efficiency at all costs to balancing efficiency with resilience.*"
- Zachary Ginsburg:

  "…other global events, such as the July CrowdStrike outage, have raised questions about whether organisations over-rely on their largest IT

DOI: 10.1201/9781003730514-6

vendors. For example, customers with a concentration of services with one vendor may face elevated risk in the event of outages, or they may face unanticipated changes in services depending on new regulations or legal decisions in the EU, U.S., or elsewhere. Because third parties, like SaaS vendors, rely on other vendors, organisations may not realise the full extent of their exposure."

MAIN COURSE

On 19 July 2024, American cyber security company CrowdStrike distributed a faulty update to its Falcon Sensor security software that caused widespread problems with Microsoft Windows computers running it. As a result, roughly **8.5 million systems crashed** and were **unable to properly restart** in what has been called **the largest outage in the history of information technology** and "historic in scale."

The **impact of this disaster was global** and very severe. More than 3,300 flights were cancelled globally, and payment and payroll systems were disrupted, while banks, healthcare providers, supermarkets and media companies were among the other businesses reporting the "blue screen of death" and network outages. **Conservatively, the cost of this outage is estimated at least A\$1.5 billion in losses** and A\$200 million in damages in New South Wales (NSW) alone, while global insured losses from that massive IT outage are likely to range from US\$400 million to US\$1.5 billion.

The world was lucky that only Microsoft devices and services were impacted, and none of the Unix/Linux derivatives were. Otherwise, the impact would have been much worse. This scenario had been predicted as early as 2003 when Dan Geer (whom I was privileged to meet at the 1989 USENIX in San Diego, CA) and his colleagues pointed to the negative impacts on cyber security caused by software monopolies like Microsoft (p. 48).[1] This theme was reiterated later in 2022 in the World Economic Forum's "Global Risks Report 2022,"[2] which is a highly recommended reading for the readers of this book.

And technically, this was not a cyber security incident (although one can argue that it was, as Availability was impacted - see Chapter 2)! The root cause of this was a **cumulative effect** of the Digital Transformation (which is discussed in this chapter) and supply chain vulnerability (see Chapter 9).

Having said that, this massive worldwide IT outage is not the result of a cyber security incident. It is important to understand what consequences a major cyber security incident can have worldwide. Humanity has just received the wake-up call and the first-hand experience of what consequences a major cyber security incident may have worldwide.

The **term "Digital Transformation" was coined in 2011** by the consulting firm Capgemini in partnership with MIT. They defined it as **"the use of technology to radically improve performance or the reach of businesses."** In short, digital transformation has emerged as the compass guiding organisations towards a more flexible, efficient, and customer-centric future. Digital transformation is a complex process that involves integrating new technologies into an organisation's operations and requires a holistic shift in how organisations work and communicate.

According to Deloitte, **"digital transformation is all about becoming a digital enterprise - an organisation that uses technology to continuously evolve all aspects of its business models."**[3]

Digital transformation is about evolving an organisation's business **by experimenting with new technologies** and rethinking the organisation's current approach to common issues. And because it's an evolution, digital transformation doesn't necessarily have a clear endpoint.

So, **digital transformation is the process of using digital technologies to transform existing traditional and non-digital business processes and services, or creating new ones,** to meet the evolving market and customer expectations, thus completely altering the way businesses are managed and operated and how value is delivered to customers. **Digital transformation is the process by which organisations embed technologies across their businesses** to drive fundamental change.

Effectively, **digital transformation is the integration of digital technology into all areas of a business,** fundamentally changing how an organisation operates and delivers value to customers. It's also a **cultural change** that requires organisations to **continually challenge the status quo, experiment, and get comfortable with failure.**

Digital transformation is the process of adoption and implementation of digital technology by an organisation to create new or modify existing products, services, and operations by means of **translating business processes into a digital format.**

As technology evolves, so should business. At this point, it's not about organisations choosing to transform; it is more about deciding how to transform. **This approach is** effectively **based on the ongoing escalation of the organisation's reliance on IT.**

We often hear the saying **"The Road to Hell is Paved with Good Intentions."** According to The Phrase Finder (https://www.phrases.org.uk/), the expression is often attributed to the Cistercian abbot Saint Bernard of Clairvaux (1090–1153), but that provenance is suspect given that the earliest reference to Saint Bernard saying this is in a work written almost 500 years later.

This saying is more-than-true today, especially for digital transformations.

Here, the focus will not be on the positives, but rather on the negatives and unintended consequences of digital transformations. So, what are the pitfalls and problems that digital transformation brings to organisations?

The original definition of digital transformation emphasised the goal of **performance improvement or business development enabled by technology, not technology itself being the goal**. But in many cases, labelling a strategic plan as a digital transformation (or sometimes, digital modernisation) has diluted the concept of a clear and compelling goal and has **created a focus on the wrong thing: on technology**. The term "digital transformation" is dangerous because it sends the wrong message.

Focusing on technology is dangerous, especially if this comes from the CEO (or their direct reports).

Even if the CEO is not pushing any specific technology, the overall mood of digital transformations creates a desire for technology innovation within the CEO's direct reports and further down the food chain, and this, in its turn, has an even higher probability of implementation of a multiplicity of various technologies without a full understanding of the holistic impact. As a result, one can often observe the following symptoms:

- Lack of strategic approach and subsequently **lack of centrally managed** business and enterprise **architecture**, resulting in a piecemeal approach and increased cyber security risks.
- Proliferation of shadow IT, when in many cases centralised IT does not have visibility and knowledge of all technological components, especially SaaS solutions (see Chapter 8) bought on a credit card and used within the organisation, and lately - shadow AI.
- An extremely high level of IT landscape complexity (see Chapter 4) that no one understands end-to-end.

These symptoms create an untenable situation for any CISO who is not able, under these circumstances, to adequately assess all cyber security risks and subsequently develop an adequate mitigation strategies and approach. This becomes even more difficult in the case (which is almost always the case) of organisations that do not articulate and document their risk appetite (see Chapter 2). If in the past, these symptoms were observed mainly in large multidivisional organisations (say, over 3,000 FTEs), today one can observe these symptoms even in smaller (just 200–300 FTEs) organisations.

The CrowdStrike incident (mentioned at the very beginning of this chapter), or, better to say, its consequences, prompted (at last) some rational thinking. Glasgow Caledonian University "smart technology" expert Matthew Anderson said, "**We need to shift our focus from prioritising efficiency at all costs to balancing efficiency with resilience.**"

In particular, one of the consequences of digital transformations is the reality of supply chains (see Chapter 9) becoming heavily dependent on technology.[4]

Advanced IT systems now enable real-time tracking, inventory management, and seamless communication across global supply chains. This has made them more efficient, transparent, and responsive. But to achieve such precision and speed, they've also become highly interdependent. Making supply chains operate efficiently hinges on the timely success of everyone and **all the technology** involved. We've now seen just how quickly things can come undone. And **the question now is** (and has been for a while!) **when, not if, the next global IT outage will occur.**

It is worth mentioning that another part of the so-called digital transformations resulted in the rapid proliferation of QR codes in general (from restaurant menus to registration at the entry point of many organisations). One should remember that **QR codes** embedded in PDFs **create additional attack vectors that are not easy to defend against.**

It is crystal clear that IT became a victim of its own success.

The weak points are the millions of components, nodes, networks, pieces of software and APIs used today by most organisations (see Chapters 4 and 5). Modern IT ecosystems are very complex and are highly interconnected (think of possible network disruptions) and interdependent.

Now, think of cyber-attacks. Terror attacks. Sabotage. Today, many organisations rely on the same Cloud and SaaS providers and the same cyber security solutions. The result is a form of **digital monoculture.** IT ecosystems dominated by a single species, technology, supplier, or strategy are commonly referred to as **monocultures.** Modern IT ecosystems with standardised hardware, software, and network configurations have evolved into what some describe as a **digital monoculture.**

However, **digital monocultures are inherently less resilient.** Lacking diversity and natural defences, a single threat or incident can have widespread and devastating effects. A good example from a non-IT area is the 19th-century potato blight pandemic in Ireland. Since all of Ireland's potatoes were genetically similar, a classic monoculture, the disease spread quickly, decimating the country's food supply and causing mass starvation. And digital monocultures are more susceptible to cyber-attacks. For instance, the 2017 WannaCry ransomware attack exploited a vulnerability in the Windows operating system. Because so many organisations used the same operating system version, the ransomware quickly infected hundreds of thousands of computers worldwide.

As explained by Senior Lecturer in Applied Ethics & Cyber Security at Griffith University, David Tuffley[5]:

> "Modern IT infrastructure is highly interconnected and interdependent. If one component fails, it can lead to a situation where the **failed component triggers a chain reaction that impacts other parts of the system.** The catalogue of possible causes reads like the script of a disaster movie."

According to Zachary Ginsburg, Senior Director, Research of Gartner Risk & Audit Practice:

> "...other global events, such as the July CrowdStrike outage, have raised questions about whether **organisations over-rely on their largest**

IT vendors. For example, customers with a **concentration of services with one vendor may face elevated risk in the event of outages,** or they may face unanticipated changes in services depending on new regulations or legal decisions in the EU, U.S., or elsewhere. **Because third parties,** like SaaS vendors, **rely on other vendors, organisations may not realise the full extent of their exposure."**

Unfortunately, people keep adding more and more extensions to the castle that has been built on a quicksand of von Neumann architecture, TCP/IP, DNS, and BGP using unsafe methods and materials with not fully understood characteristics.

It appears that organisations, users and customers are starting to question more and more the actual business value of what is being delivered as a result of the digital transformations; "where's the value" of the latest IT capability being built?[6] Couple this with the continuous stream of cyber incidents, and the user base is turning off - I know people who now reject all offers of anything they have to sign up for, simply on the basis that they don't want to share their Personally Identifiable Information (PII) more than it already has been shared and simply don't see any value anyway.

So, now, after several wake-up calls, it is the right time to urgently review how organisations rely (end-to-end) on technologies and how they can increase the resilience of their operations in the wake of a major technological outage.

QUESTIONS

These questions are important, as they prompt thinking and allow the target audience to understand the organisation's potential exposure and what they personally can do to improve the organisation's cyber security posture. To get answers to some of these questions, the target audience may need to go to their CIOs and CISOs.

1. Has anyone in the organisation ever considered the negative side effects of digital transformation? Has the organisation undertaken a detailed risk analysis of potential negative cyber security consequences of digital transformation?
2. Has anyone in the organisation ever thought of the impact on the organisation's cyber security posture, looking at all aspects of it, including Confidentiality, Integrity, Availability, Privacy, Authenticity, and Non-Repudiation?
3. What is the impact of digital transformation on the organisation's attack surface, technical debt, shadow IT, and insider threat landscape? (e.g., are these reduced or expanded?)

DESSERT

To analyse the Log4j incident, let's use a technique familiar to many readers of this book, the "5 Whys" (sometimes called "Five Whys") that was developed in the 1930s by Sakichi Toyoda, the Japanese industrialist, inventor, and founder of Toyota Industries. This technique became popular in the 1970s across many organisations. The technique is remarkably simple: when a problem occurs, you drill down to its root cause by asking "Why?" five times.[7]

As recovery from this major worldwide IT outage continued, much of the discussion was focused on CrowdStrike, human error or inadequate/insufficient testing. And this is the first "Why" that obviously does not give the answer about the root cause.

The next question one may ask is why so many organisations suffered the consequences of this massive worldwide IT outage? The answer to this question is obvious: because they are all users of CrowdStrike. This is the second "Why" that again does not give the answer about the root cause.

The next question one may ask is why so many organisations use CrowdStrike? The answer to this question is also obvious: because CrowdStrike is the market leader, as confirmed by Gartner and Forrester. This is the third "Why" that again does not give the answer about the root cause.

The next question one may ask is, why do so many organisations need to use CrowdStrike? The answer to this question is obvious and has two aspects: because they all heavily rely on IT in conducting their business, and because of the exponential growth of cyber security threats and incidents (see Andrew Jenkinson, "Ransomware and Cybercrime," CRC Press, 2022, for example). This is the fourth "Why" that again does not give the answer about the root cause.

The next question one may ask is why modern organisations, both in the private sector and government, rely so heavily on IT. And the answer to this fifth "Why" finally gives us the root cause: this is because of the so-called **digital transformation** (sometimes called **digital revolution**) that has been embraced by various organisations.

There is no doubt that digital transformations aspire to achieve multiple things, from improving customer experience and customer satisfaction to minimising waste, improving productivity, and reducing costs, to increasing efficiency and profitability of organisations. While the ROI of digital transformation depends on a variety of factors, the right technology can greatly improve an organisation's business functions and how customers engage with it.

The MIT Sloan Management Review, a publication that focuses on how management transforms in the digital age, says, "Digital transformation is better thought of as **continual adaptation to a constantly changing**

environment." MIT Sloan Management Review highlights three key areas of digital transformation:

- **Customer Experience** - working to understand customers in more detail, **using technology** to fuel customer growth and creating more customer touchpoints.
- **Operational Processes** - improving internal processes by **leveraging digitisation and automation,** enabling employees with **digital tools** and collecting data to monitor performance and make more strategic business decisions.
- **Business Models** - transforming the business by augmenting physical offerings with **digital tools and services,** introducing **digital products,** and **using technology** to provide global shared services.

Focusing on technology is dangerous, especially if this comes from the CEO. In the past, this has often created an "inflight magazine syndrome" when a CEO saw an ad in an inflight magazine and then pushed the CIO to implement this technology without any analysis of its actual suitability and its impact on the organisation. Lately, this has been more of a vendor (and/or lobbyist for the public sector) pitching.

Commercial benefits of digital monocultures include cost savings, increased efficiency, and more streamlined management, as a uniform IT environment, for example, is easier and cheaper to manage than one with diverse systems. Updates, patches, and system monitoring can be centralised so IT staff don't have to juggle diverse systems. Also, getting different systems, software, and applications to work together seamlessly (known as interoperability) is more readily achievable in monoculture-like IT environments. Finally, with standardisation, users don't need to learn multiple platforms, which shortens training times and makes it easier for employees to adapt to new software updates or system changes.

NOTES

1 https://www.tuhs.org/Archive/Documentation/AUUGN/AUUGN-V24.4.pdf.
2 https://www.weforum.org/publications/global-risks-report-2022/in-full/chapter-3-digital-dependencies-and-cyber-vulnerabilities/.
3 https://whatfix.com/digital-transformation/#:~:text=Digital%20transformation%20is%20the%20process,operated%2C%20and%20how%20value%20is.
4 https://theconversation.com/a-global-it-outage-brought-supply-chains-to-their-knees-we-need-to-be-better-prepared-next-time-235124.
5 https://www.innovationaus.com/one-small-update-crippled-millions-of-it-systems-its-a-timely-warning/.

6 https://www.cio.com/article/4040188/6-signs-of-a-dying-digital-transformation.
   html?utm_date=20250820234141&utm_campaign=CIO%20Australia%20
   First%20Look&utm_content=slotno-3-title-6%20signs%20of%20
   a%20dying%20digital%20transformation&utm_term=ANZ&utm_
   medium=email&utm_source=Adestra&aid=16578935&huid=40
   eef72f-d3d6-4c7b-971a-f71e96817901.
7 https://en.wikipedia.org/wiki/Five_whys.

Chapter 6

Agile curse

"Would you tell me, please, which way I ought to go from here?"

"That depends a good deal on where you want to get to."

"I don't much care where."

"Then it doesn't matter which way you go."

Alice's Adventures in Wonderland by Lewis Carroll

APPETISER

- A project is a temporary and unique endeavour designed to produce a product, service, or result with a defined beginning and end. The temporary nature of projects stands in contrast with business as usual (BAU) or operations.
- There's an old saying in software and systems development that goes something like, *"fast, good or cheap - pick any two"*. It is known as a triple constraint. The "agile" approach is focused on "fast" (delivery of new functionality). This ticks off one of these three. Intuitively (and this is arguably one of the selling points of the "agile" approach), the second one to tick off is "cheap." And now think about it - one can have any two out of three, and we have ticked off two already. Can the "agile" approach beat this and deliver all three, including *good in a cyber security sense?*
- Today, over 70% of US organisations are using the "agile" approach.
- One of the biggest challenges the "agile" approach poses to achieving the required strength of cyber security posture is hiding in sprints, or to be more accurate, in the duration of sprints. Sprints' duration (be it 2 weeks or 2 months) simply does not allow enough time for proper security design, independent reviews, and security testing, which creates a high probability of security gaps being hidden in the delivered product.

DOI: 10.1201/9781003730514-7

- If you are building a new house, would you prefer security for it to be delivered using "agile" methodology or a traditional "waterfall" methodology? You probably would prefer the traditional "waterfall" methodology in this case. But people keep using "agile" methodology to deliver very expensive business-critical systems and solutions, resulting in enormous cyber security exposure!
- The average cost of a cyber security breach reached US$4.9 million in 2024, and even small businesses can expect to pay US$120,000 to US$1.24M in 2025 to respond to and resolve a cyber security incident.
- About 30 years ago, I had a break-in at my house. The police officer who arrived at the "crime scene" told me, "What do you want? You live in a high-crime area." *The unparalleled level of organisations' dependency upon the Internet means that we are all in a "high crime" area now!*

MAIN COURSE

A project is a temporary and unique endeavour designed to produce a product, service, or result with a defined beginning and end (usually time-constrained and often constrained by time, funding, and/or staffing) undertaken to meet unique goals and objectives, typically to bring about beneficial changes or added value. The **temporary nature of projects** stands in contrast with **business as usual** (BAU) or **operations,** which are repetitive, permanent, or semi-permanent functional activities to produce products or services. In practice, the management of such distinct production approaches requires distinct technical skills and management strategies.

Project management is the process of supervising the work to achieve all project goals within the given constraints. This information is usually described in project documentation, created at the beginning of the development process. The primary constraints are **scope, time, and budget.** The secondary challenge is to optimise the allocation of necessary inputs and apply them to meet pre-defined objectives.

Project management is the application of knowledge, skills, tools, and techniques to project activities to achieve the successful delivery of project objectives. It's the practice of planning, organising, and executing the tasks needed to turn a brilliant idea into a tangible product, service, or deliverable. As a discipline, project management developed from several fields of application, including civil construction, engineering, and heavy defence activities.

There's an old saying in software and systems development that goes something like, "fast, good or cheap - pick any two." It is known as a **triple constraint**. This concept is familiar to anyone who has ever felt the pressure of weighing the opposing forces of scope (including quality), speed, and cost against each other. These constraints are often visualised as the "**project management triangle**" or "iron triangle," where each side represents one of these constraints. The project management triangle was popularised by Harold Kerzner in his landmark work, "Project Management: A Systems Approach to Planning, Scheduling, and Controlling."

One of the oldest, most traditional and most popular methodologies in project management is the "waterfall" methodology. This type of methodology is followed in projects where requirements are well-known and fixed, and no further changes are expected. The "waterfall" development method originates in the construction and manufacturing industries. It operates in highly regimented physical environments that are very difficult, expensive, or impossible to change or adapt once work has begun. The "waterfall" methodology is a **linear sequential** design process used in early software and systems development processes.

Traditional "waterfall" methodology is a well-established project management workflow. Like a real waterfall, each process phase cascades downward sequentially through six stages (requirements, design, build, or implementation, testing, verification/integration, deployment, and maintenance). In "waterfall," **each stage of the workflow needs to be completed before moving on to the next stage.** It is important to note that this is a **linear project management approach,** where stakeholder and customer **requirements are gathered at the beginning of the project,** and **then a sequential project plan is created to accommodate those requirements.**

Up until the late 1990s, most software projects followed a simple "waterfall" life cycle. Requirements were gathered upfront; the solution was designed, built, and tested. The release to users for user acceptance testing (UAT) occurred, followed by bug fixes, before the final production release. This approach worked well for many IT projects because they tended to be tightly scoped in both time and cost. It works with relatively fixed requirements that do not change much during the project. Often, projects were small enough for easy management of changes, often by adding an extra week or two to the project timeline. This adjustment rarely caused significant problems.

Proliferation of the Internet (and Internet applications), as well as the desire to fast-track "time to market" and the digital transformation trend, resulted in the development and subsequent proliferation of the "agile" methodology with a focus on creating working software quickly, collaborating with customers frequently, and being able to adapt to changes easily. This methodology enables teams to follow a cycle of planning, executing, and evaluating and is especially beneficial for projects that have uncertain requirements.

One can define "agile" methodology in project management as a structured approach that segments projects into manageable phases, focusing on continuous improvement. It is an iterative process that involves planning, execution, and evaluation and is about frequent delivery, rapid testing, and continuous refinement. That is great for projects that require constant updates, like selling software or evolving a website. However, it is not so good for projects that need to be built from scratch.

For this reason, "agile" methodology is often focused on short-term projects that deliver value quickly, while long-term projects remain stuck in the planning and implementation phase. The emphasis of "agile" development is on collaboration and communication throughout the project lifecycle. It involves iterative planning and changing plans during implementation. This ensures all parties work towards a common goal. **Today, over 70% of US organisations are using the "agile" approach.**

One of the biggest challenges that the "agile" approach poses to achieving the required strength of cyber security posture is hiding in sprints, or to be more accurate, in the duration of sprints. **Sprints' duration (be it 2 weeks or 2 months) simply does not allow enough time for proper security design, independent reviews, and security testing, which creates a high probability of security gaps being hidden in the delivered product.** In addition to this, **business stakeholders usually do not understand cyber security (and the potential implications of not following best practices in this space)** and always press for the delivery of functionality. The **pressure to deliver functionality often prevents software bug fixing, pushing this activity further down the track. And even if these gaps are discovered later** during security testing at the UAT stage, **the cost of closing them becomes very high.** Even if the cost is tolerable (although typically by this stage the project has already run out of money), **the organisation can rarely tolerate any additional delay to the product release.**

One other interesting real-life observation is that the "agile" approach makes it difficult to define the endpoint, as focus is mainly on the delivery of the so-called Minimum Viable Product (MVP), which is a **product with enough features to attract early-adopter customers and validate a product idea** early in the product development cycle. In industries such as software development, an MVP can help the product team receive user feedback as quickly as possible to iterate and improve the product. However, multiple real-life examples show that **projects rarely (if at all) progress beyond an MVP that is often not clearly defined** at the outset. More often than not, projects delivered using various flavours of "agile" methodology run out of either money or time, or both and stop at an (and often partially de-scoped) MVP.

Now, remember the saying: "fast, good or cheap - pick any two"? The "agile" approach is focused on "fast" (delivery of new functionality). This ticks off one of these three. Intuitively (and this is arguably one of the selling points of the "agile" approach), the second one to tick off is "cheap." And now think about it - one can have any two out of three, and we have ticked off two already. Can the "agile" approach beat this and deliver all three, including **good in a cyber security sense?** The answer is - extremely unlikely.

Now, let me ask you a question. If you are building a new house, would you prefer security for it to be delivered using the "agile" methodology or the traditional "waterfall" methodology? You probably would prefer the traditional "waterfall" methodology in this case. But people keep using "agile" methodology to deliver very expensive business-critical systems and solutions, resulting in enormous cyber security exposure!

According to IBM,[1] the average cost of cyber security breach reached US$4.9 million in 2024, a 10% increase over the previous year. This increase has a strong correlation with a continued and significant increase in the adoption and application of "agile" methodology across various fields. In 2024, the average cost of an Australian data breach hit A$4.26 million,[2] and Australian companies needed an average of 266 days to identify and contain cyber incidents. This is average, but what about maximum?

The biggest data breach costs, including fines, penalties, and settlements so far, are[3]:

- Meta (Facebook): US$1.3 Billion...
- Didi Global: US$1.19 billion...
- Amazon: US$877 million...
- TikTok: €530 million (US$600 million)...
- Equifax: at least US$575 million...
- Meta (Facebook, Instagram): US$413 million...
- Instagram: US$403 million...
- TikTok: €345 million (US$370 million)...

While the true cost of a data breach varies, on average, even **small organisations** can expect to **pay US$120,000 to US$1.24M in 2025 to respond to and resolve a cyber security incident.**

This reminded me of an almost 30-year-old incident when I had a break-in at my house. The police officer who arrived at the "crime scene" told me, "What do you want? You live in a high-crime area." The unparalleled level of organisations' dependency upon the Internet means that we are all in a "high crime" area now!

As one of the final comments, it is worth mentioning that according to some sources, "agile" development is fading in popularity in large organisations - and developer burnout is a key factor.[4]

Further proliferation of "agile" development methodology is facing significant obstacles as the tech industry goes through a wave of changes, including developer burnout, shifting working environments, and the rise of AI. One of the studies found that while smaller organisations continue to consider "agile" as a powerful productivity and organisational framework that exhibits "obvious benefits," medium-sized and larger organisations are less satisfied with what "agile" can do for them and are more likely to pick a software development strategy that uses several different frameworks.

QUESTIONS

These questions are important, as they prompt thinking and allow the target audience to understand the organisation's potential exposure and what they personally can do to improve the organisation's cyber security posture. To get answers to some of these questions, the target audience may need to go to their CIOs and CISOs.

1. Has anyone in the organisation ever considered the negative side effects of using the "agile" methodology?
2. Has anyone in the organisation ever thought of the impact of "agile methodology" on the organisation's cyber security posture?
3. What measures are taken by the organisation to ensure an adequate cyber security posture while using "agile methodology"?
4. How many "agile projects" within the organisation have been delivered on time and on budget? How many of them progressed beyond MVP?
5. How much does the organisation pay for poor software quality and delays?

DESSERT

The "waterfall" methodology is not exactly a method as much as it is an approach; however, the six distinct stages that make up this cycle are very common in most software development processes: Requirements, Design, Testing, Implementation, Verification/Integration, Deployment, and Maintenance.

- **Requirements.** During this phase, the big picture of the project's requirements is outlined. Requirements typically fall into one of two categories: Functional Requirements (FR) and Nonfunctional Requirements (NFR).
- **Design.** Once project requirements are understood, the next step is to come up with ways to design solutions that meet them. As such, the design process outlines the result and how it will be achieved.
- **Build or Implementation.** During this phase, one of multiple possible designs is selected, as well as the technology to implement it. This could involve collecting data and inspecting whether the design is able to meet the requirements.
- **Testing.** In this phase, all system components are tested. This includes an integration test, which makes sure that each part works properly with the others; a functional test, which guarantees that all functionality meets requirements; and a test of performance, which ensures that the system can handle peak loads without crashing or slowing down significantly.

- **Validation/Verification/Integration.** During this phase, what has been built and preliminary tested in the previous phases is tested to determine whether it complies with and delivers against the requirements being integrated into the target environment.
- **Deployment and Maintenance.** The project isn't over once it has gone through validation, verification, and integration. The system still needs to be deployed and maintained. Maintenance also applies to adding new features or functionality.

One of the advantages of the "waterfall" approach is that it has a **fixed timeline and budget** because the project goals are specific and defined from the start. Once the goal of the project is established, the "waterfall" methodology does not involve frequent feedback or collaboration from the client, apart from established milestones or deliverables for each phase. This makes it easier for project managers to plan and communicate with stakeholders or business partners. However, while this can help with planning, it is also only practical when there is a clear and fixed end goal. One of the disadvantages of this methodology is that addressing unexpected problems can be difficult, expensive, and time-consuming.

It is also important to remember the cost of fixing software bugs (or errors) discovered at different stages of the project. Software bugs are more than just a minor inconvenience. According to the Consortium for Information and Software Quality (CISQ), **poor software quality costs the US economy $2.08 trillion in 2020 alone.** The costs of software bugs are not just limited to the direct costs that a software developer must incur to fix software bugs. Another consequence of software bugs is productivity loss because bugs contribute to workers' downtime, disruptions, and delays. Financial loss also occurs due to a loss of reputation, because buggy software can indicate to clients that the organisation does not produce high-quality products. Furthermore, **software bugs often introduce security risks,** which can have a large financial impact in the form of cyber-attacks, data breaches, and financial theft. And there is a significant difference in the cost of fixing software bugs discovered during various stages of the so-called Software Development Life Cycle (SDLC).

In 2004, NASA published a paper illustrating the escalation of the cost of error fixing through the project life cycle. The findings in this paper are astounding! The results show the degree to which costs escalate as errors are discovered and fixed at later and later phases in the project life cycle. Let's define the cost of fixing a requirements error discovered during the requirements phase to be 1 unit; the cost to fix that same error discovered during the design phase increases to 3–8 units; at the build phase, the cost to fix the same error is 7–16 units; at the integration and test phase, the cost to fix the same error becomes 21–78 units; and at the operations phase, the cost to fix the same requirements error ranges from 29 units to more than 1,500 units. Discussion about choosing the right project management methodology must include this aspect, but, unfortunately, it is often omitted.

Another extreme example of information on error-related cost factors can be found in a book on designing cost-effective space missions.[5] These systems' cost factors represent the costs of fixing errors in electronic hardware. Depending on the phase in which the error is discovered, the resulting costs are as follows:

Phase	Resulting cost
Product Design	$1,000
Product Testing	$10,000
Process Design	$100,000
Low-Rate Initial Production	$1,000,000
Final Production/Distribution	$10,000,000

One of the perceived disadvantages of the "waterfall" approach is lengthy requirements and design stages that, in the eyes of the customer, do not produce any "tangible" outcomes, or better to say, a usable system or solution. This perceived disadvantage spawned the "agile" approach. One can argue that this perceived disadvantage is also an advantage that allows earlier identification of errors. Also, before diving into the "agile" approach, it is important to note that the **focus on upfront requirements and design in the "waterfall" approach means that security aspects can be dealt with at all six stages of the project.**

In the "agile" methodology, a project is broken down into several dynamic phases, commonly known as sprints. After every sprint, the team reflects and looks back to see if there was anything that could be improved so they can adjust their strategy for the next sprint. Within the "agile" methodology, the process consists of four main stages: Preparation, Sprint Planning, Sprint, and Sprint Retrospective.

- **Preparation:** during the preparation stage, the product owner creates a backlog of features they want to be included in the final product. Then, the development team estimates how long each feature will take to build.
- **Sprint Planning:** the sprint planning meeting is where the team decides which features from the product backlog they are going to work on during the sprint. A sprint is a set period (**usually between 2 weeks and 2 months**) during which the development team must achieve a specific goal. The team also decides how many of each type of task they can complete during the sprint. For example, the team may decide they can complete three coding tasks, two testing tasks, and one documentation task during the sprint. This information is then added to the sprint backlog.
- **Sprint:** during the sprint, the team works on completing the tasks in the sprint backlog. They may also come across new issues to address

or software bugs that need to be fixed. If this happens, they will add these issues and software bugs to the backlog and prioritise them accordingly. At the end of the sprint, the development team should have completed all features in the sprint backlog. If not, the team will carry them over to the next sprint.

- **Sprint retrospective:** after each sprint, the team holds a sprint review meeting where they demonstrate completed features to the product owner and stakeholders. They also discuss what went well during the sprint and how they could improve the next one. This feedback loop helps to ensure that each sprint is more successful than the last.

It is indisputable that the "agile" approach has succeeded in many cases in faster "time to market" and higher levels of flexibility that allow rapid modernisation of functionality. It also gave business stakeholders stronger engagement and influence on what, when, and how will be delivered.

However, there is (as always) a price to pay for this. One of the challenges, especially in larger organisations, is that development teams typically refine their backlog up to two to three iterations ahead, but in larger organisations, the product marketing team needs to plan further ahead for their commitments to the market and discussions with customers. They will often work on a very high-level, 12 to 18-month roadmap, then plan collaboratively with the teams for three months of work. The development teams will still get into detailed refinement 2–3 iterations ahead, only getting into detailed task plans for the next iteration.

Not everything can be shoehorned into a single sprint. It is time now to introduce epics. But before we do this, we need to introduce some other "agile" terminology. Stories, also called "user stories," are short requirements or requests written from the perspective of an end user. An epic is too large to be completed in a single sprint, but it is a smaller representation of work than the highest-level goals and initiatives. An epic is typically completed over the course of several sprints or longer. Initiatives are collections of epics that drive towards a common goal.

There are multiple variations of "agile" methodology, ranging from various "classical" pure "agile" to "hybrid" models mixing the "agile" approach with the traditional "waterfall" approach to requirements and design, followed by actual delivery using one of the "agile" variations. The "agile" methodology is effectively an umbrella name for several different variations. Some of the most common variations are Kanban, Scrum, Extreme Programming (XP), Adaptive Project Framework (APF), Extreme Project Management (XPM), Adaptive Software Development (ASD), Dynamic Systems Development Method (DSDM), Feature Driven Development (FDD), Crystal Methods, Disciplined Agile Delivery (DAD), Scrum@Scale, and Scaled Agile Framework.

NOTES

1 https://www.ibm.com/reports/data-breach.
2 https://securitybrief.com.au/story/average-cost-of-an-australian-data-breach-hits-aud-4-26-million.
3 https://www.csoonline.com/article/567531/the-biggest-data-breach-fines-penalties-and-settlements-so-far.html.
4 https://www.itpro.com/software/agile-development-is-fading-in-popularity-at-large-enterprises-and-developer-burnout-is-a-key-factor#:~:text=Software-,Agile%20development%20is%20fading%20in%20popularity%20at%20large%20enterprises%20%2D%20and,burnout%20is%20a%20key%20factor&text=Agile%20development%20methodology%20is%20facing,and%20the%20rise%20of%20AI.
5 https://ntrs.nasa.gov/api/citations/20100036670/downloads/20100036670.pdf.

Chapter 7

Cloud

Who owns the breach?

> "Oh, you can't help that," said the Cat: "we're all mad here. I'm mad. You're mad."
>
> "How do you know I'm mad?" said Alice.
>
> "You must be," said the Cat, "or you wouldn't have come here."
>
> *Alice's Adventures in Wonderland* by Lewis Carroll

APPETISER

- Cloud computing is a technology that allows users to store, access, and manage data and applications over the Internet.
- Cloud computing is effectively a form of outsourcing.
- As of 2024, 46 percent of organisations already have workloads in the Public Cloud.
- Worldwide spending on Public Cloud services will reach US$824.763 billion in 2025.
- Despite the cost savings promise, Cloud turned out to be expensive, and quite a few organisations now consider so-called Cloud repatriation.
- The shared responsibility model is a security framework that outlines roles and responsibilities shared between Cloud Service Providers (CSPs) and their clients to ensure security. It aims to determine accountability and responsibility so that all aspects of Cloud security are covered. Under the shared responsibility model:
  - The CSP is responsible for the *security of the Cloud*.
  - The client is responsible for *security in the Cloud*.
- The notion of shared responsibility is not well understood and often misunderstood, leading to dangerous assumptions:
  - Only 13% of organisations that experienced a breach reported that they understand *their Cloud security responsibilities*.

DOI: 10.1201/9781003730514-8

- One of the challenges of the shared responsibility model is a *clear and shared understanding* of who is responsible for what.
- In its 2024 report, CrowdStrike noted a 75% increase in Cloud intrusions.
- By 2025, 99% of Cloud security failures are forecast to come from customers.

MAIN COURSE

The term "Cloud" is one of today's most frequently used buzzwords. Whether one is talking about storage, computing, or security, people are always referencing the Cloud. This term refers to a symbol of an unknown domain. When network engineers were trying to understand what devices were on what network and how they intertwined with the Internet, they needed a way to illustrate and visualise it.

How big is Cloud usage today? According to Gartner, **worldwide spending on Public Cloud** services is forecast to grow 20.4% to a total of US$675.4 billion in 2024, up from US$561 billion in 2023, and **will reach US$824.763 billion in 2025.** As of 2024, 46 percent of organisations already have workloads in the Public Cloud, with 8 percent planning to move additional workloads to the Cloud in the next 12 months; in addition to this, 48 percent have data stored on the Public Cloud.

Today, one can define Cloud computing as a **technology that allows users to store, access, and manage data and applications over the Internet.** Instead of storing data and running applications on a local computer or server, Cloud computing allows users to access these resources from remote servers, which are managed and maintained by Cloud service providers (CSPs).

So, one can arrive at the conclusion that **Cloud computing is a form of outsourcing,** or, as per its definition, obtaining goods or services by contract from an outside supplier.

The Cloud value proposition was perceived as being so strong that in **2013, the Australian Government declared a Cloud-first strategy.** As part of its 2021 Secure Cloud Strategy, the Government has stated that moving to the Cloud will "generate a faster pace of delivery, continuous improvement cycles and broad access to services." In August, 2015 New South Wales (NSW) Government followed this trend and introduced a Cloud policy that was updated in 2020 and further complemented by a Cloud strategy that works hand-in-hand with the NSW Digital Strategy and the Federal Digital Transformation Strategy.

However, like everything, outsourcing in general, and Cloud computing in particular, has its drawbacks:

- lack of business or domain knowledge,
- language and cultural barriers,
- time zone differences,
- lack of direct control and reliance on a third party,
- contractual risks,
- supply chain/network dependency,
- etc.

Despite the cost savings promise, the Cloud turned out to be expensive, and some organisations learnt this the hard way. As a result, quite a few organisations now consider so-called **Cloud repatriation**, which involves moving applications or workloads, or data out of a Public Cloud environment.

Talking about Cloud repatriation, it is important to note that cost is not the only driver for this. For example, latency, performance, and management may be drivers - super latency-sensitive applications may not meet performance expectations in Public Cloud environments to the same degree they might on-premises or in colocation sites. Another driver may be data sovereignty demands in some markets. Countries with stricter data residency laws may force enterprises to keep data within their borders and, in some cases, out of the hands of certain companies under the purview of certain data-hungry governments. Many CSPs are looking to offer "**Sovereign Cloud**" solutions that hand over controls to a trusted domestic partner to overcome some of these issues.

Let's discuss the often-overlooked concept of shared responsibility. What does this concept mean?

The shared responsibility model is a security framework that outlines roles and responsibilities shared between CSPs and their clients to ensure security. It establishes the Cloud security obligations of the CSP and of the organisation that uses Cloud services. It aims to determine accountability and responsibility so that all aspects of Cloud security are covered. Under the shared responsibility model:

- The **CSP** is responsible for the **security of the Cloud**.
- The **client** is responsible for **security in the Cloud**.

CSPs are responsible for safeguarding the integrity of their infrastructure. This includes all elements associated with the security of the Cloud, such as maintaining network devices, updating server firmware, managing virtualisation hypervisors, and securing physical facilities like data centres. This helps build trust among clients that their mission-critical data stored on CSP's servers is safe and protected against potential loss and cyber threats.

On the other hand, clients are responsible for the safety and security of operations within their business systems, often referred to as security in the Cloud. Clients should ensure critical security elements, such as user access controls, encryption of data at rest and in transit, firewall configurations, endpoint protection, and alignment with established cyber security guidelines. However, it's important to note that data protection responsibilities vary depending on where the workloads are hosted - for example, on Software as a Service (SaaS), Platform as a Service (PaaS), Infrastructure as a Service (IaaS), or in an on-premises data centre.

Both parties must also comply with industry standards and regulations. Depending on the type of service and specific CSP, there may also be some overlapping responsibilities between the client organisation and CSP.

As they say, "The devil is in the details." The shared responsibility model for Cloud security is one of those things that seems to be simple enough on the surface but is actually very complex when put into practice. Security will tend to be an afterthought for a large portion of users deploying workloads to the Cloud. Adhering to a shared responsibility model means the clients' security team maintains responsibilities for security as they move applications, data, containers, and workloads to the Cloud, while the CSP takes some responsibility, but not much.

Unfortunately, this **notion of shared responsibility** can be (and **often is**) **misunderstood,** leading to the assumption that Cloud workloads - as well as any applications, data, or activity associated with them - are fully protected by the CSP. This can result in CSP clients unknowingly running not fully protected workloads in a Public Cloud, making them vulnerable to cyberattacks that target operating systems, data, or applications. Even securely configured workloads can become a target at runtime, as they are vulnerable to zero-day vulnerabilities (see Introduction).

Statistics demonstrate that these responsibilities are not widely understood. Although 98% of organisations reported a Cloud data breach within the past 18 months, only 13% of these organisations reported that they understand their Cloud security responsibilities. Explaining this complex landscape is especially difficult when one needs to explain it to non-technical senior executives, like, for example, CFOs, COOs, and CEOs. **Many organisations erroneously rely on their CSPs for data protection and application security.** Closing this knowledge gap is an essential step towards fulfilling Cloud security obligations.

The complexity of using the shared responsibility model in practice stems from three main sources. Firstly, CSPs' marketing machines created the impression that the Cloud is inherently secure. Secondly, the complexity of the contracts (written in the most complex form of "legalise" to protect CSPs) makes me wonder how many clients of CSPs fully understand the contracts they are signing. Thirdly, due to "grey areas" of responsibility that Cloud computing comes with, there is variation in CSPs' obligations depending upon the Cloud computing model that is being used.[1]

One of the challenges of the shared responsibility model is a **clear (and,** sorry for the pun, **shared!) understanding** of who is responsible for what. For example, it is reasonably easy to achieve this in any of the "fully shaded" areas, but it is not easy to achieve this in "half shaded" areas (see reference in the previous paragraph).

This situation is further exacerbated by the continuously growing size and complexity of the IT infrastructure (see Chapters 4 and 5). Despite all claims about enhanced security, clients gain in the Cloud, according to Gartner, "**by 2025, 99% of Cloud security failures are forecast to come from customers.**"

In the meantime, Cloud computing technology continues to be fuelled by digital transformations that can be done faster and easier using Cloud (see Chapter 5), providing organisations with everything from compute and storage to Cloud databases and development tools to advanced data analytics and AI/ML capabilities. In its 2024 report, CrowdStrike noted a **75% increase in Cloud intrusions.**

QUESTIONS

These questions are important, as they prompt thinking and allow the target audience to understand the organisation's potential exposure and what they personally can do to improve the organisation's cyber security posture. To get answers to some of these questions, the target audience may need to go to their CIOs and CISOs.

1. How much does the organisation spend on Cloud computing?
2. What percentage of an organisation's IT spend goes against Cloud computing?
3. How well is the concept of shared responsibility understood within the organisation?
4. How does the organisation measure Cloud computing cyber security risks?
5. Does the organisation have documented Cloud governance?
6. When was the last time the organisation performed an independent audit of its Cloud footprint?
7. Who in the organisation is responsible and accountable for compliance with the organisation's Cloud governance?
8. What impact does Cloud proliferation have on the size of an organisation's insider threat?
9. If the organisation's Cloud provider (Amazon Web Services (AWS), MS Azure, Google, or Oracle) is breached, does the organisation have a contract clause providing liability and a run-book?

DESSERT

The concept of Cloud computing can and should be traced back to the concept of service bureau and the Service Bureau Division within IBM that was established in 1932 (in fact, IBM had operated service bureaus in major cities beginning in the 1920s, allowing users to rent time on tabulating equipment, and later computing equipment, to solve problems which couldn't justify a full-time equipment lease).

In 1955, John McCarthy (who originally coined the term "artificial intelligence") created a theory of sharing computing time among a group of users. In 1961, he suggested that one day "Computing can be sold as a Utility, like Water and Electricity." The expression "Cloud computing" became more widely known in 1996, when Compaq Computer Corporation drew up a business plan for future computing and the Internet.

Salesforce introduced the concept of Software as a Service (SaaS) in 1999, offering customer relationship management (CRM) software over the Internet. This marked the beginning of the commercialisation of Cloud computing and set the stage for the growth of SaaS (see Chapter 8).

The true inception of the modern era Cloud happened in 2002 when Amazon Web Services (AWS) launched its Public Cloud. This was the beginning of the application of modern Cloud computing services, allowing developers to build applications independently. In 2006, Amazon Simple Storage Service (S3), the Amazon Elastic Compute Cloud (EC2), and a beta version of Google Docs were released.

The following decade saw the launch of various Cloud services. In 2010, Microsoft launched Microsoft Azure. IBM introduced its IBM SmartCloud framework in 2011, and Oracle announced its Oracle Cloud in 2012. In December 2019, Amazon launched AWS Outposts, a service that extends AWS infrastructure, services, APIs, and tools to customers' data centres, colocation spaces, and on-premises facilities.

As Cloud computing kept developing, new service models emerged. The following are the top four Cloud computing service models:

- **Infrastructure as a Service (IaaS):** this model gives customers access to virtualised computing resources, such as virtual machines, storage, and networks, enabling them to deploy and manage their software and applications. IaaS delivers on-demand infrastructure resources, such as compute, storage, networking, and virtualisation. With IaaS, CSP owns and operates the infrastructure, but customers will need to purchase and manage software, such as operating systems, middleware, data, and applications.
- **Platform as a Service (PaaS):** this model expands on IaaS by providing an all-inclusive environment for application development and deployment. Developers may build, test, and deploy their product on this platform without having to worry about managing the underlying infrastructure. PaaS delivers and manages hardware and software resources for developing, testing, delivering, and managing Cloud applications. CSPs typically offer middleware, development tools, and Cloud databases within their PaaS offerings.

- **Software as a Service (SaaS)**: this model provides whole software programs that may be accessed online. These programs can be used by users without them having to locally install or maintain any software. SaaS provides a full application stack as a service that customers can access and use. SaaS solutions often come as ready-to-use applications, which are managed and maintained by CSP.
- **Serverless computing**: this is the latest model and is also called **Function as a Service (FaaS)**. This is a relatively new Cloud service model that provides solutions to build applications like simple, event-triggered functions without managing or scaling any infrastructure.

A simple analogy to help readers understand the difference between IaaS, PaaS, SaaS, and Serverless computing (FaaS)[2] is to think of the models like eating fresh pasta. One could buy flour, eggs, sauce ingredients, etc. and make one's dish fully from scratch (on-premises data centre), where one buys all the basic ingredients to make everything (like dough and sauce) themselves. However, most of us generally don't have enough time or skills or simply don't want to spend so much time and effort to eat a bowl of pasta. Instead, one might choose one of the following options:

- **IaaS**: buying pre-packed ingredients like fresh pasta and sauce made by someone else that one uses to cook at home.
- **PaaS**: order takeaway (or takeout, as they call it in the US) or delivery (Uber Eats, Menulog, etc.) where one's meal is prepared - in this case one doesn't have to worry about the ingredients or how to cook it, but one has to worry about where to eat, the utensils, and cleaning up after your meal.
- **SaaS**: call ahead to the restaurant and order the exact meal one wants. The restaurant prepares everything ahead of time for you. So, all one must do is to show up and eat, without worrying about where to eat, utensils, and cleaning.
- **Serverless computing (FaaS)**: go out to dinner and order a pasta dish designed by you at a restaurant. One eats and pays whatever one wants, and the restaurant makes sure that there are enough ingredients and staff to create the order without a long wait.

This analogy brings us to a discussion about prices associated with various models. It is worth mentioning that in the earlier analogy, one can easily notice that **each step along the "line"** (from buying pre-packed ingredients to ordering takeaway to calling the restaurant ahead to ordering customer-designed pasta - IaaS, PaaS, SaaS, and Serverless computing (FaaS)) **comes with a higher price.**

After we have discussed Cloud service models, it is important to talk about various types of Clouds: **Public, Private**, and **Hybrid.**

Public Clouds deliver resources, such as compute, storage, network, develop-and-deploy environments, and applications over the Internet. They are owned and run by CSPs like AWS, Microsoft Azure, and Google Cloud.

Private Clouds are built and run for use by a single organisation. Sometimes, it is not easy to draw a line between Private Clouds and managed services that provide greater control, customisation, and data security but come with similar costs and resource limitations associated with traditional IT environments.

Environments that mix at least one private computing environment (traditional IT infrastructure or Private Cloud) with one or more Public Clouds are called **Hybrid Clouds**. They allow leveraging resources and services from different computing environments and choosing the most optimal for the workloads.

When talking about types of Cloud deployments, one may also hear the term **Multicloud** environment. Industry research shows that many organisations considered, using a Multicloud approach, meaning they combine Cloud services from at least two different CSPs, whether public or private. Adopting a Multicloud approach gives greater flexibility to choose the solutions that best suit specific business needs and may also reduce the risk of vendor lock-in, **but comes with increased complexity and cost.**

As **Cloud computing is a form of outsourcing,** let's have a quick look at multiple drivers for outsourcing, including:

- lower costs (due to economies of scale or lower labour costs),
- increased efficiency,
- variable capacity and scalability (up and down),
- increased focus on strategy/core competencies,
- access to skills or resources,
- increased flexibility to meet changing business and commercial conditions,
- accelerated time to market,
- lower ongoing investment in internal infrastructure,
- access to innovation, intellectual property, and thought leadership,
- etc.

Among the benefits specific to Cloud computing, the following are usually mentioned: cost reduction, maintenance, skillset shortage avoidance, productivity, performance, speed of provisioning, availability, scalability, elasticity, and security. Let's have a quick look at each of these publicly declared benefits.

Cost reduction is an interesting area, so let's have a closer look at it. **Public Cloud delivery model converts capital expenditure** (e.g., buying servers) **to operational expenditure.** This was a great value proposition for those organisations that were cash-strapped but needed a technology refresh, as this was taking away the need for immediate capital outlay. Purportedly, it was lowering entry barriers, as infrastructure is typically provided by a third party and need not be purchased for one-time or infrequent intensive computing tasks, especially for fixed-term projects. However, transition to operational expenditure takes away any flexibility in delaying capital outlay for technology refresh – one can't delay it to the next financial year, and whether one wants this or not, one has to pay for the use of committed Cloud resources.

Capital avoidance, from first glance, looks very attractive at the point in time when it needs to be invoked. However, if one looks through the lenses of Total Cost of Ownership (TCO), say over 10 or 15 years, financial benefits become far less attractive. Moreover, organisations that choose to use Cloud services effectively enter a one-way door and become a captive audience of CSP that can arbitrarily increase prices of various services. For example, Microsoft announced that as of 1 September 2023, the price of MS 365 subscriptions in Australia will increase by 9%, which is significantly higher than Consumer Price Index (CPI)! For European countries, price increases (effective 1 April 2023) for Microsoft Cloud ranged from 9% for the UK to 11% for Denmark, Norway, and the Eurozone, to 15% for Norway. On 9 December 2025, Microsoft announced that it will raise the prices of its Microsoft 365 software subscriptions — which include apps such as Word, PowerPoint, and Excel — for most of its business, enterprise, and government customers on 1 July 2026, including in Australia. Also, don't forget about the loss of flexibility mentioned at the end of the previous paragraph.

Another factor to consider in TCO analysis is network costs, like, for example, the cost of Microsoft ExpressRoute. Public Cloud might look cheaper, but this is not always the case. Ingress-egress fees, data transfer fees - they all add up. And as the workload grows, organisations may realise that it's actually cheaper to run these workloads in on-premises environments or in a Private Cloud. For example, one organisation known to me could have decreased its costs (on the same footprint) by 45% by moving from AWS Public Cloud to a Private Cloud.

Then, it is important to note that many large CSPs charge their customers in US$, and by doing this, expose their clients to currency exchange rate variations (and hedging costs money), which, in turn, makes it difficult to make accurate financial forecasts.

Also, in the absence (which is very often the case) of strong Cloud governance, clients' footprints in the Cloud tend to grow, continuously increasing clients' costs. One of the Australian universities faced a dilemma during their first encounter with Cloud computing when the actual cost eclipsed the projected one by a factor of three. Cloud costs can be far more unpredictable than on-premises equivalents, especially in the case of suboptimal configurations combined with a lack of spending controls in place.

From a cost point of view, Public Cloud is great for projects where Cloud resources are required for a finite duration of time, especially if one can stand them up in the morning and shut down in the evening, maximising the benefits of the "pay per use" model. But for workloads that require 24/7 operation, Public Cloud is often not the cheapest option, especially if it is looked at through TCO lenses based on the expected lifetime of the workload.

Despite the cost savings promise, the Cloud turned out to be expensive, and some organisations learnt this the hard way. As a result of this, quite a few organisations now consider so-called **Cloud repatriation**. Cloud repatriation involves moving applications or workloads, or data that were once in a Public Cloud environment, either back to on-premises infrastructure, colocation infrastructure, or a different (usually Private) Cloud environment with an alternative CSP.

For example, between 2013 and 2016, Dropbox pulled a significant amount of data back from AWS, and this worked out significantly cheaper and gave Dropbox more control over the data the company hosted.

More recently (in 2023), web company 37signals (which runs project management platform Basecamp and subscription-based email service Hey) announced the two services were migrating off from AWS and Google Cloud. This move boosted 37signals' profit by US$1 million, and the expectation was to save US$7 million in 5 years!

Popular search engine optimisation (SEO) tools developer Ahrefs revealed that its decision to use its own hardware over the AWS Public Cloud will save it $400 million over 3 years. The company calculated the costs of having its equivalent hardware and workloads entirely within AWS's Singapore region over the last 2 years and estimated the cost would be $440m, versus the $40m it actually paid for 850 on-premises servers during that time.

Let's talk now about the pros and cons of some other benefits attributed to Cloud usage.

Maintenance of Cloud environments is perceived to be easier because of the servers and storage maintained by the Cloud service providers. Although this may be the case in many situations with the benefit of not struggling with the search for skilled personnel, the price one pays for this is threefold: loss of full control, loss of full visibility (and often loss of understanding) of the entire environment end-to-end, as well as potential security issues that will be discussed later.

Skillset shortage avoidance looks like a great benefit. However, it is important to remember that organisations inevitably need as many (if not more) people to manage increasingly complex and intertwined Cloud environments as they did for on-premises, and some companies may prefer to just keep things in-house or use a managed services provider.

Productivity, performance, and availability are questionable benefits, as they can be achieved both within and outside Cloud services and are significantly linked to the overall applications, data and network architecture, and implementations. When talking about availability, one must be mindful that replication and/or hot-hot data replication is a double-edged sword, and if the primary database becomes poisoned, the same is true for its real-time replica. About 10 years ago, I had the questionable privilege of managing one such incident that closed NSW motor registries across the state for 3 days in a row.

Speed of provisioning is an unquestionable benefit of using Cloud computing, as one can stand up new environments in a matter of several (1–8) hours and sometimes, even minutes. This is especially useful for projects and experimentation.

Scalability and elasticity are great benefits if one remembers that **applications have to be written with these in mind** and that "lift-and-shift" of legacy applications into the Cloud is unlikely to result in such benefits. It is also important to remember that dynamic provisioning of resources is not a "free for all" but comes with a reservation price.

Security is the most interesting and controversial aspect that deserves deeper discussion. A typical argument one can hear is that Public Cloud CSPs (and the biggest players like Microsoft, AWS, Google and Oracle) can offer much better levels of protection than an organisation that is 1/1000 of their size or even smaller, as the big players can attract and keep professionals of the highest qualifications. This is true, but, unfortunately, this is not the full picture due to two factors: the concept of shared responsibility and the fact that the complexity of achieving security is greatly increased when data is distributed over a wider area or a greater number of devices (further exacerbated by numerous APIs), as well as in multi-tenant systems shared by unrelated users. In addition, user access to security audit logs may be difficult or impossible. Private Clouds are in part driven by clients' desire to retain control over the infrastructure and avoid losing control of information security.

NOTES

1 https://blog.r2ut.com/shared-responsibility-model-what-is-it and https://www.wiz.io/academy/shared-responsibility-mode.
2 https://www.fedbar.org/wp-content/uploads/2016/09/CACD-pdf-1.pdf.

Chapter 8

SaaS sprawl

"Why, sometimes I've believed as many as six impossible things before breakfast."

Through the Looking Glass, and What Alice Found There by Lewis Carroll

---

APPETISER

- In 2024, organisations maintained an average of over 125 different SaaS applications (up from 80 in 2021).
- According to Zylo, the average organisation has approximately 269 SaaS applications. For large organisations, this number skyrockets to an average of 650 and is increasing by six new SaaS applications every 30 days.
- The central IT Department and CISO typically are aware of only a third of those.
- Result: fragmented SaaS ecosystem.
- What organisation can sustain this pace of growth without compromising its cyber security?
- What organisation can successfully manage this level of complexity?
- It was expected that in 2025, SaaS applications would account for 85% of the organisations' tech stack.
- Shadow IT: *38% of technology purchases are defined, managed, and controlled by business leaders of various business units* rather than by the Central IT Department - nearly half of all IT spend "lurks in the shadows."
- SaaS became the biggest category of shadow IT.
- SaaS sprawl is the proliferation of multiple unapproved, duplicate, redundant, and poorly integrated SaaS solutions.
- One recent survey found that over 30% of businesses reported duplicated work due to multiple SaaS applications. The average company *wastes more than US$135,000 on unused, underused, or duplicate SaaS tools.*

DOI: 10.1201/9781003730514-9

- On average, seven out of ten employees waste up to an hour of their workday just hopping between business tools.
- 46% of workers report that their job is chaotic because of juggling between apps, a phenomenon currently represented by the expression "app fatigue." As a result, up to 80% of productivity is lost.
- SaaS sprawl brings with it numerous cyber security and compliance risks: 51% of organisations experienced an attack that targeted their SaaS data, and 52% of these attacks were successful.
- According to a recent survey, 75% of respondents believe that the most significant risk of SaaS sprawl is in the area of cyber security, as SaaS sprawl dramatically increases the attack surface.
- The SaaS provider is not responsible for ensuring the data security of the organisation's data!
- Is the organisation's data encrypted at rest and in transit?

MAIN COURSE

The notion of Software as a Service (SaaS) was introduced earlier in Chapter 7 and goes back to the 1990s. Proliferation of SaaS continued with various verticals like construction collaboration solutions, as SaaS is very well suited for collaboration between multiple geographically distributed organisations.

Typically, SaaS offerings are hosted in the Cloud with 24/7 availability via an independent software vendor (ISV) or, more frequently now, via a third-party Cloud Service Provider (CSP) such as AWS (Amazon Web Services), Microsoft Azure, or Google. So, SaaS is a software deployment model in which a third-party provider builds applications using Cloud infrastructure and makes them available to customers via the Internet. This means software can be accessed from any device with an Internet connection and a web browser.

Some of the most well-known examples of SaaS are email, calendaring, and office tools (such as Microsoft 365). When Microsoft launched Office 365 (now Microsoft 365 or MS 365) in 2011, this was the real tipping point for SaaS.

In 2021, the average organisation used 110 SaaS applications, up from 80 in 2010 (+38%). Gartner reported that, in 2024, "organisations maintained an average of over 125 different SaaS applications totaling US$1,040 per employee annually and that IT typically is aware of only a third of those due to decentralised ownership and sourcing." From first glance, US$1,040 per employee annually looks like a reasonably small number, until one realises that for an organisation with 15,000 employees and contractors, this translates into a total cost exceeding US$15 million per year!

Early in 2025, the Australian Federal Government's volume sourcing agreement with Microsoft reached A$954 million in value as it was renewed for another year. The new contract, now spanning 7 years, has reached almost ten times the original A$96 million value of the contract signed in 2019[1]

It was expected that in 2025, **SaaS applications would account for 85% of the organisations' tech stack.**

While the subscription-based pricing model of SaaS can be a benefit, it can also be a disadvantage. Over the long term, the cost of using SaaS may be higher than traditional licensing models, especially for organisations that have many users or require specific features.

As it is easy to see in the earlier example of the Australian Federal Government Microsoft spend, the pay-per-use model and a reasonably low-looking per-user cost do not result in a low total bill.

Apart from benefits associated with the use of SaaS solutions, there are also disadvantages to relying on SaaS solutions, and organisations should be aware of potential limiting factors, security concerns, and cost issues. While leveraging the "pros" of SaaS can open up capabilities and boost efficiencies, every organisation should also review the list of potential "cons" of using SaaS, as there are cons.

Let's have a closer look at SaaS sprawl. Let's deduce the common misconception: SaaS sprawl is not similar to shadow IT. In short, shadow IT is a broader notion, and SaaS sprawl is just one of the components of shadow IT. In essence, **SaaS sprawl** refers to the **proliferation of multiple unapproved, duplicate, redundant, and poorly integrated SaaS solutions.**

According to Wikipedia, **shadow IT** refers to information technology (IT) systems, devices, software, applications, services and other IT resources deployed by departments other than the central IT department to bypass limitations and restrictions that have been imposed by the central IT department and without explicit central IT department approval. Shadow IT has grown exponentially in recent years with the adoption of Cloud-based applications and services. While shadow IT can promote innovation and improve employee productivity, it often introduces significant cyber security risks to organisations through data leaks and potential compliance violations, especially when such systems are not aligned with corporate governance. Cloud services, and especially SaaS, have become the biggest category of shadow IT. The number of services and apps has increased, and staff members routinely purchase them using credit cards and install and use them without involving the central IT department. But shadow IT isn't always the result of employees acting alone - according to Gartner, **38% of technology purchases are defined, managed, and controlled by business leaders of various business units rather than by the central IT department.**

Shadow IT has become increasingly prevalent in recent years because of digital transformation efforts (see Chapter 5). In 2019, an Everest Group study estimated that **nearly half of all IT spending "lurks in the shadows."**

Notably, these figures were pre-pandemic. A sudden influx of remote workers due to COVID-19 restrictions has likely increased the size of shadow IT even further. And now one needs to add to this proliferation of shadow AI, as people are sneaking AI into work.

Now, ask yourself, would you like electrical work in your house to be done by an unlicensed electrician? Or plumbing done by an unlicensed plumber? Or even worse - your house built without a licensed independent certifier approving each and every step during its construction? Shadow IT and SaaS sprawl are exactly in this space. Why is this happening? Maybe because of KPIs (see Chapter 13). And this is another example of the **cumulative effect**.

As mentioned earlier, SaaS sprawl refers to the proliferation of multiple unapproved, duplicate, redundant, and poorly integrated SaaS solutions. Lack of strong governance, coordination or oversight from the central IT department results in SaaS sprawl, or in other words, a **fragmented SaaS ecosystem**. It's like a garden where each plant grows independently, without any planned arrangement or guidance. Without a clear strategy or framework in place, teams are left to their own devices, making individual decisions about which SaaS applications to adopt.

A scary picture has been painted by Zylo.[2] Zylo's SaaS Management Index report showed that **organisations often underestimate the number of applications they use by two to three times the actual number**. This is in part because the central IT department now only manages, on average, 17% of an organisation's SaaS. This means the remaining 83% are being managed and purchased by business units and individual employees. The repercussions of this are that it becomes difficult (if possible at all) for the central IT department to manage and optimise the organisation's SaaS assets. According to Zylo, **the average organisation has approximately 269 SaaS applications. For large organisations, this number skyrockets to an average of 650**. What's even scarier is that Zylo's research has shown that the **average organisation adds six new SaaS applications every 30 days**. Ask yourself: **"Can the organisation sustain this pace of growth without compromising its cyber security? Can an organisation successfully manage this level of complexity?"**

One of the side effects of SaaS sprawl can be **erosion of trust in the central IT department** as other departments (outside the central IT department) influence and control outcomes, and the central IT department is often left picking up the pieces without having contributed to the fragmentation.

One may ask, what are the consequences of SaaS sprawl? It is likely to result in inefficiencies and duplicated efforts, as different departments or teams use different applications to perform similar tasks. When it comes to integration, user experience suffers as employees navigate through a maze of systems, and data quality takes a hit with redundant, sometimes conflicting inputs.

This can lead to data silos and confusion, negatively impacting productivity and collaboration, and increasing cyber security risks.

A recent survey found that **over 30% of businesses reported duplicated work** due to multiple SaaS applications. The **average company wastes more than US$135,000 on unused, underused, or duplicate SaaS tools**. According to a RingCentral and CITE Research survey of 2000 knowledge professionals, **seven out of ten employees waste up to an hour of their workday just hopping between business tools**. Moreover, 50% of employees claim that they find it challenging to look for resources in the jungle of applications in their office, and **46% of workers report that their job is chaotic because of juggling between apps,** a phenomenon currently represented by the expression "app fatigue." As a result, **up to 80% of productivity is lost,** as are various other workplace difficulties such as stress, knowledge loss, and a drop in output quality. Add to this integration complexities and vendor management challenges:

- Integrating multiple SaaS applications can be challenging, especially when they are not designed to work together. This can hinder data flow and collaboration among different systems and people, and result in multiple unsynchronised sources of data.
- Managing relationships with multiple SaaS providers, including contract negotiations, renewals, support, and updates, can become complex, expensive, and time-consuming.

Apart from the above-mentioned issues, SaaS sprawl brings with it numerous cyber security and compliance risks, as each SaaS application may have its own security protocols and compliance requirements. Without proper oversight, organisations may expose sensitive data or violate regulatory standards. SaaS sprawl typically increases security risks, as data can be stored in unsecured systems or shared with unauthorised individuals, and this is supported by the following (scary) statistics:

- **51% of organisations experienced a ransomware attack that targeted their SaaS data, and 52% of these attacks were successful.**
- 43% of organisations agree that security misconfigurations lead to security incidents. To minimise these risks, companies must implement proper security measures and monitor SaaS usage within their organisations.

According to a recent survey, **75% of respondents believe that the most significant risk of SaaS sprawl is in the area of cyber security**. It is given that SaaS applications hold a large amount of sensitive data, consumer financial data, records, and other information. Security is heavily impacted by **SaaS sprawl, as it dramatically increases the attack surface.**

When an organisation starts looking at a SaaS solution, it should remember that the **SaaS provider** (despite all marketing claims) **is not responsible for ensuring the data security of the organisation's data.** SaaS providers and

SaaS customers each have their roles and responsibilities for data security in a third-party SaaS product (see Chapter 7). SaaS providers are primarily responsible for the security of the infrastructure and the application itself, while SaaS customers are responsible for configuring the application's security settings, managing user access, and educating users about security practices. While SaaS providers secure the application itself, strict measures should be taken by the SaaS customer regarding sensitive data. One thing SaaS customers (and especially smaller organisations) need to be aware of is that they cannot assume that their data is secure or retrievable in case of ransomware, disasters, or misconfiguration of user privileges. These are situations when having an off-site backup copy is absolutely important. Organisations that take data security seriously should think about the encryption of both data at rest and data in transit.

One of the risks associated with SaaS data security (especially with no data encryption at rest) is a scenario in which an employee of the SaaS provider with the right level of access is incentivised (or threatened with harm to their family) to harvest and farm out sensitive customer data that can be monetised or used in the interest of a nation-state actor. Another risk associated with SaaS solutions is that **SaaS providers often rely on shared infrastructure to deliver their services to multiple customers,** and this can be very attractive to cyber-criminals or nation-state actors.

As we touched on the topic of data security, it is important to mention some obvious considerations, such as data residency and privacy - residency of customers' data and compliance with privacy laws is important for some organisations that prefer to maintain data sovereignty (see Chapters 7 and 9). Concerns around privacy and security are one of the major disadvantages of SaaS for many customers. Some organisations simply aren't comfortable handing over their confidential data to a third party. A similar situation may occur with regulatory compliance requirements - some organisations may find it difficult to meet regulatory requirements while using SaaS solutions. Organisations using SaaS solutions have limited control over the software and the SaaS provider's operational processes and practices. This makes it difficult for organisations to conduct audits and ensure that the SaaS provider is following best practices. Statements like "Trust me, I am a doctor!" do not fly in this case. Additionally, SaaS providers most likely will not provide detailed logs or information about the software operation, which can make it difficult for organisations to troubleshoot issues or identify potential security breaches.

QUESTIONS

These questions are important, as they prompt thinking and allow the target audience to understand the organisation's potential exposure and what they personally can do to improve the organisation's cyber security posture.

To get answers to some of these questions, the target audience may need to go to their CIOs and CISOs.

1. What percentage of an organisation's IT spend is directly controlled by the central IT department?
2. What is the size of the organisation's shadow IT (e.g., decentralised business technology solutions that are not supported or even registered by the Central IT department)? Are the organisation's CIO and CISO aware of its size?
3. What is the size of the organisation's SaaS sprawl? Are CIO and CISO aware of its size?
4. When was the last time the organisation performed an independent audit of its SaaS solutions? How many of them are duplicates, redundant, and not fit for purpose?
5. What controls does the organisation have in place to contain shadow IT and SaaS sprawl?
6. Does the organisation have documented SaaS governance?
7. Who is responsible and accountable for compliance with SaaS governance?
8. How does the organisation measure cyber security risks associated with SaaS?
9. What impact does SaaS sprawl have on the size of an organisation's insider threat?
10. Every new SaaS tool adds how much to the organisation's annual cyber insurance premium?

DESSERT

Software as a Service (SaaS) was introduced earlier in Chapter 7, and these are some examples of the very early SaaS applications that were introduced in the mid-late 90s:

- WebEx (launched in 1995), which provided an early example of web conferencing software.
- NetSuite (launched in 1998), which provided accounting and enterprise resource planning (ERP) software.
- Salesforce (launched in 1999), which provided a web-based customer relationship management (CRM) solution allowing a very wide spectrum of organisations to manage their customer relationships more efficiently and with greater scalability.

In the early 2000s, advancements in technology made it possible for SaaS solutions to become a reality for businesses, and the initial pitch was to smaller businesses that did not have a "critical mass" (or, better to say, enough money, expertise, or time, or all of the above) to build, implement, deploy and maintain either in-house developed or COTS (commercial-off-the-shelf) applications. Larger organisations can be attracted to SaaS technology for short-term projects or applications that aren't needed after the project has been delivered. Over the next two decades, SaaS applications started progressive replacement of on-premises software - it was seen as more cost-effective, easier to deploy and maintain, and all around more flexible.

The idea of a SaaS model is not new. Software vendors have been selling subscription-based software for years, allowing customers to pay only for the services they use. The main difference with SaaS is that this model reduces or eliminates the costs of upfront purchasing, installing and maintaining software (and hardware to run this software on). In theory, SaaS can greatly reduce an organisation's IT budget with a subscription plan that meets the current and future needs of the organisation with flexibility and scalability.

SaaS is one of the four Cloud computing service models. It is a web-based software delivery model that has become an industry standard worldwide. It encompasses an array of applications, spanning accounting, applicant tracking, customer relationship management (CRM), document creation/editing and management, email management, photo editing/design and many others. This model provides whole software programs that may be accessed online. These programs can be used without users having to locally install or maintain any software. SaaS provides a full application stack as a service that customers can access and use. SaaS solutions often come as ready-to-use applications, which are managed and maintained by SaaS providers.

SaaS provides a complete software solution that one typically purchases on a pay-as-you-go basis from a SaaS provider. Having said this, there are multiple variations of charging models for SaaS, and sometimes some of them are in the form of an obscured licence agreement or a combination of licence agreement and pay-as-you-go (like, for example, Service Now offering). In the past, the Team Binder charging model was based on the dollar value of the project it was being used for, which was another variety of SaaS charging model.

Global circumstances have helped accelerate the adoption of SaaS solutions, with the GFC of 2007–2009 driving businesses to reduce expenses and the COVID-19 pandemic making Cloud-based applications essential in a remote-first environment since 2020. The COVID-19 pandemic impacted the global industry in several significant ways. One major development was how it created workflows that promoted safety and flexibility with remote access for employees. Pandemic shutdowns forced organisations' leaders to seek solutions to protect and adapt their businesses' operations. And SaaS was one such solution that emerged, where businesses gained a significant competitive advantage amid the chaos of the changing global economy.

SaaS providers declared many pros to using SaaS in the organisation, including focus on core capabilities (especially important for smaller organisations), shorter implementation time (or, in other words, reduced time to benefit), scalability, reduced maintenance cost and effort, automated updates, pay-per-use or subscription pricing model, ubiquitous access, business continuity, duplication, and automated backups. However, when one digs into the details of these positives, one may (and will) uncover that these pros are not as "black and white" as they are being marketed.

Let's, for example, have a look at **shorter implementation time.** When speaking about shorter implementation time, one needs to remember another factor that has a significant impact on the implementation timeline. The majority (especially vertical) SaaS solutions are designed and built along Henry Ford's saying, "**Any customer can have a car painted any colour that he wants, so as long as it is black.**"[3] Yes, it is possible to configure SaaS solutions to reflect the customer's organisation's org structure, cost centres, users, direction, origination and destination of various workflows, etc., but this does not require any changes in the code or any new coding. However, some of the SaaS solutions allow customisations, sometimes very heavy customisations, by introducing new code developed for the specific customer or by changing the core code of the SaaS solution. The moment the organisation decides to pursue this type of customisation path, it can "Kiss Goodbye" any hopes of shorter implementation time, as this decision moves implementation into the space of development of custom-built software. I saw numerous initiatives (especially around the Salesforce platform) that took years to develop, build and implement, on par with any in-house or outsourced software development, and massive problems some years later when the need to upgrade such a solution arrives, or some elements of the SaaS solution used in this customisation become unsupported.

Another interesting (and partially related) example is **automatic updates.** Although automated updates are typically seen as a benefit of SaaS, in some cases, when customers, for whatever reason, don't want this to happen, automated updates become a drawback of using SaaS. Sometimes mandatory updates may even cause damage due to a lack of compatibility with existing older software that the organisation may need to use for whatever reason, or open new vulnerabilities (at APIs, for example). And yes - forget about automated updates if the organisation has a heavily customised SaaS solution. For example, one organisation that uses a heavily customised Salesforce SaaS solution based on Salesforce Process Builder faced an 18-month and $6 million project to perform migration to Flow Builder (as Salesforce confirmed in May 2025 that it will fully retire and will no longer be supporting Workflow Rules and Process Builder as of December 31, 2025). It also often has a negative impact on security, especially when complex real-time integration is required.

Another heavily promoted pro of using SaaS is the **pay-per-use or subscription pricing model**. Typically, this benefit is centred around several aspects: no capital investment required, leveraging costs over a large user base, avoiding capital expenditure by moving to a pay-per-use model that takes away the need for capital expenditure every 3–5–7 years when a hardware upgrade is required, moving to a recurrent (e.g., perceived more predictable) cost model, and automated software updates.

As much as this is true in many cases, the picture is not as "black-and-white" as it is often portrayed, and costs should be looked at through the lenses of Total Cost of Ownership (TCO) over the lifetime of the solution (say, 10–15 years). When looked at through these lenses, the picture often becomes less obvious, especially considering recent price hikes by SaaS providers like, for example, Microsoft. It is probably right to bring here an analogy of using renting instead of buying, which is an attractive business model but ultimately costs more, ties companies into long-term contracts and has dire consequences on security, as rarely is any diligence taken by the customer, as assumptions are made in the absence of a good understanding of the shared responsibility model (see Chapter 7).

Apart from benefits associated with the use of SaaS solutions, there are also disadvantages to relying on SaaS solutions, and organisations should be aware of potential limiting factors, security concerns, and cost issues. While leveraging the "pros" of SaaS can open up capabilities and boost efficiencies, every organisation should also review the list of potential "cons" of using SaaS, as there are several cons.

The problem with outsourcing technology or buying it as a service in the form of SaaS is that development and upgrading remain in the hands of another party. If anything unforeseen happens to this party, such as an M&A, a disaster, a receivership, or another event, the customer's organisation is vulnerable. It is important to remember that with the SaaS model, customers' organisations never actually own the service it is using, leaving control of important business functions with a third party. Even if the organisation is super diligent and owns its data and performs regular data escrows (read - additional cost), what can it do with this data if the SaaS provider disappears from the surface of the Earth?

Transitioning to using SaaS is, in a sense, a one-way door, as the cost of reversing such a transition is typically very high. An organisation moving to use an SaaS solution becomes heavily dependent on this solution, and in case something goes wrong - be it an automated update/patch, or an Internet outage, or an SaaS service provider going out of business (or selling it to another company) - the organisation's business operation may be in jeopardy. It is also important to mention that organisations using SaaS solutions are a **captive audience** and have **no ability to accurately predict their costs over time**. For example, after the 1st of September 2023, MS 365 subscription renewals for Australia increased by 9%, which is a significant number and is much higher than Consumer Price Index (CPI). These are some obvious disadvantages associated with the use of SaaS solutions:

- **Vendor lock-in** is the limited ability to negotiate terms or change vendors. Since the vendor controls the software, they also control the terms of the contract, leaving customers with limited bargaining power, if any at all. This is especially true for smaller companies, which often face a dilemma of "take it or leave it." In addition, organisations that use SaaS solutions are often dependent on a single vendor for their software needs, which can make it difficult to switch to another provider if needed. This can be a costly problem if the vendor's service is poor or if the business needs to migrate to another solution.
- **Opaqueness of the SaaS solutions,** as customers get only vague ideas about infrastructure and software implementation architectures and maintenance processes of the SaaS provider. The main issue here is a **lack of transparency,** as there tend to be contradictions between the sales pitch and achievable, practical results.
- **Lack of control** is a major disadvantage of SaaS solutions, since organisations rely on the SaaS provider for updates and new features - software is hosted in the Cloud, updates and new features are controlled by the SaaS provider, and customers have little control over when and how these updates and features are implemented.
- **There is no guarantee about how long the SaaS will be available,** and if needed, the cost of migration elsewhere or the cost of re-development can be more than building the organisation's solution in the first place.
- Despite (or in line with) various marketing claims about using the best practice, in reality use of SaaS solutions (especially in "out of the box" mode without customisations) is likely to result in **staying with the pack, instead of getting ahead of the curve,** as it's not easy to stay ahead of the curve with SaaS - majority of SaaS solutions are typically designed to be one-size-fits-all, and users have limited ability to customise or configure the software to their specific needs, which, as discussed earlier, comes with its own problems. SaaS empowers, but it is also an equaliser, and an organisation may lose its competitive advantage/distinction by conforming to "standard (allegedly the best) practice" and face a "customisation dilemma."
- **No customisation** potentially results in loss of competitive advantage/ distinction but maximises numerous benefits of using a SaaS solution; customisations have their disadvantages, as was discussed earlier and in the next bullet point.
- **Customisation** results in a loss of numerous benefits of using a SaaS solution and most likely leads to higher costs, but offers the ability to differentiate from others (at a price).
- **System features can change** and may cause dysfunction in the customer's organisation, and the **customer's organisation has limited ability**

to manage the SaaS provider's priorities for new/changed functionality or around decisions to stay with an older version of the software because the organisation is not ready to retrain its personnel (or for any other reason, like compatibility with the organisation's other software). Similarly, the customer may end up waiting for a long time to get new functionality (important for their organisation) implemented in the SaaS solution.

- **A typical organisation needs more than one SaaS solution to address all the organisation's needs, which often increases architectural and integration complexity** (see Chapter 4) and creates additional challenges in securing the organisation's data.
- One of the biggest drawbacks of SaaS is its **dependence on Internet connectivity**. Since the software is hosted in the Cloud, **users need a fast, stable, and reliable Internet connection to access it** – a degraded or downed Internet connection significantly impacts the SaaS solution and subsequently the organisation's ability to operate. A bad Internet connection causes slow response times, service disruptions, or a total outage.
- Providers of SaaS solutions typically offer service-level agreements (SLAs) for uptime and performance. These SLAs guarantee a certain level of service (and sometimes offer compensation if the vendor fails to meet their obligations). However, **as SaaS solutions are totally dependent upon Internet connectivity and SaaS service providers are accountable only for their Cloud-based solutions, one should take their SLAs with a grain of salt** - they are necessary to have in place, but, unfortunately, are not sufficient to give customers full peace of mind. For example, Microsoft Office 365 guarantees a 99.9% uptime SLA, but this is meaningful only if Internet connectivity is fast, stable, and reliable.
- **Loss of control** as the SaaS model turns much of that control over to the SaaS provider (while with the traditional perpetual software licence sales model, applications were largely controlled by the organisation that used them), and the customer (unless they have very strong SaaS governance processes) may not be aware of the increased usage (be it number of users, storage, or something else).
- **Performance of SaaS solutions may deteriorate over time** - many SaaS solutions get slower over time, especially if they get a lot of adoption and, as a result, a high number of users; they just get too loaded and heavy. They are likely going through optimisation cycles on the SaaS provider's side, but even so, these cycles typically do not improve their performance all that much.
- It can be **difficult to terminate (or scale down) services** that an organisation doesn't want any more, as some SaaS providers - especially at the enterprise level - have long lead times for termination or allow organisations to terminate only once per year.

- One of the major unintended consequences of the growing popularity of SaaS is the so-called "SaaS sprawl," which can be defined as the uncontrollable proliferation of SaaS solutions across organisations, resulting in increased cost, a disjointed user experience, difficulties in managing and organising data, and increased cyber security exposure. This topic deserves a more detailed discussion below.
- Security is a big topic when it comes to SaaS. Marketeers are often claiming better security offered by SaaS solutions, but is this really the case? Let's talk about it in more detail below.

It is worth noting that digital transformation initiatives brought with them the adoption of DevOps (DevOps combines development (Dev) and operations (Ops) to unite people, process, and technology in application planning, development, delivery, and operations), which became a major driver for the proliferation of shadow IT. Cloud and DevOps teams like to run fast and without friction. However, obtaining visibility and management levels that security teams require often leads to setbacks and delays within the development cycle. When a developer spawns a Cloud workload using their personal credentials, they do so not as a matter of preference or out of malice but because going through the proper internal channels may delay work and cause the entire team to miss the deadline.

As discussed earlier, SaaS solutions have a lot of benefits, but some unique risks exist as well. One of the risks associated with SaaS solutions is that **SaaS providers often rely on shared infrastructure to deliver their services to multiple customers,** and this can be very attractive to cyber-criminals or nation-state actors. The bigger the service and the more sensitive the data, the more attractive it becomes to attackers, who can gain access to multiple customers' data in one place.

NOTES

1 https://www.itnews.com.au/news/governments-microsoft-sourcing-deal-hits-954m-614515.
2 https://zylo.com/blog/too-many-apps/.
3 https://www.amazon.com.au/My-Life-Work-Henry-Ford/dp/B08JDYXN75/ref=sr_1_3?adgrpid=86175837079&dib=eyJ2IjoiMSJ9.kZgbdutEEAA8JUiKjS6iaPUNovlVha1xeNuburMTpY2orrkEA3DoWIaSfVjXn06p08boh uH42wdDT1YsnZU_iSHebaYr6u0oYQkujLtt1LOpaeu69OklZmNOE_FfDLY9kxXyc0LGBCYLVe-ipoARmfguh9ij67CKsE8roIgfWJX_cThy-aTH7 BmUZgbC9M0SH1EJtq46ENUwBEip6x9urypeLv9JnQOX5FDDWCxwYaL6 jtjmtIaEKgz9FbpxpLYeNjtBDupCBWLG8aKYt2Ee8XRLc8MxTAxHQgc0Eaiv Ums.qsZpogMHJDsTMI7UAxOPmwKJAFEe5kQRXkbw_XGFF3E&dib_tag= se&hvadid=583877744094&hvdev=c&hvlocphy=9071822&hvnetw=g& hvqmt=e&hvrand=10538069048362079336&hvtargid=kwd-315165338053& hydadcr=15327_329664&keywords=henry+ford+autobiography&mcid=eb4 ee384ddee30438513392e58c83373&qid=1763759487&sr=8-3.

Chapter 9

Supply chain challenges

"If everybody minded their own business, the world would go around a great deal faster than it does."

Alice's Adventures in Wonderland by Lewis Carroll

APPETISER

- A supply chain attack is a cyber-attack that seeks to damage an organisation by targeting less secure elements in the supply chain.
- SolarWinds supply chain attack affected 18,000+ organisations, including government agencies and major corporations.
- Some other well-known supply chain attacks include Target USA (2014 - 70 million customers impacted, 40 million debit and credit card details stolen), Panama Papers (2016 - tax evasion tactics of over 214,000 companies and high-ranking politicians exposed), Equifax (2017 - 147 million customers impacted, sensitive data, like social security numbers, driver's licence numbers, DOBs, and addresses stolen), Paradise Papers (2017 - 13.4 million investment records of the wealthy 1%).
- Supply chain attacks may have several types: software supply chain attack, firmware supply chain attack, hardware supply chain attack, and service provider supply chain attack.
- The biggest supply chain attack threat organisations face today is the software supply chain.
- Recently, software supply chain attacks moved from the periphery of concerns to the forefront.
- In 2024, approximately 183,000 organisations were affected by supply chain attacks worldwide.
- Supply chain attacks are the most difficult threats to prevent!

DOI: 10.1201/9781003730514-10

- Supply chain compromises will continue. They are extremely difficult to protect against, highlighting the need for security to be considered as part of the vendor selection process.
- How many software suppliers and service providers are used by the organisation? Have the organisation's software supplier(s) or service provider(s) been targeted? What is the risk here?

MAIN COURSE

Approximately at 3:30 pm local time on Tuesday, September 17, 2024, pagers belonging to Hezbollah fighters, collaborators, and civilian supporters exploded across Lebanon. According to the New York Times, the pagers received a message that appeared to have come from the group's leadership. It was this message that is believed to have activated the explosions. This attack targeted approximately 5,000 pagers and resulted in at least 12 people killed and nearly 3,000 injured. The following day, Wednesday, September 18, 2024, was marked by another round of blasts, when exploding walkie-talkies killed at least 25 and injured more than 600 people.

Why are we talking about this in a book on cyber security? These explosions were the result of **supply chain interference.** An American official, who spoke on condition of anonymity, said Israel briefed the US on the operation, where small amounts of explosives hidden in the pagers were detonated. The Lebanese government and Iran-backed Hezbollah also blamed Israel for the deadly explosions. The Israeli military declined to comment. Whether devices have been rigged with explosives and a switch that could remotely detonate the device or hacked to cause batteries' thermal runaway, in either case, we have witnessed a **supply chain attack.** And this is **arguably the most impactful and most widely publicised supply chain attack** that opened a new chapter in what can be used as warfare.

Now, back to cyber security. The most well-known supply chain attack was the SolarWinds attack of 2020. In December 2020, the SolarWinds attack sent shockwaves around the world. Attackers gained unauthorised access to SolarWinds' software development environment, **injected malicious code** (see Chapter 3) into Orion platform updates, and created Sunburst **malware,** potentially compromising national security. This **attack affected 18,000+ organisations, including government agencies and major corporations** (those impacted included a significant number of the US federal agencies, such as the Department of Homeland Security, the State Department, the Department of Energy, the National Nuclear Security Administration, the Department of Commerce and the Department of the Treasury and private companies like AT&T, Microsoft, Cisco and Deloitte), and the malicious actors responsible for the breach may have been preparing to carry out the attack since 2019.

The SolarWinds supply chain attack was unique in that the hackers didn't initiate remote control immediately. Rather, the malware should have laid dormant for 2 weeks before initiating contact with a command-and-control server (a remote session manager for compromised systems also known as C2) via a backdoor.

As it was reported by Krebs, the SolarWinds attack was so extensive that communications at the US Treasury and Commerce Departments were reportedly compromised. More than 425 of the Fortune 500 use SolarWinds, and over 18,000 SolarWinds Orion customers have downloaded the software with the Trojan. This attack allowed attackers to penetrate FireEye and steal tools used by the company's Red Team, the team simulating the attacker during penetration testing.

As a backdrop to the SolarWinds attack, one should remember that in July 2020, Microsoft issued CVE-2020-1350 (SIGRed), a critical vulnerability in Windows DNS (see Chapter 10) servers with a Common Vulnerability Scoring System (CVSS) score of 10 out of 10. SolarWinds, which relies on Microsoft DNS infrastructure, may have been unknowingly exploited via this flaw. Another example of the cumulative effect...

One may ask: "Why did this attack impact so many organisations?" The answer is very simple - because of the widespread adoption of best-of-breed tools, such as the SolarWinds Orion management platform or the Microsoft suite. One may recall the earlier-mentioned prediction made by Dan Geer and his colleagues in 2003 about the negative impacts on cyber security caused by software monopolies like SolarWinds and Microsoft, and reiterated later in 2022 in the World Economic Forum's "Global Risks Report 2022," which is highly recommended reading for the readers of this book (see Chapter 5).

Some other well-known supply chain attacks include Target USA (2014 - 70 million customers impacted, 40 million debit and credit card details stolen), Panama Papers (2016 - tax evasion tactics of over 214,000 companies and high-ranking politicians exposed), Equifax (2017 - 147 million customers impacted, sensitive data, like social security numbers, driver's licence numbers, DOBs, and addresses stolen), and Paradise Papers (2017 - 13.4 million investment records of the wealthy 1%, including Donald Trump, Justin Trudeau, Vladimir Putin's son-in-law and even Queen Elizabeth, exposed).

So, what is a supply chain attack? A supply chain attack is a cyber-attack that seeks to damage an organisation by targeting less secure elements in the supply chain. A supply chain attack can occur in any industry, from the financial sector or the oil industry to the government sector. A supply chain attack can happen in software, firmware, or hardware.

Typically, cyber-criminals tamper with the manufacturing or distribution of a product by installing hidden malware or firmware-based or hardware-based spying components. Symantec's 2019 Internet Security Threat Report states that **in 2018, supply chain attacks increased by 78 percent.** Although "supply chain attack" is a broad term, in reference to cyber security, a supply chain attack can involve physical tampering with electronics (computers, ATMs, power systems, factory data networks) to install undetectable malware for the purpose of bringing harm to a player further down the supply chain network. Alternatively, the term can be used to describe attacks exploiting the software supply chain, in which an apparently low-level or unimportant software component used by other software can be used to inject malicious code into the larger software that depends on this component.

A supply chain attack is a type of cyber-attack that targets trusted third-party vendors and/or suppliers who offer services or software vital to the supply chain instead of directly targeting a specific organisation. Supply chain attacks exploit trust relationships between different organisations. All organisations have some degree of trust in other organisations when they install and use software on their networks or collaborate as part of vendor or contractor agreements. Supply chain attacks target the weakest link in the chain of trust. Even if the target organisation is well-defended and has a strong cyber security posture, if a trusted vendor is not secure, attackers will target that vendor to bypass whatever security is in place in the primary target organisation. By gaining a foothold in the provider's network or the provider's software, an attacker can exploit this trust to gain access to a more secure network.

A supply chain attack (also known as a **third-party attack, value-chain attack** or **backdoor breach**) is when a cyber-criminal accesses an organisation's network via third-party vendors or through the supply chain. **Supply chains are often massive and complex, which is why some attacks are so difficult to trace.** Many organisations work with dozens of suppliers for everything from ingredients or production materials to outsourced work and technology. This is why it's so important to protect the supply chain and ensure the organisations one's organisation is working with are as committed to security as the client's organisation.

Supply chain attacks are a type of cyber-attack that is often overlooked. This type of attack can cause catastrophic damage over time and can be more difficult to detect and prevent if the organisation's vendors and outsourced service providers aren't maintaining a strong cyber security posture (which is difficult to control by the client's organisation). Usually, supply chain attacks work by delivering malicious software via a supplier or vendor. For example, a software update, like in the SolarWinds case, or a key-logger placed on a USB drive can make its way into a large retail organisation, which then logs keystrokes to determine passwords to employees' accounts.

As USB drives were mentioned, we should point to another well-known supply chain attack called Stuxnet that was discovered in 2010 and allegedly used USB drives to deliver malware into a very secure air-gapped (e.g., not physically connected to any network) environment, causing substantial damage to Iran's nuclear program.[1] There are numerous YouTube documentaries describing this attack, and it is highly recommended to watch at least one of them.[2]

One form of a supply chain attack is an attack on a non-IT service provider (like an outsourced overseas Qantas call centre (see Chapter 2)).

Although the recent unsuccessful CrowdStrike update that crashed approximately 8.5 million systems (see Chapter 5) and was called the largest outage in the history of IT and "historic in scale" was not a deliberate supply chain attack, it clearly shows the full potential and disastrous consequences of this type of attack.

The biggest supply chain attack threat organisations face today is the software supply chain. Software supply chains are highly susceptible to attack because in **modern development organisations software, is not created from scratch and uses many off-the-shelf components such as third-party APIs, open-source code, and proprietary code from software vendors. Any of these could be exposed to security threats and vulnerabilities.** The average **software project today has 203 dependencies!** If a popular app includes one compromised dependency, every organisation that downloads from this software vendor is compromised as well, so the number of victims can grow exponentially. **And the risk grows with the never-ending growth of the IT ecosystem** (see Chapters 4 and 5).

Remember the Log4j story (see Introduction)? Again, although this was not a result of malicious activity, it clearly demonstrated the scale of potential disaster and the cost and time it takes to fix this type of problem. As software is reused, a vulnerability in one application can live on beyond the original software's lifecycle.

Today's software is very complex, and an attempt to create protection against software supply chain attacks resulted in the creation of the notion of Software Bill of Materials (SBOM). Unfortunately, the practical use of SBOM as an ongoing, pragmatic, and easy-to-use tool, rather than a one-off tick box, turned out to be an unattainable dream.

Another example of the **cumulative effect** is a result of the combination of complexity (see Chapter 4) and the supply chain: the recent "widespread data theft" from Salesforce customers.[3]

Another aspect to consider is the possibility of an **insider threat** viewed through a potential supply chain attack lens. Is it possible to incentivise a software developer to build in malware in their code (or data)? Of course, it is possible. And if the money is not a strong enough motivation (though a sufficient enough financial inducement that will set the person for life will typically do it), then a threat to harm next of kin will definitely achieve this goal. Again, the question is, "What does this mean?" This means that **at no point in time can anyone be confident that software used by the organisation does NOT contain timebomb malware that can go off at some point in the future.** And this is before we start talking about vulnerabilities that slipped through code reviews, testing, etc.

Recently, **software supply chain attacks moved from the periphery of concerns to the forefront.**

According to Verizon's "2024 Data Breach Investigations Report," the use of vulnerabilities to initiate breaches surged by 180% in 2023, compared to 2022. Of those breaches, 15% involved a third party or supplier, such as software supply chains, hosting partner infrastructures, or data custodians. In the first quarter of 2023, over 60,000 organisations reported being impacted by supply chain attacks. **In 2024, approximately 183,000 organisations were affected by supply chain attacks worldwide. In June 2024,** BlackBerry revealed that **more than 75 percent of software supply chains have experienced attacks in the previous 12 months.** In today's interconnected digital landscape, the security of the software supply chain has become a paramount concern for cyber security professionals. **Rapidly increasing reliance on third-party software vendors and suppliers** introduces numerous vulnerabilities and **keeps raising risks associated with supply chain attacks.**

Supply chain attacks such as those perpetrated on Blackbaud, Accellion, Microsoft Exchange servers, and - most notably - SolarWinds, represent a unique challenge and key shift in attack vectors for malicious actors around the world. The SolarWinds attack demonstrated to organisations that they must always have their guard up when it comes to their supply chains. It displayed some particular vulnerabilities of manufacturing in the software supply chain and how they can pose a risk for high-profile, highly protected companies such as Cisco, Intel, and Microsoft.

It also shows IT security leaders that once a bad actor has infiltrated one part of the supply chain, they've infiltrated the whole thing. Security researchers state that **supply chain attacks are some of the most difficult threats to prevent** because they take advantage of inherent trust. Beyond that, they're difficult to detect, and they can have longer-lasting residual effects. Mitigating and remediating a supply chain attack isn't as simple as installing an antivirus or resetting an operating system. As Lucian Constantin said, supply chain attacks "are some of the hardest types of threats to prevent because they take advantage of trust relationships between vendors and customers and machine-to-machine communication channels, such as software update mechanisms that are inherently trusted by users." This was echoed by Jake Williams (SANS Institute): "**Supply chain compromises will continue. They are extremely difficult to protect against, highlighting the need for security to be considered as part of the vendor selection process.**"

Often, organisations don't even have full visibility (and thus full understanding) of their supply chain. What visibility does the organisation have of the supply chain of the organisation's service provider(s) and of the supply chain further down the track? To which N-th degree organisation can and should go to ensure that its supply chain is interrogated end-to-end? How often can organisations afford to do it? Will the organisation discover that one of its service providers is using deprecated TLS 1.0 and TLS 1.1? How many organisations understand that 13 root Internet servers are part of their supply chain?

QUESTIONS

These questions are important, as they prompt thinking and allow the target audience to understand the organisation's potential exposure and what they personally can do to improve the organisation's cyber security posture. To get answers to some of these questions, the target audience may need to go to their CIOs and CISOs.

1. Does the organisation have full end-to-end visibility and a full understanding of its supply chain?
2. How many suppliers (IT and non-IT) are used by the organisation? How many suppliers are listed in the organisation's vendor master, and what percentage have been actively in use within the last 12–18 months?
3. Is there anyone in the organisation who is accountable for cyber security of the IT and non-IT supply chain? Who is responsible for ensuring the ongoing cyber security of the IT and non-IT supply chain?
4. How many suppliers have access to the organisation's systems and data?
5. Does the organisation use specific clauses in supplier agreements covering supply chain cyber security exposure?
6. Does the organisation proactively govern and manage suppliers' compliance with cyber security obligations through their agreements?
7. Does the organisation classify suppliers according to cyber security risk exposure (through detailed cyber security assessments) and maintain a list of suppliers through whom a supply chain attack can occur?
8. Is supply chain attack risk reflected in the organisation's risk register?
9. What measures, if any, does an organisation take to protect itself against supply chain attacks?
10. Does the organisation have a playbook for recovery from various supply chain attacks?
11. What impact do the size and complexity of the supply chain have on an organisation's insider threat size?

DESSERT

In April 2023, it was disclosed that the **US Department of Justice detected the SolarWinds breach in May 2020, 6 months before the official announcement,** and informed SolarWinds of the anomaly. During the same period, Volexity traced a data breach at a US think tank to the organisation's Orion server. In September 2020, Palo Alto Networks identified anomalous activity related to Orion. **In each case, SolarWinds was notified but found nothing suspicious.**

Considering the huge size and complexity of today's IT ecosystem, one should remember that supply chain attacks may have several types:

- **Software Supply Chain Attack**: a software supply chain attack only requires one compromised application or piece of software to deliver malware across the entire supply chain. Attacks will often target an application's source code, delivering malicious code into a trusted app or software system. **Cyber-criminals often target software or application updates as entry points.** Software supply chain attacks are incredibly difficult to trace, with cyber-criminals often using **stolen certificates** to "sign" the code to make it look legitimate.
- **Firmware Supply Chain Attack**: inserting malware into a computer's booting code is an attack that only takes a second to unfold. Once a computer boots up, the malware is executed, jeopardising the entire system. Firmware attacks are quick and often undetectable if one is not looking for them; they are incredibly damaging.
- **Hardware Supply Chain Attack**: hardware attacks depend on physical devices, much like the USB keylogger or pagers mentioned earlier. Cyber-criminals will target a device that makes its way through the entire supply chain to maximise its reach and damage.
- **Service Provider Supply Chain Attack**: penetrating one of the service providers that has access to the organisation's systems and/or data.

Let's have a look at the most serious (and the most denied) case of hardware supply chain attack that allegedly happened in 2015.

On October 4, 2018, Bloomberg Businessweek published a story, which is the culmination of years of investigative work and cites nearly 20 anonymous sources from both the US government and private companies reportedly involved in the affair. This **report alleged that the Chinese government directly interceded to insert small microchips into motherboards** from a company called Supermicro, which are in use in servers everywhere from the adult film industry to the US military and the US Intelligence Community data centres, making them vulnerable and opening them up to remote hacks. The report said that American authorities first became aware of the existence of the microchips in 2015, that the classified probe is still ongoing, and that US officials have identified an unspecified unit of China's People's Liberation Army (PLA) as being responsible for sneaking the malicious hardware into the servers. The report said the following: "Nested on the servers' motherboards, the testers found a tiny microchip, not much bigger than a grain of rice, that wasn't part of the boards' original design. Amazon reported discovery to US authorities, sending a shudder through the intelligence community." According to unnamed US officials cited in the report, spying hardware was designed by a unit of the PLA and was inserted into equipment manufactured in China for the US-based Supermicro Computer Inc.

"Think of Supermicro as the Microsoft of the hardware world," a former US intelligence official told Bloomberg. "Attacking Supermicro motherboards is like attacking Windows. It's like attacking the whole world," he said. By 2015, the San Jose-based firm had sold thousands of servers to more than 900 customers in around 100 countries. The customer base included the Central Intelligence Agency, various elements of the US military, the Department of Homeland Security, NASA, and the US Congress, as well as big-name tech firms such as Apple.

The basic concept behind the alleged plan was pretty straightforward. The PLA unit in question allegedly infiltrated Supermicro's China-based subcontractors who make the motherboards and added its own hardware, reportedly no bigger than a grain of rice or the tip of a pencil. These chips themselves don't do much on their own, but what they do is immensely important. The small amount of computer code they contain instructs the completed servers to be open to outside modifications and to be ready to receive further code from other computers remotely, creating a backdoor for hackers to access the information they contain. It could potentially have other functions as well, including acting as a remotely operated kill-switch to just shut down a system entirely on command. Hackers could also potentially use it as a gateway to feed false or confusing information into a target system as well.

The issue reportedly only became apparent in 2015 after Amazon sent systems produced by a company called Elemental, which included Supermicro servers, for a deep security inspection, according to Bloomberg. Elemental manufactured equipment for the Department of Defense data centres, the CIA's drone operations, and onboard networks of Navy warships. The report said that "Elemental also started working with American spy agencies. In 2009, the company announced a development partnership with In-Q-Tel Inc., CIA's investment arm, a deal that paved the way for Elemental servers to be used in national security missions across the U.S. government."

Amazon Web Services was looking to acquire Elemental, which specialised in hardware to support online video-streaming services, to help with its own projects, such as Amazon Prime Video. The unnamed third-party security firm located the chips, after which Amazon reportedly informed the FBI, prompting the still ongoing (at the time of publication) investigation. One of Bloomberg's anonymous sources said that US officials identified at least 30 private companies, including Apple, that had the sabotaged servers. It is important to note, however, that Amazon, Apple, and Supermicro have all vociferously, publicly, and categorically denied Bloomberg's report. The three companies say they have never located a piece of malicious hardware on the servers, contacted the US government about such an issue, or been aware of any investigation. The Chinese government, not surprisingly, issued a vague and indirect response when the outlet asked for comment. Following the report, Supermicro moved manufacturing out of China. That being said, in 2016, Apple did stop buying products from Supermicro entirely, citing a security incident that it said was unrelated to any hardware tampering.

After this story had looked like it was long forgotten, it resurfaced in 2021, when several publications insisted that this story was actually true.[4]

A software supply chain attack is a highly effective way of breaching security by injecting malicious libraries or components into a product without the developer, manufacturer, or end client realising it. It's an effective way to steal sensitive data, gain access to highly sensitive environments, or gain remote control over specific systems.

Software supply chain attacks typically piggyback on the legitimate processes in order to gain uninhibited access into an organisation's ecosystem. This attack begins with infiltrating a software vendor's security defences. This process is usually much simpler than attacking a victim directly due to the unfortunate myopic cyber security practices of many organisations. Penetration could occur via multiple attack vectors. Once injected into the software vendor's ecosystem, malicious code needs to embed itself into a digitally signed process of its host. This is the key to gaining access to a software vendor's client network. A digital signature verifies that a piece of software is authentic to the manufacturer, which permits the transmission of the software to all networked parties. By hiding behind this digital signature, malicious code is free to ride the steady stream of software update traffic between a compromised software vendor and its client network. For example, the malicious payload that compromised the US government was injected into a SolarWinds Dynamic Link Library (.dll) file. This file was a digitally signed asset of SolarWinds Orion software, the disguise that nation-state hackers needed to gain access to SolarWinds' client base.

Compromised software vendors unknowingly distribute malware to their entire client network. The software patches that facilitate the hostile payload contain a backdoor that communicates with all third-party servers; this is the distribution point for the malware. A popular software vendor could infect thousands of businesses (18,000+ in the case of SolarWinds) with a single update, helping malicious actors achieve a higher magnitude of impact with a lot less effort. When a victim installs a compromised software update from a software vendor, malicious code is also installed with the same permissions as the digitally signed software, and the cyber-attack is initiated. Once installed, a Remote Access Trojan (RAT) is usually activated to give cyber-criminals access to each infected host for sensitive data exfiltration. And all this is possible because many, many moons ago we chose von Neumann computer architecture (see Chapter 3).

Another interesting case that deserves discussion is the October 2023 Okta breach, as it demonstrated the chain reaction mechanism of theft, rather than direct compromise of an organisation that uses certain software through malware covertly pushed into this organisation's environment(s).

As discussed earlier, supply chain attacks involve a compromised software vendor that has been breached, and the data stolen is then used to compromise the software vendor's customers. In this case, attackers breached Okta's support ticket system using a compromised service account. From there, the **attackers stole the HTTP Archive (HAR) file**. HAR file is a file used to log web browser interactions with a website that captures details like network requests, responses, headers, timing information, etc.) files uploaded by Okta's customers, which **contain Okta's customers' credentials**.

Cloudflare, being an Okta customer, responded to the initial breach by rotating 5,000 exposed credentials. Sadly, their efforts fell short. In an extensive report, Cloudflare described how a few weeks after the incident, **Okta attackers used two credentials that were not rotated** (remember that complexity is your enemy, as discussed in Chapter 3) to compromise their Atlassian suite: a token and service account credentials, both belonging to integrations within Cloudflare's Atlassian environment, and were used to gain administrative access to Cloudflare's Jira, Confluence, and Bitbucket.

Compromised production, the Atlassian suite contained Cloudflare's internal Confluence wiki (14,099 pages), Jira bug tracking (2 million tickets) and Bitbucket source code (11,904 repositories), all of which the attackers had access to. This was a devastating attack on one of the largest SaaS (see Chapter 8) companies that severely highlighted the risks of supply chain attacks, especially for SaaS solutions (see Chapter 8). Although not initially their fault, Cloudflare's most sensitive data was leaked. This attack demonstrated again how **cyber-attackers abuse non-human access, which usually goes unmonitored, to achieve privileged access** to internal systems. Another noteworthy point is that the attackers targeted Cloud, SaaS, and also on-premises solutions to expand their access. This emphasises the **growing need for a holistic approach to securing non-human identities across the entire organisation**.

As we started to talk about software supply chain attacks, it is important to discuss the Software Bill of Materials (SBOM). **Today's software is very complex** and consists of multiple components, including newly written code, historical and reused code, libraries, etc.

According to the US Cybersecurity & Infrastructure Security Agency (CISA), a Software Bill of Materials (SBOM) is a nested inventory, a list of ingredients that make up software components. Effectively, SBOM is a list of all the components, libraries, metadata, and other dependencies used in a software application. SBOM also lists the licenses that govern those components, the versions of the components used in the codebase, and their patch status, which allows security teams to quickly identify any associated security or licence risks. The idea of SBOM is derived from the term "Bill of Materials" (BOM) that has its origins in the world of manufacturing, where a BOM is an inventory detailing all the items included in a product. In the automotive industry, for example, **manufacturers maintain a detailed BOM for each** vehicle.

Numerous supply chain attacks resulting in high-profile security breaches prompted President Biden to issue a cyber security executive order (EO) detailing guidelines for how federal departments, agencies, and contractors doing business with the government must secure their software. Among the recommendations was a requirement for SBOMs to ensure the safety and integrity of software applications used by the federal government. Although the EO is directed towards organisations doing business with the government, these guidelines, including SBOMs, are likely to become a de facto baseline for how all organisations build, test, secure, and operate their software applications. CISA recently released their secure software development attestation form, and any providers of software for use in the critical infrastructure were given 90 days to provide a completed form, and all other providers of software to the US government were given 180 days to do the same.

So, any organisation that builds software needs to maintain an SBOM for its codebases. Organisations typically use a mix of custom-built code, commercial off-the-shelf code, and open-source components to create software. As one principal architect of a leading software supply chain provider noted, "We have over a hundred products, with each of those products having hundreds to thousands of different third-party and open-source components." The idea of SBOM is that it allows organisations to track all the components in their codebases. This is in theory. In practice, the size of SBOM is often measured in several megabytes or more! Is this complex (see Chapter 4)? For sure it is! Think about how easy it is to maintain and update it!

The International Standards Organisation (ISO) began establishing a standard for marking software components with machine-readable IDs. Software Identification tags (SWID tags), as they're now known, are structured with metadata embedded in software and contain information such as the name of the software product, version, developers, relationships, and more. SWID tags can aid in automating patch management, software integrity validation, and vulnerability detection and permit or prohibit software installs, like software asset management. In 2012, ISO/IEC 19770-2 was confirmed, and it was modified in 2015.

It is not enough just to prepare (and maintain) the SBOM. **It needs to be secured with a digital signature.** A digital signature is exactly what it sounds like: an electronic version of the traditional pen and paper signature. It checks the **validity and integrity** of digital communications and documents using a sophisticated mathematical approach. It ensures that a message's content is not tampered with while in transit, assisting in overcoming the problem of impersonation and tampering in digital communications. Digital signatures have increased in adoption over time and are a cryptographic standard. A digitally signed SBOM provides a checksum, which is a long string of letters and numbers that represents the sum of a piece of digital data's accurate digits and can be compared with, and this allows finding faults or changes. A checksum is like a digital fingerprint. On a regular basis, it checks for redundancy using a cyclic redundancy check (CRC) - a mathematical technique that provides a way to detect errors in transmitted data by appending a special code, called a checksum, to the original information. Changes to raw data in digital networks and storage devices are detected using an error-detecting code and verification function. As a digital signature is meant to serve as a validated and secure way of proving authenticity in transactions - that is, once signed, a person cannot claim otherwise - it holds all signatories to the procedures and actions laid out in the bill.

As one of the core purposes of digital signatures is verification, an unsigned SBOM is not verifiable. One can think of it as a contract: if a contract hasn't been signed by participating parties, there's no real way to enforce it. Similarly, an unsigned SBOM is just an unsigned document: the customer cannot hold the supplier accountable. This can also lead to further problems down the road, as an unsigned SBOM can also pose risks for an organisation's security. Anything that might have otherwise been protected by a signed SBOM is now not protected, and therefore, data and information can be sent or replicated anywhere. One of the main purposes of signed SBOMs - accountability - is lost when the SBOM is unsigned, as changes can then be made to it without knowledge of the creator or the client.

SBOM is very complex. More importantly, as software evolves (and it constantly evolves, unless one uses software that is beyond its end of life (EOL) date), SBOM needs regular reviews and updates.

Now, let's look at the practicalities. Do you think you will be able to see SBOM for any of Microsoft's products? Or SAP? Or Salesforce? Or SolarWinds? Or for any other major software vendor? The answer is - with 99.999% probability - "No," unless your organisation is something like the CIA, NSA, or FBI. But more importantly, even if you could, the SBOM that you would see is a point in time (most likely the time of the original deployment or, at best, at the time of the last major release). Now, with quarterly (monthly? weekly?) patches and twice-a-year updates, how much effort would it take to validate each next iteration of SBOM?

Now, think about an organisation with, say, 400 people that has more applications than bums on seats - how much effort would it take to analyse each SBOM update? Or an organisation with 4,000 applications. **The effort required to analyse each SBOM change is simply astronomical** and thus **cannot be implemented in practice,** as no client organisation can afford to do it every time the software vendor provides a patch or an update. What does this mean? This means that **at no point in time can any organisation, especially those that embark on the digital journey** (see Chapter 5), **be confident in the third-party software it uses.**

NOTES

1 https://en.wikipedia.org/wiki/Stuxnet.
2 https://www.youtube.com/watch?v=Fqk_VUMzY_M.
3 https://www.itnews.com.au/news/widespread-data-theft-hits-salesforce-customers-via-third-party-619871?eid=1&edate=20250828&utm_source=20250828_AM&utm_medium=newsletter&utm_campaign=daily_newsletter.
4 https://www.theregister.com/2021/02/12/supermicro_bloomberg_spying/ and https://www.bloomberg.com/features/2021-supermicro/ and https://www.datacenterdynamics.com/en/news/years-later-bloomberg-doubles-down-disputed-supermicro-supply-chain-hack-story/.

Chapter 10

The fifth column just got bigger

Internet protocols

"Curiouser and curiouser!"

Alice's Adventures in Wonderland by Lewis Carroll

APPETISER

- The Internet is the fabric of today's business interactions, and it is based on insecure foundation protocols like TCP/IP, DNS, and BGP.
- The TCP/IP protocol suite, developed under the sponsorship of the US Department of Defense (DoD), was *designed to work in a trusted environment.*
- Each of the protocols in the TCP/IP protocol suite has its own specific insecurities. To better understand the insecurities of the Internet, one should read the article by Stu Sjouwerman, "How the NSA Killed Internet Security in 1978."
- The focus was on solving technical challenges of moving information quickly and reliably, *not on securing it.* TCP/IP designers never envisioned the Internet as it exists today.
- The *fundamental flaw* in TCP/IP design is that it was invented with the idea of *connecting everything.* Unfortunately, when one connects everything, one ends up with an invitation for hackers, cybercriminals, and nation-state actors for international espionage and/or sabotage.
- The TCP/IP security problem arises because *TCP/IP uses the address of a connected device to serve the dual purpose of identifying that device as well.*
- The inherent insecurity of the Internet due to TCP/IP insecurities was further exacerbated by the Domain Name System (DNS) and the Border Gateway Protocol (BGP).
- DNS is the phonebook of the Internet. DNS was designed in the early 1980s when the Internet was much smaller, and security was not a primary consideration in its design.

DOI: 10.1201/9781003730514-11

- DNS vulnerabilities are buried in its original design. DNS architects were concerned about *reliability and functionality, not security.*
- The problem is that DNS is too important to do without, but it's difficult to defend. One may ask: "How come DNS has survived?" The answer is very simple: because it is extremely useful.
- Andy Jenkinson said that "options to abuse DNS are endless as DNS touches everything." "As businesses *continue to digitally transform* and the interconnected ecosystem on which they depend expands, *DNS attacks will only become more frequent and more damaging.*"
- DNS experts Dr Paul Mockapetris and Dr Paul Vixie stated, "Over 95% of all Cyberattacks, Malware, and Bots rely upon DNS."
- 88% of organisations have suffered DNS attacks, and 76% of DNS attacks caused application downtime, and the average attack took over 5 and a half hours to mitigate, with organisations encountering an average of seven attacks per year at a cost of $942,000 per attack.
- In 2024, the average cost of DNS attack recovery has grown to $1.1 million, and DNS attacks lead to application outages in 82% of businesses and data theft in 29% of those cases.
- Security of BGP is non-existent as BGP largely relies on the Internet equivalent of word of mouth for organisations.
- BGP does not directly include security mechanisms and is based largely on trust between network operators.
- As admitted by one of the BGP Fathers, security at that time of BGP design "wasn't even on the table."
- The most significant issue for BGP is its lack of effective security measures, which makes the Internet vulnerable to different forms of attacks.

MAIN COURSE

The word "Internet" was heavily used in the previous chapters. And it is not surprising, as neither Cloud nor SaaS would have been possible without it. The Internet is also the main mechanism used for malware distribution in software supply chain attacks.

The Internet's predecessor, ARPANET, was established by the Advanced Research Projects Agency (now DARPA) of the United States Department of Defense. It was the first wide-area packet-switched network with distributed control and one of the first computer networks to implement the TCP/IP protocol suite. Both technologies became the foundation on which the Internet runs today. The first successful test of ARPANET occurred in October 1969. ARPANET was then showcased in October 1972 at the first International Conference on Computer Communications (ICCC).

It is important to remember not only how ARPANET was funded but also the fact that despite multiple claims that ARPANET's purpose was always more academic than military, at the time it was not about a general-purpose network but about a special-purpose military/academic network with the **main focus on Availability (survivability) and then on Integrity (guaranteed or almost guaranteed delivery) with significantly less (if any at all) focus on Confidentiality (as it was assumed that multiple packet delivery routes would prevent interception of the whole message).** As David D. Clark, an MIT scientist whose air of genial wisdom earned him the nickname "Albus Dumbledore," mentioned much later, **"It's not that we didn't think about security. We knew that there were untrustworthy people out there, and we thought we could exclude them."** Vinton Cerf, who in the 1970s and 1980s designed key building blocks of the Internet, later said, **"We didn't focus on how you could wreck this system intentionally. You could argue with hindsight that we should have** but getting this thing to work at all was non-trivial."

How wrong was this judgement! What started as an online community for a few dozen researchers is now accessible to an estimated 5.64 billion people. That's more than the population of the entire planet in the early 1960s, when the first talk of building a revolutionary new computer network began.

So, what is TCP/IP? TCP/IP, which stands for Transmission Control Protocol/Internet Protocol is a suite of communication protocols that enable devices to connect and exchange data over the Internet and other networks. The foundational protocols in the suite are the Transmission Control Protocol (TCP), the User Datagram Protocol (UDP) and the Internet Protocol (IP). **TCP/IP is the foundation upon which the Internet operates,** providing the rules and procedures for how devices send and receive information. **The term "Internet" was adopted in 1983,** at about the same time that TCP/IP came into wide use.

One of the major and long-lasting features of TCP/IP was the introduction of the concept of IP address. An IP address works like a postal address, allowing data to be routed to the chosen destination. The initial version of this scheme is called IPv4 and uses a 32-bit address field capable of uniquely addressing about 4.3 billion devices.

By 1992, it became evident that this would not be enough, and the world was already running out of IP addresses, which resulted in the introduction in 1994 of Network Address Translation (NAT) - an interim solution allowing for dealing with the shortage of IPv4 addresses.

It is important to note that **IPv4 suffered from several significant security vulnerabilities** and limitations. These include a **lack of built-in security features and susceptibility to various types of attacks,** like IP address spoofing and Distributed Denial of Service attacks. Additionally, the use of NAT can hinder security monitoring and intrusion detection.

To fundamentally solve the problem of an insufficient number of IP addresses, IPv6 was first introduced in the mid-1990s, and the standard was published in 1998. IPv6 uses a 128-bit address field capable of uniquely addressing about 340 undecillion (2 to the power of 128) devices. It is important to understand that NAT is not going to disappear overnight, as Google reported a slow 5% annual increase in IPv6 traffic, with global adoption likely to surpass 50% by the end of 2024.

Although **IPv6** resolved the problem of IP address exhaustion, it came with its problems and **introduced new security challenges and vulnerabilities.** These stem from the protocol's **complexity** (see Chapter 4) and the potential for misconfigurations (especially while transitioning from IPv4) and inadequate security measures. The larger address space of IPv6 and new features make it more challenging to configure, manage, and secure, potentially leading to misconfigurations and an increased attack surface. While IPv6 inherited vulnerabilities of IPv4, IPv6 has its own vulnerabilities, such as router advertisement attacks and issues with Neighbor Discovery Protocol (NDP), not to mention that IPv6 traffic may bypass traditional IPv4 security devices like firewalls and intrusion detection systems if they are not configured to handle IPv6 traffic. Many existing security tools and practices are not yet fully adapted to address IPv6-specific vulnerabilities, requiring updates and adjustments. Also, IPv6's stateless address autoconfiguration (SLAAC) can make it easier to track devices and users, raising privacy concerns.

By now, you have likely concluded that the TCP/IP protocol suite is pretty complex and maybe even confusing. And you are right, as it is a result of evolutionary development that has happened over the last 60 years!

As we can see, TCP/IP (and the Internet) were created out of fear that a military strike from the Soviet Union could knock out the whole copper wire-based telephone network that was used at that time for military communications. The collaborative effort that produced unprecedented levels of communication and massive leaps in technology and resulted in the creation and proliferation of TCP/IP (and subsequently the Internet) also resulted in numerous problems. These problems emanate from the architecture that runs the Internet itself. The **fundamental flaw in TCP/IP design is that it was invented with the idea of connecting everything. Unfortunately, when one connects everything, one ends up with an invitation of hackers, cybercriminals and nation-state actors for international espionage and/or sabotage.** Despite its remarkable success, TCP/IP has experienced a patchwork development process. As the protocol was designed many years ago, **TCP/IP was not conceived with the current scale and complexity of the Internet in mind.** For example, the need for improved congestion control, error recovery and flow control mechanisms led to the development of TCP/IP extensions, such as Selective Acknowledgments (SACK) and Explicit Congestion Notification (ECN).

One of the fundamental flaws of TCP/IP is in its inherent openness, which consequently results in a lack of security. This openness is largely a result of the address-based nature of TCP/IP. In simple terms, the **security problem arises because TCP/IP uses the address of a connected device to serve the** dual purpose of identifying that device as well. This creates a network vulnerability that is very visible and spoofable to users with malicious intent all over the world. With identity being used simultaneously as a device's address, hackers can simply mock a valid IP address to gain access to an organisation's network, where they can steal data, disrupt service, and wreak large-scale technological havoc. One of the best examples of this was the very first Internet attack - the Morris worm that raged in November 1988, crashing thousands of computers and causing millions of dollars in damage. The worm was using the Internet's essential nature - fast, open and frictionless - to deliver malicious code (see Chapter 3) along communication lines designed to carry harmless files or emails. A couple of other examples from the same era include IP address spoofing, TCP ISN guessing: Mitnick vs. San Diego Supercomputer Center (SDSC) (December 1994), and TCP SYN denial-of-service attacks: Panix (September 1996).

Certain steps have been taken to prevent this type of attack, and Morris worm-type attacks should not succeed on a properly configured system today - rsh is normally disabled on untrusted networks, fixes have been made to sendmail and finger, there is the introduction of widespread use of network filtering and improved awareness of the dangers of weak passwords. But these virus and worm outbreaks have demonstrated that networked computers continue to be vulnerable to new attacks, despite the widespread deployment of antivirus software and firewalls.

The TCP/IP protocol suite, developed under the sponsorship of the US DoD, was designed to work in a trusted environment. The model was developed as a flexible, fault-tolerant set of protocols that were robust enough to avoid failure if one or more nodes went down. The focus was on solving the technical challenges of moving information quickly and reliably, not on securing it. The designers of this original network never envisioned the Internet as it exists today.

The problem is that weakness is inherent in the design itself, and eradicating it is difficult. Many early TCP/IP protocols are now considered insecure and vulnerable to various attacks, ranging from password sniffing to denial of service. The fact that TCP over IP is a low-level protocol means that all the higher-level protocols (e.g., HTTP, Telnet and Simple Mail Transfer Protocol (SMTP)) are vulnerable by inheritance (e.g., hijacking a Telnet connection). And I have recently seen a government organisation that still allows HTTP traffic!

Despite the numerous improvements made to TCP/IP, security remains a significant concern. One of the most critical issues is the lack of encryption in certain applications and protocols, such as Simple Mail Transfer Protocol (SMTP). This exposes email communications to eavesdropping, interception, and tampering by malicious actors. Additionally, the core design of TCP/IP lacks inherent security features, which resulted in the development of various security protocols and mechanisms as "add-ons." Examples include the Secure Sockets Layer (SSL) and its successor, Transport Layer

Security (TLS), which provides encryption for web traffic. While these security measures have improved the overall safety of Internet communications, the reliance on external solutions exposes the protocol to potential vulnerabilities and necessitates constant vigilance to stay ahead of emerging threats.

The **TCP/IP protocol suite is vulnerable to a variety of attacks** ranging from password sniffing to denial of service. **Software to carry out most of these attacks is freely available on the Internet. These vulnerabilities** - unless carefully controlled - **can place organisations connected to the Internet at considerable risk.** In 1999, B. Harris and R. Hunt wrote an article, "TCP/IP security threats and attack methods," that was published in Computer Communications, Vol. 22, Issue 10, pp. 885-897[1] that describes various TCP/IP insecurities. This article describes a range of known attack methods, focusing in particular on SYN flooding, IP spoofing, TCP sequence number attack, TCP session hijacking, RST and FIN attacks, and the Ping of Death (PoD). **More recent coverage of security flaws in TCP/IP** can be found in the paper "Security Flaw in TCP/IP and Proposed Measures" published by Springer in Lecture Notes in Networks and Systems 896 "Cyber Security and Digital Forensics, Select Proceedings of the International Conference, ReDCySec 2023" (pp. 93-107). **Each of the protocols in the TCP/IP protocol suite** (TCP, UDP, IP, ICMP, etc.) **has its own specific insecurities.** For more details and examples of TCP/IP-related attacks, please read Chapter 11 in "Cyber Insecurity: Examining the Past, Defining the Future," published by CRC Press in 2025.

Those who want to better understand the insecurities of the Internet should read the article by Stu Sjouwerman, **"How the NSA Killed Internet Security in 1978."**

Now, let's have a look at how the inherent insecurity of the Internet due to TCP/IP insecurities was further exacerbated by the Domain Name System (DNS) and the Border Gateway Protocol (BGP). Let's start with DNS.

Every device connected to the Internet has its own IP address, which is used by other devices to locate the device. But it is important to remember that an IP address also enables identification and communication. Today, IP addresses are considered personally identifiable information (PII) that is defined as any information connected to a specific individual that can be used to uncover that individual's identity, such as their social security number, full name, date of birth, email address, or phone number.

DNS turns domain names into IP addresses, which browsers use to load Internet pages. DNS servers make it possible for people to input normal words into their browsers, such as https://www.microsoft.com, without having to keep track of the IP address for every website. DNS was designed in the 1980s when Internet access was restricted to government agencies, scientists, and the military. **DNS architects were concerned about reliability and functionality, not security.** As a result, DNS has always been vulnerable to a broad spectrum of attacks.

DNS is the phonebook of the Internet.[2] Humans access information online through domain names, like https://www.google.com or https://www.microsoft.com. Web browsers interact through IP addresses. **DNS translates domain names to IP addresses,** so browsers can load Internet resources. As discussed earlier, each device connected to the Internet has a unique IP address, which other machines use to find the device. DNS servers eliminate the need for humans to memorise IP addresses such as 192.168.1.1 (in IPv4) or more complex, newer alphanumeric IP addresses such as 2400:cb00:2048:1::c629:d7a2 (in IPv6).

Initially, ARPANET did not have DNS - it was not required due to its small size. Then, later, the concept of domains was developed. It was suggested that domains should be based on the type of organisation the computer belongs to. For example, computers at educational institutions have the domain.edu, while commercial organisations have the domain .com, non-profit organisations have the domain .org and organisations with a global presence have the domain.net. In 1983, Paul Mockapetris, who at the time was at the University of Southern California, created the DNS. One of the main disadvantages of DNS is the **potential for DNS hijacking and DNS spoofing attacks.**

The Internet can't survive without DNS. However, DNS creates numerous insecurities. Probably this is one of the best (if not the best!) descriptions of DNS insecurities[3]:

> "Imagine proposing a new application project to your boss. It's a distributed network database that runs across millions of nodes on the Internet. Everyone would own and run their own server, but would need to coordinate data storage, retrieval, and updates with all the others. This cooperation would be based on a published document describing the relationship - but that's all! There would be no organisation and no master control server in charge, just some simple hierarchies and some registration authorities that keep track of who holds what records. Anyone could query this database anonymously, and the whole distributed system would work out the answer and return it to the requestor. Oh, and the whole thing would run over the fire-and-forget, unreliable User Datagram Protocol (UDP), which can be easily spoofed. Your boss would probably laugh you out of the room for proposing such an unworkable system. Yet, in 1983, the Internet Engineering Task Force proposed a solution and the following year, the first Domain Name System (DNS) server was coded at UC Berkley. This was back in the days when everyone on the net (called ARPANET back then) trusted each other completely, and none of the participants were motivated to cause problems. Somehow, good old DNS survived this sheltered childhood and thrives today in our modern swamp of vipers and leeches, that is, the Internet. It hasn't been without some scars, as DNS still bears some fundamental weaknesses that are still exploited today."

One may ask: "How come DNS has survived?" The answer is very simple because it is extremely useful.

Firstly, it's the strong inertia of being the first such system with deep legacy and dependence sunk into the Internet's infrastructure, combined with the enormous potential cost and complexity of its replacement with something else.

Secondly, it's cheap and easy to run and query, with many different services available in both commercial and open-source implementations.

And thirdly, of course, it's something that is proven and works well on a global scale of interconnected disparate networks because it is distributed, and no one controls it.

It's obvious that DNS is a critical piece of Internet infrastructure. As security guru Dan Geer said in 2012,[4] "Risk is a consequence of dependence. We are stuck with DNS and the future of the Internet depends on it."

So, the problem is that **DNS is too important to do without, but it's difficult to defend** - in fact, DNS services are an excellent target for an attack. Remember that **DNS was designed in the early 1980s** when the Internet was much smaller, **and security was not a primary consideration in its design.** As a result, DNS design allows many types of attacks, which we are about to have a brief look at.

In his excellent article,[5] Andy Jenkinson highlighted that the first warning about DNS came in 1999, when Daniel J. Bernstein (DJB) warned the world about the exposure and vulnerabilities of DNS servers. Unfortunately, his concerns were largely ignored. Then, nearly a decade later, **in 2008, Dan Kaminsky demonstrated how DNS security flaws left the entire Internet vulnerable to attacks.** Microsoft and others responded with temporary fixes, but these were mere patches and failed to address the underlying issues. **In 2013, Edward Snowden exposed how the NSA, along with its allies, had long exploited the Internet's weaknesses, including DNS** and Public Key Infrastructure (PKI), to carry out mass surveillance. This became the modus operandi for cyber wars and cybercrime.

Rather than spurring real action to address and improve DNS security, Snowden's and Kaminsky's revelations armed adversaries with knowledge of these vulnerabilities, as the NSA sought to cover up and keep their methods secret. Despite Kaminsky's warnings and Snowden's disclosures, the majority still ignore or dismiss these critical vulnerabilities. Adversaries continue to exploit these weaknesses, and the Internet remains dangerously exposed. As Dan Kaminsky concluded, "DNS should not have been capable of this much damage - it was - but why?"

DNS attacks picked up in 2018, when large numbers of US federal agencies suffered DNS attacks. This served as the catalyst for Cybersecurity and Infrastructure Security Agency (CISA) to reluctantly issue its first Emergency Directive - M-19-01 on DNS Tampering and Abuse.

The DNS system is vulnerable to numerous cyber threats due to its design limitations and lack of security measures. Such hazards include spoofing, amplification, DoS, and the interception of private information. Moreover, DNS attacks are often used as a distraction tactic with other cyber-attacks, making it harder for a security team to focus on a potentially more significant threat. With these vulnerabilities, it is essential to have strong DNS security to prevent DNS attacks and protect business continuity.

The list of DNS vulnerabilities is quite long. No wonder that attacks like these have affected so many organisations, including, but not limited to, The New York Times, LinkedIn, Dell, Harvard University, Coca-Cola, and many others.

Another unpleasant side effect of using DNS is DNS tracking/logging. Whenever a domain name is resolved, a DNS server is queried for information. In doing so, information about the user is sent to the Internet Service Provider in charge of that server, which records the user's IP address and thus the user's approximate location. TLS/SSL certificates encrypt the communication so that hackers are not able to read the content, but this doesn't hide the user's IP address when a user visits a domain name. If someone is able to track an IP address, they can potentially relate it to other stored information like name, address, bank details, and much more. Hackers can potentially collect and correlate this information to perpetrate their attacks. In the past, some Internet Service Providers have accumulated this information to resell it to third parties, often advertisers, enabling them to implement their strategies in a targeted manner. Users in Europe enjoy greater protection due to the introduction of the General Data Protection Regulation (GDPR).

For those interested in DNS abuse, it is recommended to look at multiple of Andy Jenkinson's publications on this topic (and start following him on LinkedIn), in which he highlights the lack of understanding of DNS that has led and continues to lead to multiple misconfigurations and exposures. As he once said that, **"options to abuse DNS are endless as DNS touches everything."** Quoting Andy Jenkinson again: **"As businesses continue to digitally transform and the interconnected ecosystem on which they depend expands, DNS attacks will only become more frequent and more damaging."** Dr Paul Mockapetris and Dr Paul Vixie (both are Internet Hall of Fame inductees and DNS experts) state, **"Over 95% of all Cyberattacks, Malware and Bots rely upon DNS."** It may also be of interest for some to follow DNS Abuse SIG[6] and read this report.[7]

Summarising, this is why DNS is inherently vulnerable to cyber-attacks:

- **Insufficient Security Measures**: historically, DNS was designed with a focus on functionality rather than security. While efforts such as Domain Name System Security Extensions (DNSSEC) aimed to address some of these security shortcomings, adoption remains relatively low, leaving many DNS transactions vulnerable to interception and manipulation.

- **Protocol Complexity:** the DNS protocol itself is complex, with various components and interactions between servers. This complexity increases the likelihood of implementation errors and vulnerabilities that can be exploited by attackers.
- **Attack Surface:** DNS is a critical component of Internet infrastructure, making it an attractive target for attackers seeking to disrupt services, steal sensitive information, or launch large-scale attacks, such as Distributed Denial of Service (DDoS) attacks.
- **Centralisation and Hierarchical Structure:** the hierarchical structure of DNS involves multiple levels of authority, from the root servers down to individual domain name servers. This structure creates multiple potential points of failure and opportunities for attackers to exploit vulnerabilities at various levels.
- **Lack of Authentication:** traditional DNS lacks built-in authentication mechanisms, making it susceptible to various types of attacks. Without cryptographic validation of DNS responses, attackers can manipulate DNS data to redirect users to malicious websites or intercept sensitive information.
- **Weaknesses in Infrastructure:** DNS infrastructure, including DNS servers and resolvers, is often poorly configured or outdated, leaving it vulnerable to exploitation. Additionally, many organisations fail to implement security best practices, such as regular software updates and patch management, further exacerbating the vulnerabilities in DNS infrastructure.
- **Human Factors:** human errors, such as misconfigurations or weak password practices, can also contribute to DNS vulnerabilities. Attackers often exploit these weaknesses through social engineering tactics or by targeting individuals with access to DNS infrastructure.

Overall, the combination of protocol complexity, lack of authentication, weaknesses in infrastructure, and the attractiveness of DNS as a target makes it susceptible to cyber-attacks and hacking. The result of this is that, according to IDC's 2022 Global DNS Threat Report, on a global scale, **88% of organisations have suffered DNS attacks, and 76% of DNS attacks caused application downtime,** and the average attack took over five hours to mitigate - with **organisations encountering an average of seven attacks per year** at a cost of $942,000 per attack. In addition to financial losses, other serious consequences of DNS attacks include data theft, reputation damage, website downtime, and malware infections. **In 2024, the average cost of DNS attack recovery has grown to $1.1 million, and DNS attacks lead to application outages in 82% of businesses and data theft in 29% of those cases. 80% of organisations consider DNS security crucial for their protection.**

In July 2024, another DNS insecurity was described in the blog titled "Ducks Now Sitting (DNS): Internet Infrastructure Insecurity."[8] It is called "The Sitting Ducks attack."

Just another example of a DNS-related problem. Due to a DNS setting error (which the security researcher who discovered it said was almost certainly a cut-and-paste problem), Mastercard had a DNS record with a missing character for almost 5 years. That error would have allowed attackers to potentially take over the subdomain, create a bogus site that mimics the legitimate Mastercard site and then trick customers into revealing sensitive details and credentials.[9] What is frightening about this mistake is not how much damage cyber thieves could have done, but how easy it is to make and how difficult it is to discover. CIP CEO Andy Jenkinson reviewed the Mastercard problem and labelled it "appalling."

The fragility of and risks associated with DNS were recently demonstrated again.[10] Rogue digital certificates vouching for the authenticity of a crucial piece of Internet infrastructure were issued in error during internal testing by a third-party authority and missed by the network security company Cloudflare. Three TLS credentials wrongly issued by the Financial Agency (Fina) in Croatia were reported and created consternation among engineers, as the certificates were for the Cloudflare public DNS server located at the Internet Protocol address 1.1.1.1. As digital certificates are used to validate the identity of services, concerns arose that this was an attempt to maliciously impersonate Cloudflare's 1.1.1.1 DNS offering. Adding to the concern, Cloudflare discovered in its investigation of the event that Fina had issued a total of 12 certificates for 1.1.1.1, covering 15 domains. And this points to the supply chain risks (see Chapter 9).

One may wonder why DNS and BGP are discussed together in the same chapter. To begin with, the **security of BGP is non-existent**. But, as in the case with DNS, we all rely on BGP every day. For everything. DNS, as well as BGP, are both other insecure layers built on top of the already inherent insecurities of TCP/IP.

In September 2022, AWS lost control of its Cloud-based IP address pool for more than 3 hours, which allowed cyber criminals to steal $235,000 in cryptocurrency from users of one of AWS's customers. Using BGP hijacking (a form of attack that exploits known weaknesses in this core Internet protocol), hackers gained control over a pool of 256 IP addresses. So, as some people say in this type of situation, "It's always DNS (unless it's BGP)." Early in 2023, Microsoft experienced a 3-hour outage of its core MS 365 offering due to Azure network issues, wiping out some of its most popular services. It was obvious that Microsoft impacted the internal network with a configuration change. The change didn't immediately cause problems, but issues slowly rippled across the infrastructure. This had all the hallmarks of a dodgy DNS config or a broken BGP update. So, as some people say in this type of situation, "It's always DNS (unless it's BGP)."

For decades, cyber criminals, hackers and agencies like the NSA (especially after 9/11) have abused DNS. These techniques have been explained in detail in multiple articles, including these two articles by Andy Jenkinson: "How the Domain Name System (DNS) and the Hypertext Transfer Protocol

(HTTP) Are Exploited by Cyber Criminals" and "Domain Name System (DNS) Abuse," in which he highlighted the risks of DNS abuse and pointed out that DNS is possibly the most abused and the most manipulated area of Internet assets. And, as they say, better late than never: DNS abuse is any activity that makes use of domain names or the DNS protocol to carry out harmful or illegal activity. And after some 30+ years of running BGP, it would be nice to believe that we've learnt from this rich set of accumulated experience, and we now understand how to manage the operation of BGP to keep it secure, stable, and accurate. But no, that is not where we are today. Despite its crucial function in routing wholesale amounts of data across the globe in real time, **BGP still largely relies on the Internet equivalent of word of mouth for organisations** to track which IP address rightfully belongs to which autonomous system number (ASN)!

So, what is BGP? **BGP is a standardised exterior gateway protocol designed to exchange routing and reachability information among autonomous systems (AS) on the Internet. An AS is a very large network or group of networks with a single routing policy.** In practice, one can think of **AS as a collection of routers controlled by a single organisation** that uses one or more interior gateway routing protocols and common metrics to route packets among themselves. An interior gateway protocol (IGP) or interior routing protocol is a type of routing protocol used for exchanging routing table information between gateways (commonly routers) within an AS.

The origins of BGP can be traced back to 1989 when Kirk Lougheed, Len Bosack and Yakov Rekhter were sharing a meal at an Internet Engineering Task Force (IETF) conference. They famously sketched the outline of their new routing protocol on the back of napkins, hence it is often referred to as the "Two Napkin Protocol." It was first described in 1989 and has been in use on the Internet since 1994. IPv6 BGP was first defined in 1994, and it was later improved in 1998. The current version of BGP is version 4 (BGP4), which was first published in 1994 and subsequently updated in 1995 and then in 2006. BGP used for routing **within the AS** is called Interior Border Gateway Protocol (iBGP). In contrast, the Internet application of the protocol is called Exterior Border Gateway Protocol (eBGP). As later admitted by one of the BGP Fathers, **security at that time "wasn't even on the table."**

Similar to DNS, BGP is not secure and allows it to be abused. The challenge with BGP is that **BGP does not directly include security mechanisms and is based largely on trust between network operators** that they will secure their systems correctly and will not send incorrect data.

Mistakes happen, though, and problems could arise if malicious attackers were to try to affect the routing tables used by BGP. The task of trying to build a secure BGP system is a bit like trying to stop houses from burning. We could try to enforce behaviours of both the building industry and the furniture and fittings industries, and behaviours that make it impossible for a house to catch fire. Or we could have a fire brigade to put out the fire as quickly as possible. Unfortunately, for many years, we've opted for the latter option as an acceptable compromise between cost and safety.

There are parallels here with BGP security. It would be an ideal situation where it would be impossible to lie in BGP. Any attempt to manufacture falsified BGP information could be readily identified and discarded as being bogus. But this is a very high bar to meet. And some 30 years of effort are showing just how hard this task really is.

It's hard because no one is in charge. It's hard because BGP can't be audited, as there is no standard reference data set to compare it with. It's hard because it is impossible to arbitrate between conflicting BGP information, as there is no standard reference point. **It's hard because there are no credentials that allow a BGP update to be compared against the original route injection,** as BGP is a hop-by-hop protocol. And **it's hard because BGP is the aggregate outcome of a multiplicity of opaque local decisions.** There is also the problem that **it is just too easy to be bad in BGP. Accidental misconfiguration in BGP appears to be a consistent problem,** and **it's impossible to determine the difference between a mishap and a deliberate attempt to inject false information into the routing system.**

It is extremely challenging to identify a "correct" routing system, and it is much easier to understand when and where an anomaly arises and react accordingly. This situation could be characterised as: we know what we don't want when we see it, but that does not mean that we can recognise what we want even when we may be seeing it! This is partially due to the observation that **the absence of a recognisable "bad" does not mean that all is "good"!**

BGP security is a very tough problem. The **combination of the loosely coupled, decentralised nature of the Internet and a hop-by-hop routing protocol** that has limited hooks on which to hang credentials relating to the veracity of the routing information being circulated unites to **form a space that resists most conventional forms of security.** It's a problem that has its consequences, in that all forms of Internet services can be disrupted, and users and their applications can be deceived in various ways, where they are totally oblivious to the deception.

Let's have a look at some statistics on BGP incidents in 2024. The number of BGP Route Leaks in Q2 2024: 3,044 (vs 3,017 in the previous quarter). At the same time, the number of perpetrated BGP Hijacks: 13,626 (vs. 15,000 in the previous quarter).

The most significant point of concern in BGP is its **lack of effective security measures,** which makes the Internet vulnerable to different forms of attacks. Many solutions have been proposed to combat BGP security issues, but not a single one is deployable in a practical scenario.

One may ask: "Why is securing BGP so hard?" Reasons are very similar to those mentioned in the explanation of why DNS is inherently vulnerable to cyber-attacks, plus several other reasons related to the nature and design of BGP, including no one being in charge, routing by rumour, and routing being relative (e.g., not absolute).

One important factor in many aspects of the Internet is the ability to support a "piecemeal" deployment. Indeed, this loosely coupled nature of many aspects of the Internet is now so pervasive **that central orchestration of many deployed technologies in the Internet is practically impossible. The Internet is just too big, too diverse, and too loosely coupled to expect any quick change.** Any activity that requires some general level of coordination of actions across a diversity of networks and operational environments is a forbidding prospect.

However, recently, BGP insecurity has attracted the attention of the White House, and in early September 2024, it indicated that it hopes to sort out the weak security of Internet routing and specifically of BGP. Earlier in June 2024, the US Justice Department (DoJ) and the Defense Department (DoD) wrote to the FCC regarding the communications agency's decision to look into secure Internet routing. Endorsing the need to address BGP risks, the DoJ and DoD pointed to the way that China Telecom Americas (CTA) advertised erroneous traffic routing in 2010, 2015, 2016, 2017, 2018, and 2019 to send American network traffic to China. CTA had its FCC license revoked in 2021.

As you have seen, the Internet insecurity stemming from insecurity of its foundational protocol (TCP/IP) has been further negatively impacted by two other insecure components (DNS and BGP) lumped on top of it. It is important to remember and understand that these protocols were developed 30–40 years ago and that the world has dramatically changed since then.

QUESTIONS

These questions are important, as they prompt thinking and allow the target audience to understand the organisation's potential exposure and what they personally can do to improve the organisation's cyber security posture. To get answers to some of these questions, the target audience may need to go to their CIOs and CISOs.

1. How heavily do the organisation's business and operations depend upon the Internet?
2. Does anyone in the organisation understand the risks associated with TCP/IP, DNS, and BGP?
3. Does the organisation have a documented business continuity plan for the Internet loss scenario? How frequently is it being tested? When was the last time it was tested?
4. What protocols are used by the organisation? Are there any obsolete and totally insecure versions of protocols (like HTTP) still in use by the organisation?
5. Who manages the organisation's DNS? What is the organisation's level of trust in its DNS provider?

DESSERT

How secure is the Internet and its use? To answer this question, we need to go back in time to the 1960s, when a system called SAGE (Semi-Automatic Ground Environment) had been built. SAGE was using computers to track incoming enemy aircraft and to coordinate military response. The system included 23 "direction centres," each with a massive mainframe computer that could track 400 planes, distinguishing friendly aircraft from enemy bombers. The system required 6 years and US$61 billion to be implemented. The weak point of SAGE was communications links connecting its nodes - if one cuts these communications links, SAGE would become useless. At the height of the Cold War, military commanders were seeking a computer communications system without a central core, with no headquarters or base of operations that could be attacked and destroyed by enemies, thus blacking out the entire network in a single hit.

This required a significant paradigm shift from using point-to-point links (that can be easily disrupted) or switching communication channels (or circuits, as they are called) to what is called packet switching, and as a result of this paradigm shift, the Advanced Research Projects Agency Network (ARPANET) was created. Packet switching is a very simple concept that can be illustrated using the following analogy.

The traditional method of using point-to-point links or switching communications channels is no different from loading the whole assembled article (be it a plane or a missile) after it was manufactured on a train or truck for delivery to its destination (say, to an airfield or to a missile silo). The problem with this is that if the train line or chosen highway is blown, then it is impossible to deliver this article to its destination in a timely manner. Packet switching is similar to disassembling a manufactured article into components and sending each of these components via a different route - be it a rail line, a highway, or any combination of both. In this case, even if one component is not delivered to its destination due to the disruption of one of the transport arteries, it is much easier to ship another similar component rather than the whole article. Eventually, when all components arrive at their destination (and the sequence in which they arrive at their destination is not important in this case), they can be assembled into the article again.

As packet switching benefits were recognised, multiple attempts were undertaken to create proprietary packet switching protocols or to create one that would become a worldwide standard. Examples of proprietary efforts include IBM SNA (1974),[11] Digital Equipment Corporation (DEC) DECnet (1975),[12] Honeywell BULL DSA, and Univac DCA. Probably quite a few people have never heard the names of these companies and protocols. In 1975, five nations (Canada, France, Japan, the UK, and the US) began discussions about standardising the host-network interface for public packet switching networks. The result was the protocol CCITT Recommendation X.25, which was adopted by all the nations involved.

At the core of a packet-switching network is a networking device called a router that receives and forwards data packets between computer networks. It acts as a traffic director, managing the flow of information and ensuring data reaches the correct destination. A router is a device that connects two or more packet-switched networks or subnetworks. It serves two primary functions: managing traffic between these networks by receiving and forwarding data packets to their intended IP addresses, and allowing multiple devices to use the same Internet connection. Routers are essential for connecting multiple devices to the Internet.

However, whether this was the case of X.25 being a victim of the "camel syndrome" ("a camel is a horse designed by a committee"), or a failed competition with TCP/IP, or all of the above, or something else can be debated, but TCP/IP won the race.

The TCP/IP protocol suite enables end-to-end data communication, specifying how data should be packetised, addressed, transmitted, routed, and received. This functionality is organised into four abstraction layers (and thus is not 100% fully mappable onto the 7-layer reference Open Systems Interconnection (OSI) model from ISO[13]), which classify all related protocols according to each protocol's scope of networking:

- **Application layer** includes several protocols like SMTP (Simple Mail Transfer Protocol), FTP/SFTP (File Transfer Protocol/Secure File Transfer Protocol), SSH (Secure Shell), HTTP/HTTPS (Hypertext Transfer Protocol/Hypertext Transfer Protocol Secure), DHCP (Dynamic Host Configuration Protocol), and Telnet.
- **Transport layer** includes several protocols like connection-orientated TCP (Transmission Control Protocol), connectionless UDP (User Datagram Protocol), the newer SCTP (Stream Control Transmission Protocol), real-time RTP (Real-time Transport Protocol), and QUIC (Quick UDP Internet Connections).
- **Internet layer** includes several protocols like IP (Internet Protocol), ICMP (Internet Control Message Protocol), and IGMP (Internet Group Management Protocol).
- **Link layer** includes protocols used to describe the local network topology, like ARP, RARP, NDP, PPP, PPPoE, PPPoA, SLIP, LLDP, and DLCI.

An implementation of the layers for a particular application forms a protocol stack. The technical standards underlying the Internet protocol suite and its constituent protocols are maintained by the Internet Engineering Task Force (IETF).

TCP/IP provides standards for assigning addresses to networks, subnetworks, hosts and sockets, and for using special addresses for broadcasts and local loopback. IP addresses are made up of a network address and a computer (or host or local) address. This two-part address allows a sender to specify the network as well as a specific host on the network.

Remember ARPANET, which was mentioned earlier in this chapter? It did not have DNS. The beginnings were small-scale and did not require any sophisticated or automated tools to remember and manage the addresses of connected computers. So, Stanford Research Institute (now SRI International) maintained a text file named HOSTS.TXT that mapped computer names to the numerical addresses of computers on the ARPANET. Addresses at that time were assigned manually, and computers, including their hostnames and addresses, were added to the primary file by contacting the SRI Network Information Centre (NIC) via telephone during business hours. Later, the WHOIS directory was set up on a server in the NIC for the retrieval of information about resources, contacts, and entities.

Then the NIC team developed the concept of domains. It was suggested that domains should be based on the type of organisation the computer belongs to. For example, computers at educational institutions have the https://www.domain.edu, while commercial organisations have the https://www.domain.com, non-profit organisations have the https://www.domain.org and organisations with a global presence have the https://www.domain.net.

These were what are called top-level domains or generic top-level domains (gTLD). By the early 1980s, maintaining a single, centralised host table had become slow and unwieldy, and the emerging network required an automated naming system to address technical and personnel issues. In 1983, Paul Mockapetris, who at the time was at the University of Southern California, created the DNS. In 2012, Paul Mockapetris, who was inducted into the Internet Hall of Fame, admitted that he got the job because "nobody else wanted to do it." The first version of DNS, named Berkeley Internet Name Domain (BIND), was created in 1984 at UC Berkeley.

DNS vulnerabilities are buried in its original design. Let's have a look at one of the DNS design aspects. A Canonical Name (CNAME) record is a type of resource record in DNS that maps one domain name (an alias) to another (the canonical name). CNAME records must always point to another domain name, never directly to an IP address. So, CNAME records are a type of DNS record that allows one domain name to be an alias for another domain name. This can be convenient when running multiple services (like an FTP server and a web server, each running on different ports) from a single IP address. An address record (A) maps a domain name to an IP address. So, if this IP address ever changes, one only has to make this change in one place within the network: in the A record. Essentially, when one types a domain name into a browser, the A record is used to find the corresponding IP address, allowing this browser to connect to the correct server. **While CNAME records offer flexibility and convenience** in managing domain names, **they also come with certain disadvantages in terms of cyber security.**

One of the main disadvantages of using DNS CNAME records is the **potential for DNS hijacking and DNS spoofing attacks.**[14] **DNS hijacking occurs when an attacker gains unauthorised access to a DNS server and redirects legitimate traffic to malicious websites.** By creating a CNAME record pointing to a malicious domain, an attacker can effectively redirect users to a fake website that resembles the original, tricking them into providing sensitive information such as login credentials or financial details. This can lead to identity theft, financial loss, or other forms of cybercrime.

Additionally, **CNAME records can create** dependencies and **potential points of failure.** If a CNAME record points to a domain that is temporarily or permanently unavailable, it can disrupt the resolution of the original domain name. This can lead to service disruptions, broken links, or other accessibility issues for users trying to access resources associated with the original domain. It is **essential to regularly monitor and maintain CNAME records to ensure their continued availability** and prevent potential disruptions.

Another **disadvantage of CNAME records is the impact on DNS resolution time.** When a DNS resolver server receives a query for a domain with a CNAME record, it needs to perform an additional lookup to resolve the final domain name. This can introduce latency and increase the time it takes to resolve the DNS query. In scenarios where performance is critical, such as high-traffic websites or real-time applications, the additional lookup caused by CNAME records can have a noticeable impact on user experience.

So, in summary, while DNS CNAME records offer flexibility and convenience in managing domain names, they also introduce certain cyber security risks and performance considerations.[15] DNS hijacking, increased resolution time, troubleshooting complexities, and potential points of failure are among the disadvantages associated with the use of CNAME records.

DNS is maintained by a distributed database system, which is based on a client-server model. The nodes of this database are the name servers. A DNS server is a computer with a database containing the public IP addresses associated with the names of the websites that an IP address brings a user to. Once the DNS server finds the correct IP address, browsers take the address and use it to send data to content delivery network (CDN) edge servers or origin servers. Once this is done, the information on the website can be accessed by the user. The DNS server starts the process by finding the corresponding IP address for a website's uniform resource locator (URL). The DNS protocol uses two types of DNS messages, queries, and responses.

DNS resolution takes place transparently in applications such as web browsers, email clients, and other Internet applications. In a usual DNS query, the URL typed in by the user must go through four servers for the IP address to be provided. The four servers work with each other to get the correct IP address to the client, and they include the DNS recursor (or DNS resolver), which receives the query from the DNS client (as it does this, it makes queries that get sent to the other three DNS servers: root nameservers, gTLD nameservers and authoritative nameservers), Root nameserver designated for the Internet's DNS root zone (its job is to answer requests sent to it for records in the root zone), gTLD name server that keeps the IP address of the second-level domain contained within the gTLD name, Authoritative nameserver that gives the real answer to your DNS query. This is done to improve efficiency, reduce DNS traffic across the Internet and increase performance in end-user applications. To add to this already complex setup, DNS is also supported by distribution across Internet open resolvers (operated by various entities, including Internet Service Providers, universities, public DNS server providers and other organisations), and DNS also supports DNS cache servers, which store DNS query results for a period of time determined by the configuration (time-to-live) of the domain name record in question.

Looks complex? Yes, because it is complex! And it is even more complex to maintain this distributed system operating properly and in sync!

Some of the well-known types of major DNS attacks include DNS Denial of Service (DoS), DNS Distributed Denial of Service (DDoS), DNS Pseudo-Random Subdomain (PRSD), DNS TCP SYN Flood, DNS NXDOMAIN, DNS Amplification, DNS Distributed Reflection Denial of Service, tsu-NAME DDoS, DNS Hijacking (varieties include Local, Using a Router, Man-in-the-Middle (MITM), Rogue DNS), DNS Rebinding, DNS Spoofing or DNS Cache Poisoning (variation – via Spam), DNS Forgot Password, DNS Tunnelling, DNS Fust Flux, DNS Smoke Loader C2 Campaign, DNS Domain Generation Algorithm (DGA), DNS Domain Squatting, DNS Phishing, and Vulnerabilities due to Bugs in DNS Implementations Data Exposure in Managed DNS, Unauthorised DNS Changes, and DNS Data Leakage.

An AS is a collection of connected IP routing prefixes under the control of one or more network operators on behalf of a single administrative entity or domain that presents a common and clearly defined routing policy to the Internet. Each AS is assigned a unique ASN, which is a number that identifies the AS for use in BGP routing. ASNs are assigned to Local Internet Registries (LIRs) and end-user organisations by their respective Regional Internet Registries (RIRs), which in turn receive blocks of ASNs for reassignment from the Internet Assigned Numbers Authority (IANA). The IANA also maintains a registry of ASNs that are reserved for private use (and should therefore not be announced to the global Internet). Up until 2007, AS numbers were defined as 16-bit integers, which allowed for a maximum of 65,536 assignments. Since then, the IANA has begun to also assign 32-bit AS numbers to RIRs.

Common types of BGP security risks include route hijacks (when a router advertises bogus routes that are more attractive than the legitimate ones), route leaks (when a router advertises routes that it should not), and route instability (when a router changes its routes frequently or withdraws them abruptly, and this is one of the most important and pathological problems of the Internet). Other threats related to BGP include: BGP wrong peering setup or changes, BGP route flapping, BGP manipulation, and BGP DoS.

BGP vulnerabilities are well known and recognised, and by 2007, several BGP enhancement proposals were developed with a view to improving BGP security: secure-BGP (sBGP), secure-origin BGP (soBGP) and pretty-secure-BGP (psBGP). These enhancements came with certain advantages, as well as some limitations.

NOTES

1 https://www.sciencedirect.com/science/article/abs/pii/S014036649900064X.
2 https://www.cloudflare.com/learning/dns/what-is-dns/.
3 https://www.f5.com/labs/articles/threat-intelligence/dns-is-still-the-achilles-heel-of-the-internet-25613.
4 https://www.usenix.org/system/files/login/issues/august2012.pdf.
5 https://www.linkedin.com/posts/andy-jenkinson-96210727_in-1999-when-many-of-todays-security-professionals-activity-7248316498883047424-bVnJ?utm_source=share&utm_medium=member_ios.
6 https://www.first.org/global/sigs/dns/.
7 https://www.first.org/global/sigs/dns/DNS-Abuse-Techniques-Matrix_v1.1.pdf.
8 https://eclypsium.com/blog/ducks-now-sitting-dns-internet-infrastructure-insecurity/.
9 https://www.csoonline.com/article/3808152/mastercards-multi-year-dns-cut-and-paste-nightmare.html.
10 https://www.itnews.com.au/news/cert-authority-issued-multiple-rogue-tls-credentials-for-cloudflare-dns-620105?eid=1&edate=20250908&utm_source=20250908_AM&utm_medium=newsletter&utm_campaign=daily_newsletter.
11 https://www.ibm.com/docs/en/zos-basic-skills?topic=implementation-what-is-systems-network-architecture-sna.
12 https://en.wikipedia.org/wiki/DECnet.
13 https://en.wikipedia.org/wiki/OSI_model.
14 https://www.imperva.com/learn/application-security/dns-hijacking-redirection/.
15 https://et.eitca.org/cybersecurity/eitc-is-cnf-computer-networking-fundamentals/domain-name-system/introduction-to-dns/the-disadvantage-of-the-dns-cname-records/.

Chapter 11

Compliance ≠ Security

"Then you should say what you mean," the March Hare went on.

"I do," Alice hastily replied; "at least - at least I mean what I say - that's the same thing, you know."

"Not the same thing a bit!" said the Hatter. "You might just as well say that 'I see what I eat' is the same thing as 'I eat what I see'!"

Alice's Adventures in Wonderland by Lewis Carroll

APPETISER

- Conformity and compliance play distinct roles.
- Conformity refers to *meeting the specifications or criteria set by a standard or test method*, which is *often voluntary*.
- Compliance refers to *adhering to external regulations, laws, or mandates set forth by governing bodies or authorities*. Compliance pertains to meeting *mandatory* statutory and regulatory requirements imposed by local, state, federal, and international authorities.
- Compliance and security *are not the same thing*. Just because an organisation is compliant with a certain standard or regulation does not mean it is fully protected against cyber threats.
- Examples of organisations that have suffered breaches despite being compliant:
  - *Target:* in 2013, Target suffered a data breach that compromised the credit and debit card information of 40 million customers. Target was compliant with the Payment Card Industry Data Security Standard (PCI DSS).
  - *Equifax:* in 2017, Equifax, one of the largest credit reporting agencies in the US, suffered a data breach that exposed the personal information of 143 million consumers. Equifax was compliant with the Payment Card Industry Data Security Standard (PCI DSS).

DOI: 10.1201/9781003730514-12

- *Microsoft Exchange Server:* in March 2021, it was discovered that multiple vulnerabilities in Microsoft Exchange Server had been exploited by state-sponsored attackers. The breach affected at least 30,000 organisations in the US and around the world. Microsoft was compliant with various regulations.
- *Fidelity Investments:* in August 2024, Fidelity Investments revealed that it suffered a breach that resulted in the personal data of over 77,000 customers being exposed. At the time, Fidelity held an ISO/IEC 27001 information security management system certification from National Quality Assurance (NQA), accredited by the ANSI National Accreditation Board (ANAB).

MAIN COURSE

It is not unusual for people to use the words "compliance" and "conformance" (often also called "conformity," and we will use this term) interchangeably. The common habit of using the two terms interchangeably means that many are unaware of the subtle differences between them. This is a common mistake many of us are prone to. At first, it may seem that "to conform" and "to comply" essentially mean the same thing, notably, to agree to do something or to follow certain rules. However, the strict definitions of these two terms illustrate something entirely different. Let's have a closer look.

Virtually every organisation, regardless of the industry, conducts its activities under set standards, guidelines, and regulations. In some cases, these guidelines detail internal procedures that must be adhered to to ensure that the organisation's products/services keep meeting the standards considered satisfactory to the consumer.

In other cases, these guidelines are prescribed by the external regulatory bodies, and deviations come with strict penalties.

The distinction between internal and external requirements creates the need to differentiate between compliance and conformity.

In general English, the term "conformity" is often simply considered to be the harmonisation between a person's behaviour and the standards of a particular group. For example, a person conforms when they seek to adopt the same behaviour, beliefs, attitudes, and practices of those in the group or the wider society. The conformity for taking a party photograph is that everyone should be smiling and making friendly gestures to the camera. As opposed to a state of compliance, conformity is not prescribed by a legal body. In fact, refusal to conform is viewed as an act of independence or rebellion. If a person does not conform to certain social norms or conventions, they face rejection. And so is the case with the use of conformity in Management Systems Standards. Conformity pertains to aligning with established standards, guidelines, or specifications, often set by international bodies like, for example, the International Standards Organisation. Conformity encompasses meeting the prescribed criteria, whether they are industry standards, organisational policies, customer requirements, or other relevant benchmarks. Organisations may conform to the various standards, specifications, industry best practices, or customer-specific requirements to improve their products' or services' quality and reliability. Effectively, **conformity refers to meeting the specifications or criteria set by a standard or test method, which is often voluntary. It implies that a product, service, or process has met the requirements and specifications defined by a certain standard, albeit not legally mandated.**

The term "compliance" implies a more formal, serious type of act. It is defined as the act or process of adhering to and fulfilling a given order or command. Compliance recognises a situation where certain rules or orders have been met. In ISO 37301:2021 - Compliance management systems, compliance is defined in clause 3.26 as "meeting all the organisation's compliance obligations." **"Compliance" typically refers to adhering to external regulations, laws, or mandates set forth by governing bodies or authorities. Compliance pertains to meeting mandatory statutory and regulatory requirements imposed by local, state, federal, and international authorities.** It involves aligning operations with legal mandates to ensure adherence to applicable laws and regulations. In essence, it involves meeting these applicable mandatory requirements to avoid legal repercussions or penalties. **Effectively, compliance indicates an adherence to legal and regulatory requirements.** It's about fulfilling an external authority's legislative and contractual requirements.

In ISO/IEC Guide 2: Standardisation and related activities - General vocabulary (2004), conformity is defined as the fulfilment of a product, process, or service of specified requirements. These requirements are typically specified in a standard or specification as either part of a conformance clause or in the body of the specification. A conformity clause is a section of a specification that states all the requirements or criteria that must be satisfied to claim conformance to the specification. An example of conformity is when an organisation can demonstrate that it conducts a Management Review. So, **conformity is very much linked to the achievement of the requirements within the applicable ISO/IEC Standard.**

ISO/IEC compliance is the adherence to international standards and guidelines set forth by International Standards Organisation (ISO) and International Electrotechnical Commission (IEC). These standards are designed to ensure that products, services, and processes meet certain requirements and are consistent across different countries and organisations. The intent of ISO/IEC compliance is to ensure that products and services are safe, reliable, and of the required quality. **Demonstration of** compliance with ISO/IEC standards is usually achieved through certification and auditing activities, which involve assessment of management systems and testing and verification of products and services to ensure they meet the standards set forth.

Conformity and compliance play distinct roles. While conformity revolves around voluntary adherence to standards, enhancing quality and efficiency, compliance is anchored in meeting legal, statutory, and regulatory requirements and obligations that are often based on international or national standards. As such, conformity audits evaluate adherence to standards, while compliance audits assess adherence to legal, statutory, and regulatory requirements.

Within ISO and ISO/IEC standards, there is a clear view that:

- Conformity refers to when an organisation seeks to meet the requirements of a standard. Conformity can be seen as formal and/or informal requirements that an organisation commits itself to meet (corporate, business specifics, customer specifics, product/process/service specifics, industry guidelines, etc.).
- Compliance relates to a situation in which the organisation fulfils a compliance obligation or legal requirement stipulated by a legal or higher authority. Compliance can be seen as a mandatory requirement for an organisation to always meet applicable local, state, national/federal, and international laws and regulations.

So, conformance is what an organisation commits itself to (formally or informally), and compliance is what is required from the organisation based on local (i.e., state, federal), national, and international laws and regulations.

As conformance and compliance are not the same, one needs to understand the difference between a certificate of conformity (CoCf) and a certificate of compliance (CoC):

- A certificate of conformity is a declaration issued by an organisation, confirming that a product has been produced in accordance with specified requirements and standards. It serves as evidence that the product meets the agreed-upon specifications, management system (e.g., quality, information security, etc.) standards and contractual obligations.
- A certificate of compliance is a document issued by a regulatory body or authorised third party, verifying that a product meets specific regulatory standards or requirements. It attests that the product complies with applicable laws, regulations or industry standards, ensuring safety, quality, etc.

A certificate of compliance focuses on regulatory compliance, verifying that a product, service, or process meets legal or industry-specific requirements. In contrast, a certificate of conformity pertains to the products', services', or systems' adherence to agreed-upon specifications, management systems standards, and contractual obligations.

A certificate of compliance is typically issued by a regulatory authority or authorised third party, while a certificate of conformity is issued by the organisation itself. Self-declaration of conformity is formally allowed by ISO/IEC 1750:2004 - Suppliers' declaration of conformity as one of the methods of attestation of conformity assessment that relates to first-party or self-declaration of conformity.

It is important to understand that compliance and security are not the same thing. Just because an organisation is compliant with a certain standard or regulation does not mean it is fully protected against cyber threats. Security is the implementation of technical controls, cultural norms, and procedures that protect digital assets from threats - security helps to manage risks. Compliance is meeting the requirements of a third party for business or legal reasons.

One of the biggest myths is that being compliant is being secure. Compliance is not security. Compliance does not result in good security, but good security often results in compliance. An organisation could be secure without being compliant and vice versa. Security doesn't equal compliance, nor vice versa. However, being non-compliant typically ensures large fines. And this drives the behaviour.

Incidentally, similar problems do relate to conformity to management system standards; that is, a certificate of conformity to ISO 9001 does not guarantee that the organisation is producing high-quality products.

Equating security with compliance is a common misconception that can lead to a false sense of security. Believing that compliance alone is sufficient for security can make organisations complacent, underestimating the need for continuous monitoring, constant vigilance, and improvement of security practices across the organisation. Compliance and security are two pillars upon which organisations base their operational and strategic decisions. However, prioritising one at the expense of the other may lead to vulnerabilities and inefficiencies in the organisation. The main difference is in how compliance and security are measured. In many cases, compliance is a yes-or-no answer, like, for example, does the organisation have X policy in place? When it comes to security, there are many shades of grey.

Various cyber security specialists commented on this topic. One example is what was said by Gary Hibberd, Professor of Communicating Cyber at Cyberfort Group:

> "Being compliant limits your approach to security to the narrow confines of the standard you are using. [It is] like looking through 'rose-tinted-glasses', everything will appear okay because that is the lens you are using. But in fact, your approach could be one-dimensional and miss important aspects of cyber security. The result is that you may be compliant but not necessarily secure."

To illustrate that **compliance is not equal to security**, let's have a look at some of the examples of organisations that have suffered breaches despite being compliant:

- **Target:** in 2013, Target suffered a data breach that compromised the credit and debit card information of 40 million customers. Target was compliant with the Payment Card Industry Data Security Standard (PCI DSS) but failed to detect and respond to the breach in a timely manner.
- **Equifax:** in 2017, Equifax, one of the largest credit reporting agencies in the US, suffered a data breach that exposed the personal information of 143 million consumers. Equifax was compliant with the Payment Card Industry Data Security Standard (PCI DSS) and other regulations, but the breach occurred due to a vulnerability in a web application.
- **SolarWinds:** in December 2020, it was discovered that SolarWinds, a leading IT management software company, had been hacked. The breach affected at least 18,000 customer organisations, including numerous US federal agencies. SolarWinds was compliant with various regulations, but the breach occurred due to a vulnerability in its software supply chain.
- **Microsoft Exchange Server:** in March 2021, it was discovered that multiple vulnerabilities in Microsoft Exchange Server had been exploited by state-sponsored attackers. The breach affected at least 30,000 organisations in the US and around the world. Microsoft was compliant with various regulations, but the breach occurred due to a vulnerability in its software.
- **Fidelity Investments:** in August 2024, Fidelity Investments revealed that it suffered a breach that resulted in the personal data of over 77,000 customers being exposed. At the time, Fidelity held an ISO/IEC 27001 information security management system certification from NQA, accredited by the ANSI National Accreditation Board (ANAB).

Every organisation wants to be secure in the long term, but compliance might order an organisation to focus on implementing certain safeguards within a short period of time. Given this situation, some organisations might elect to focus on compliance now and look at security later. This approach can be a slippery slope, as compliance frameworks and standards are always changing. Subsequently, organisations might need to spend additional budget to align with those new versions each time they become publicly available, and this can be a costly exercise.

There are many reasons why relying only on compliance can be problematic.

- **Compliance frameworks create a "rose-tinted-glasses" effect, especially among those without a deep understanding of security.** Typical thinking in this case is that as frameworks are developed by groups of professionals, they are comprehensive, and nothing has been left out. But - there is always a but - these frameworks effectively ignore inherent holes like von Neumann architecture, TCP/IP, DNS, and BGP (see Chapter 10) and focus on prevention and mitigation of the next level risks and thus **create a false perception of achieving security through being compliant.**

- **Compliance controls are not always comprehensive or clear.** Frequently, controls within compliance frameworks aren't prescriptive and can be interpreted in many ways, leading to ambiguity. It is important to remember that compliance standards are often (if not usually) designed for a broad range of organisations, and as a result, they might not fully address the unique security needs and risk profiles of a particular organisation.
- **Most compliance requirements are a point-in-time snapshot of the organisation's environment.** Just because all requirements are being met at that time doesn't mean they always will be.
- **Compliance frameworks don't cover all possible vectors of attacks.** This allows for significant gaps, especially in a rapidly evolving environment of emerging new threats.
- **Compliance frameworks are not always up to date.** The threat landscape is continually evolving, with attackers developing new techniques and exploiting novel vulnerabilities. While compliance standards are updated periodically, they can't always keep pace with the rapidly evolving threat landscape (see Chapter 15). As a result, organisations meeting current standards can still be vulnerable to new and more sophisticated attacks. Compliance standards cannot always anticipate or adapt to these changes quickly enough.
- **The compliance approach** quite **often leads to a checkbox mentality,** as it is easy to adopt a checklist mentality, **focusing on meeting specific compliance requirements without a full understanding of the underlying security principles.** This approach can lead to serious gaps in security posture, leaving the organisation open to cyber-attacks. **It can also result in a false sense of security. Believing that compliance alone is sufficient for security can make an organisation complacent,** underestimating the need for continuous monitoring, constant vigilance, and improvement of security practices across the organisation.
- Unfortunately, **many organisations practice checkbox compliance.** This is where **they implement what's necessary in a compliance framework, not because they see any value in it, but because they are mandated to do so to operate.** They tick off the required policies and use those compliance efforts to claim that they're secure and protected against a variety of threats. This is problematic for a few reasons. Firstly, no compliance framework is a comprehensive or accurate representation of what organisations are deploying across their entire networks, for that matter. That's because technology and the digital threat landscape

are always changing. Secondly, checkbox compliance sends a specific kind of message. Organisations essentially tell regulators that they understand the importance of security, but are just unwilling to prioritise it. So, they'll just take certain measures and nothing else. This limits organisations' ability to explain what they've implemented and why to regulators and/or customers in the event of a breach.

- **Compliance frameworks don't account for the human factor,** like, for example, insider threats. Compliance frameworks can mandate controls to mitigate insider threats, but they cannot eliminate the risk posed by malicious or negligent insiders. Operational risks are a major contributor to cyber security breaches.
- **Compliance frameworks don't account for technological limitations and dependencies, like, for example, reliance on legacy systems or the introduction of new technologies.** Many organisations often rely on legacy systems that may not fully support modern security controls, making full compliance challenging while leaving security gaps. The rapid pace of technological innovation can outstrip the guidelines set by compliance frameworks, leaving many vulnerable to exploitation through new technologies. As Caryll Arcales, a global security specialist, said, "Due to the changes in technology, one limitation of compliance is that it does not align or lag behind the latest trends in cyber security."
- **Compliance framework measures may not be sufficient to defend against Advanced Persistent Threats (APT), which involve sophisticated stealth attackers targeting specific organisations for extended periods of time.**

There are plenty of very good real-life examples of why compliance is not equal to security.[1]

QUESTIONS

These questions are important, as they prompt thinking and allow the target audience to understand the organisation's potential exposure and what they personally can do to improve the organisation's cyber security posture. To get answers to some of these questions, the target audience may need to go to their CIOs and CISOs.

1. How well do the organisation's top three tiers of leadership and management below the Board understand the difference between conformity and compliance?
2. How heavily do organisations rely on compliance in the area of security?

3. Does the organisation have a profound "tick in a box" mentality and culture?
4. Will a compliance certificate still leave the organisation exposed to civil suits?
5. How does the organisation look at supply chain security? Is this based on compliance certificates from suppliers, vendors, or service providers?

DESSERT

The terms "conformity" and "compliance" are closely related to standards created by the International Standards Organisation (ISO) and the International Electrotechnical Commission (IEC). These international standards are called ISO/IEC standards and provide a set of specifications, guidelines, and best practices for a wide range of products, services, and processes.

Unfortunately, ISO and IEC are giving too many different definitions of these two important terms, which are provided in ISO and IEC terminology databases for use in standardisation:

• ISO Online browsing platform[2];
• IEC Electropedia.[3]

As conformance and compliance are not the same, one needs to understand the difference between a certificate of conformity (CoCf) and a certificate of compliance (CoC):

• A certificate of conformity is a declaration issued by an organisation, confirming that a product has been produced in accordance with specified requirements and standards. It serves as evidence that the product meets the agreed-upon specifications, management system (e.g., quality, information security, etc.) standards and contractual obligations.
• A certificate of compliance is a document issued by a regulatory body or authorised third party, verifying that a product meets specific regulatory standards or requirements. It attests that the product complies with applicable laws, regulations or industry standards, ensuring safety, quality, etc.

A certificate of compliance focuses on regulatory compliance, verifying that a product, service, or process meets legal or industry-specific requirements. In contrast, a certificate of conformity pertains to the products', services', or systems' adherence to agreed-upon specifications, management systems standards, and contractual obligations.

A certificate of compliance is typically issued by a regulatory authority or authorised third party, while a certificate of conformity is issued by the organisation itself. Self-declaration of conformity is formally allowed by ISO/IEC 1750:2004 - Suppliers' declaration of conformity as one of the methods of attestation of conformity assessment that relates to first-party or self-declaration of conformity.

NOTES

1 https://www.linkedin.com/pulse/compliance-security-our-false-sense-keshri-sekhon.
2 https://www.iso.org/obp.
3 https://www.electropedia.org/.

Chapter 12

Standards and frameworks

"The Duchess! The Duchess! Oh, my dear paws! Oh, my fur and whiskers! She'll get me executed, as sure as ferrets are ferrets!"

Alice's Adventures in Wonderland by Lewis Carroll

APPETISER

- Standards and frameworks are designed with a continuous improvement cycle in mind.
- Compliance with standards and frameworks makes it harder for adversaries to compromise systems. The question is: how much harder?
- NIST CSF is designed as a guide, whereas the ISO/IEC 27000 series is designed as a standard.
- The NIST CSF and the ISO/IEC 27000 series have some similarities. Both frameworks and standards are based on risk management principles, are aligned with other international standards and best practices, and can be tailored to any organisation regardless of size, sector, or geography.
- NIST CSF is a voluntary framework developed by the NIST and consists of five core functions, 23 categories, and 108 subcategories.
- The ISO/IEC 27000 family of international standards, also known as the ISMS family of standards or, more simply, ISO/IEC 27K, covers a broad range of information security standards. At the core of the ISO/IEC 27000 family is ISO/IEC 27001.
- The ISO/IEC 27000 family of standards consists of 97 individual standards.
- The ISO/IEC 27000 family of standards is still significantly based on "pre-Internet era" paradigms.
- The goal of an ISMS is not necessarily to maximise information security, but rather to reach an organisation's desired level of information security.

- The practicality and usefulness of ISMS are heavily dependent on what is called the Statement of Applicability (SoA). SoA is a document that lists applicable controls, as in Annex A of ISO/IEC 27001, that the organisation will implement to meet the requirements of the standard. Annex A contains 93 controls.
- A properly and well-defined SoA is a foundation of meaningful and useful ISMS, while a wrongly defined SoA may result in a waste of time, money, and resources without delivering expected benefits to the organisation.
- How can a client organisation rely on a supplier's ISMS certificate without a full understanding of the risks and controls covered by the supplier's ISMS?!
- Australian Signals Directorate (ASD) website on Essential 8: "While no set of mitigation strategies is guaranteed to protect against all cyber threats, organisations are recommended to implement eight essential mitigation." strategies from the Strategies to Mitigate Cyber Security Incidents as a baseline.
- The Essential 8 strategies are primarily focused on MS Windows-based Internet-connected networks.
- Is achieving a certain level of maturity a sustainable state, or is it just measured at a certain point in time? The hypothesis is that using a sustainable state approach is unachievable without exceptions for any organisation, especially for larger organisations.

MAIN COURSE

NIST and ISO/IEC

Previous discussion of conformity and compliance logically leads us to the topic of security standards and frameworks, and this scene is dominated by the National Institute of Standards and Technology (NIST) and ISO/IEC. It is also worth mentioning SOC 2, but our focus will be on NIST's Cyber Security Framework (CSF) and the ISO/IEC 27000 series, as they represent two main approaches, standards, and frameworks, to ensure protection of the integrity and safety of the organisation and customer data.

NIST CSF is a voluntary framework developed by the NIST in collaboration with the private sector, academia, and government agencies. It provides a common language and a set of best practices for identifying, protecting, detecting, responding to, and recovering from cyberthreats. It is designed to be flexible, adaptable, and scalable for any organisation, regardless of size, sector, or maturity level. **NIST CSF consists of five core functions, 23 categories, and 108 subcategories** that describe the desired outcomes of effective cyber security.

The ISO/IEC 27000 series is a family of international standards developed by ISO and IEC. This family of standards specifies the requirements and guidelines for establishing, implementing, maintaining and improving an information security management system (ISMS). An ISMS is a systematic approach to managing the confidentiality, integrity, and availability of information assets. The ISO/IEC 27000 series includes 97 standards; the most relevant ones for cyber security are ISO/IEC 27001 and ISO/IEC 27002. ISO/IEC 27001 defines the requirements for an ISMS, while ISO/IEC 27002 provides a code of practice for information security controls. Without questioning the importance and quality of each of these standards, the **sheer number** of them raises questions about the ability of any organisation to digest and implement them all, especially for small organisations.

While both NIST CSF and the ISO/IEC 27000 series support a formalised approach to security, they aren't interchangeable. The **NIST CSF is designed as a guide**, whereas the **ISO/IEC 27000 series is designed as a standard**. The difference here is that **NIST CSF serves as an instruction manual, and ISO/IEC 27001 is more of a test that requires certain measures to pass.** There is no certification or audit process in the NIST CSF. It's a guide that organisations can use to establish their cyber security. There are no proof points that show an organisation is adhering to the NIST CSF. However, organisations can self-report that they've used this framework.

Both the NIST CSF and ISO/IEC 27001 have their benefits, and choosing one (or both) comes down to the organisation's priorities, needs, and compliance requirements. Here are a few things to consider:

- The NIST CSF is best for organisations in the early stages of their cyber security journey or those looking for an organised, intentional approach. ISO/IEC 27001 is best for strengthening an existing cyber security program.
- ISO/IEC 27001 will help organisations by demonstrating trust through a standardised certification. It's common for large organisations to require an ISO/IEC 27001 certification from the vendors they do business with, while the NIST CSF is rarely a noted requirement from customers.

ISO/IEC 27000 family of standards

This chapter will mainly focus on the ISO/IEC 27000 family of standards and, in particular, ISO/IEC 27001.

ISO/IEC 27000 recommends best practices - best practices for managing information risks by implementing security controls - within the framework of an overall ISMS. It is very similar to standard management systems such as those for quality assurance and environmental protection. ISO/IEC purposely broadened the scope of the ISO/IEC 27000 series so it covers security, privacy, and IT issues as well, so that organisations of all shapes and sizes can benefit from it. The information security controls should be selected and tailored to the needs of each organisation so that they can treat the risks as they deem appropriate.

ISMS provides a structured and systematic approach for managing the information security of an organisation and involves putting policies, procedures, and controls into writing to create a documented system that instructs, monitors, and improves information security. An ISMS will also cover topics such as how to protect sensitive information from being stolen or destroyed and detail all the mitigation necessary to achieve information security goals. Information security encompasses certain broad policies that control and manage security risk levels across an organisation. It is comprised of a set of policies, processes and procedures for systematically managing an organisation's information assets, including, but not limited to, sensitive data. The goal of an ISMS is to minimise risks and ensure business continuity by proactively limiting the impact of a security breach. An ISMS also typically addresses employees' behaviour and processes, as well as data and technology. It can be targeted towards a particular type of data, such as customer data, or it can be implemented in a comprehensive way that becomes part of the organisation's culture.

At the core of the ISO/IEC 27000 family (which **consists of 97 individual standards**[1]) is ISO/IEC 27001; the latest version of this key standard was published on the 25th of October 2022. The main body of ISO/IEC 27001 consists of ten sections (i.e., clauses). The first three clauses provide general introductory information, terms, and definitions. Clauses four to ten contain mandatory requirements that organisations must follow to become ISO/IEC 27001 compliant. To achieve "continuous improvement" within the information security management system, the ISO/IEC 27001:2022 standard specifies that organisations should address seven main areas - also known as "clauses":

- Context of the organisation
- Leadership
- Planning
- Support
- Operation
- Performance evaluation
- Improvement

Immediately after the ten clauses, Annex A contains 93 information security controls (this number has decreased from 114 in the previous version of ISO/IEC 27001:2013 to 93 in ISO/IEC 27001:2022, including 11 new controls introduced in this version of the standard). The organisation is not expected to implement each of these controls.

When an organisation performs the information security risk treatment process (defined in clause 6), the organisation needs to go through Annex

A to determine what controls this organisation needs and then verify that no necessary controls have been omitted. So, Annex A in ISO/IEC 27001:2022 is a part of the standard that lists a set of classified security controls that an organisation uses to demonstrate compliance with ISO/IEC 27001.

The controls are broken down into four numbered sections. These sections correspond with Clauses five to eight of a linked ISO 27002 standard, which provides more detailed guidance on how ISO/IEC 27001:2022 controls can be implemented. The four categories are as follows:

- Clause 5: Organisational (37 controls),
- Clause 6: People (8 controls),
- Clause 7: Physical (14 controls),
- Clause 8: Technological (34 controls).

A summary of Annex A controls can be found in endnote 2.[2]

It is important to note that the **practicality and usefulness of ISMS is heavily dependent on what are called the Statement of Applicability (SoA)**, as defined in clause 6.1.3 of the main requirements for ISO/IEC 27001:2022, which is part of the broader clause 6.1, focused on actions to address risks and opportunities. **In ISO/IEC 27001:2022, an SoA is a document that lists the Annex A controls that the organisation will implement to meet the requirements of the standard. It is a mandatory step for anyone planning on pursuing ISO/IEC 27001 certification.** The organisation's SoA should contain four main elements:

- A list of all controls that are necessary to satisfy information security risk treatment options, including those contained within Annex A
- A statement that outlines why all the above controls have been included
- Confirmation of implementation
- The organisation's justification for omitting any of the Annex A controls

The SoA is therefore an integral (and the most important!) part of the mandatory ISO/IEC 27001:2022 documentation. **A properly and well-defined SoA is a foundation of meaningful and useful ISMS,** while a **wrongly defined SoA may result in a waste of time, money, and resources without delivering expected benefits to the organisation.** The **correct definition of SoA is based on the correct identification of information assets and risks to them.** As such, failure to properly identify information assets and associated risks results in an ill-defined SoA. In the past, (having been an ISMS auditor for SAI Global), I have witnessed first-hand numerous organisations with ill-defined SoAs and, as a result, multiple ISMS implementations with very questionable value. Now, if you ask any of your suppliers whose compliance with ISO/IEC 27001 is certified by an independent and properly accredited auditor to share with you their SoA, most likely the answer will be "No." But **how can a client organisation rely on a supplier's ISMS certificate without a full understanding of the risks and controls covered by the supplier's ISMS?!**

The **goal of an ISMS is not necessarily to maximise information security but rather to reach an organisation's desired level of information security.** Depending on the specific needs of the industry and organisation, these levels may vary. For example, since healthcare is a highly regulated field, a healthcare organisation must develop a system to ensure sensitive patient data is fully protected.

However, it is important to remember that due to its origins, the ISO/IEC 27000 family of standards is still significantly based on "pre-Internet era" paradigms, and though the standards have dramatically evolved, their foundation is still significantly based on the "perimeter security" paradigm.

Essential 8

Discussion about standards and frameworks would have been incomplete without mentioning Essential 8.

In 2017, the Australian Cyber Security Centre (ACSC), then a division of the Australian Signals Directorate (ASD), released the Information Security Manual (ISM). This comprehensive guide offered practical advice on safeguarding systems and data and provided guidance and standards for the protection of information and information systems from unauthorised access, use, disclosure, disruption, modification, or destruction. ISM's intended audience included Chief Information Security Officers (CISOs), Chief Information Officers, cyber security professionals, and information technology managers. The ISM is based on industry standards and best practices and is intended to be used in conjunction with an organisation's risk management framework. It is organised into four key activities:

- Govern
- Protect
- Detect
- Respond

ISM provided guidance on governance, physical security, personnel security, and information and communications technology security topics. It is not required by law, unless specifically mandated by legislation or other lawful authority. If the ISM conflicts with legislation or law, the latter takes precedence. The ISM does not provide a comprehensive consideration of legislative and legal considerations, and organisations are encouraged to familiarise themselves with relevant legislation, such as the Archives Act 1983, Privacy Act 1988, and Telecommunications (Interception and Access) Act 1979.

Initially introduced in 2010 and later updated in 2017 and again in 2023 (maturity model changes), the ACSC released a set of prioritised strategies to help organisations mitigate and protect against various types of cyber threats. These strategies are based on the ACSC's experience responding to cyber security incidents, conducting vulnerability assessments, and performing penetration testing on Australian government organisations. The ACSC's strategies are designed to address a range of cyber threats, including targeted cyber intrusions (also known as advanced persistent threats), ransomware attacks and other external adversaries (that destroy data and prevent operation of computers/systems/networks), malicious insiders who steal data, and malicious insiders who destroy data. ACSC strategies are further classified into five relative security effectiveness ratings:

- Essential
- Excellent
- Very good
- Good
- Limited

The ACSC considers the strategies with an "essential" rating to be the minimum baseline for all organisations to follow in order to effectively protect against cyber threats. The ACSC has also released additional guidance on implementing these strategies and on measuring the maturity of their implementation.

Essential 8 is the "essential" minimum baseline security for organisations and is a subset of the Strategies to Mitigate Cyber Security Incidents. It provides practical guidance on how to protect organisations' systems and data from cyber threats, how to implement mitigation strategies in a phased approach and how to measure the maturity of implementation.

It is important to understand that the **Essential 8 strategies are primarily focused on MS Windows-based Internet-connected networks** and are designed to complement each other to provide coverage against a range of cyber threats. While the principles behind Essential 8 can be applied to other systems, such as Cloud services and enterprise mobility, alternative guidance may be more appropriate for these environments.

Essential 8 is a set of cyber security controls developed by ASD, with a key role in this initiative played by ACSC. These controls are designed to provide a practical framework for organisations to improve their cyber resilience and security posture. Essential 8 covers a range of key security controls, including application whitelisting, patching operating systems, and mitigating techniques against phishing and ransomware attacks.

One should remember that although the eight mitigation strategies specified in Essential 8 are useful strategies, they are not bulletproof and mainly target (and thus are limited to) Microsoft environments. These eight strategies include:

- **Application control:** only allowing approved applications to run on a system - great in theory, but **does not protect against supply chain attacks.**
- **Patching applications:** applying updates and patches to software to fix vulnerabilities - great in theory, but **does not protect against supply chain attacks.**
- **Configuring Microsoft Office macro settings:** applying least privileges to Microsoft Office macros - **not always possible to achieve,** for example, in cases when the Finance Department uses thousands of macros.
- **User application hardening:** disabling, removing, restricting and monitoring applications to limit the ability for compromise - **not always possible to achieve** for legacy applications, especially when the source code is not available.
- **Restricting administrative privileges:** limiting the number of users with administrative privileges on a system - **not always possible to achieve,** especially for legacy applications.
- **Patching operating systems:** applying updates and patches to the operating system to fix vulnerabilities - great in theory, but **does not protect against supply chain attacks.**
- **Multi-factor authentication:** requiring more than one form of authentication to access systems or data - **greatly improves security but still does not provide a 100% guarantee,** as discussed later in this chapter.
- **Regular backups:** regularly backing up important data to protect against data loss - **may be of no use if backup copies are not stored off-site or test restores are not performed.**

Essential 8 adds upon the Strategies to Mitigate Cyber Security Incidents by defining four maturity levels. Maturity levels are designed based on the level of adversary tradecraft (tools, tactics, techniques, and procedures) and the targeting that an organisation is aiming to mitigate.

- **Maturity level 0:** there are weaknesses in the organisation's cyber security posture that could be exploited by adversaries.
- **Maturity level 1:** focuses on mitigation strategies against adversaries that use widely available tools and techniques to gain access to systems.
- **Maturity level 2:** focuses on mitigation strategies against adversaries that are willing to invest more time and effort in their attacks and use more advanced tools and techniques to bypass security controls and evade detection.

- **Maturity level 3**: focuses on mitigation strategies against threat actors with advanced capabilities that are willing to invest significant time, money, and effort in their attacks and may use customised tools and techniques to compromise a target.

NSW Government mandated implementation of Essential 8:

> "ACSC has developed and published the Essential 8 strategies for mitigating cyber incidents. The Essential 8 are embedded in Mandatory Requirements 3.3 to 3.10. Agencies must implement the Essential 8 in applicable ICT environments with a minimum requirement of Level 1 maturity, as part of the baseline set in the Mandatory Requirements. Mitigation strategies for Level 2 and Level 3 maturity should then be considered alongside other mitigation strategies based on the threats and risks identified by the agency as part of the threat-based requirements."[3]

It is interesting that technically **this mandate has an "out of jail" ticket in the form that it is directed only towards "applicable ICT environments."**
Some people may be confused between Essential 8 and ISO/IEC 27001 and ask, "Why do we need both?" Essential 8 focuses on eight key areas, while ISO/IEC 27001 provides a comprehensive set of controls and processes for information security management. ISO/IEC 27001 is more comprehensive and detailed, while Essential 8 is lightweight and easier to implement. It appears (at least in my opinion) that the introduction of Essential 8 was possibly an attempt to deal with the complexity and cost of implementing and maintaining ISO/IEC 27001-compliant ISMS by simplifying the approach and shifting focus on some foundational hygiene, capabilities, and controls.
As ISO/IEC 27001 was mentioned in the previous paragraph, it would be remiss not to mention NIST CSF here. Although there are a lot of similarities between Essential 8 and NIST CSF, there are also some differences between them:

- **Essential 8 focuses** on **prevention** of cyber security threats **and post-incident recovery, while NIST CSF offers a holistic approach** to cyber security, **including prevention, detection, response, and recovery.**
- **Essential 8 is a set of eight security controls, while NIST CSF is a framework** that includes **five core functions and associated components.**
- The **Essential 8 focuses** on the **implementation of security controls,** while the **NIST CSF focuses** on the **implementation of a risk management process.**
- **Essential 8 is tailored for Australian organisations, while NIST CSF is designed to be applicable to organisations of any size and industry in any country.**

- Essential 8 is designed to be implemented in a short period of time, while **NIST CSF** is designed to be implemented over a longer period.

Let's have a closer look at Essential 8. The very first warning can be found on the ASD website:

"**While no set of mitigation strategies is guaranteed to protect against all cyber threats,** organisations are recommended to implement eight essential mitigation strategies from the Strategies to Mitigate Cyber Security Incidents as a baseline. This baseline, known as **Essential 8, makes it much harder for adversaries to compromise systems.**"[4]

As always, the devil is in the details - how "much harder" is "much harder"? Let's explore each of the eight areas of Essential 8. In the first place, one should remember that, as mentioned earlier, Essential 8 is primarily focused on MS Windows-based Internet-connected networks (what about other operating systems?). Put this aside; except for multi-factor authentication, seven out of eight Essential 8 focus areas are just good IT Service Management (ITSM) practices that should be practised by any good IT manager. Over 30 years ago, I was managing a medium-sized software development environment and practised all of them that were relevant in those days.[5] Including regular backups that deserve separate discussion, as a lot of organisations do not understand this aspect.

Firstly, **regular backups without regular restores are useless,** as there is no level of confidence that, in case of necessity, successful restoration will happen. I saw **only one organisation** that was diligently doing a quarterly "switch" exercise: full restoration on the disaster recovery site and operation from this site for the next quarter. And then "switch" back after the next quarter. About 10 years ago, I was managing a major incident (instead of a test database, somebody by mistake executed an SQL script on the production database and noticed the mistake several hours later, when the database was already buggered) that impacted motor-registry offices. The system was supposed to be fault-tolerant and operated in a hot-hot mode, and thus both databases (primary and secondary) got corrupted at the same time. There was a backup, and it failed to restore. There was a bit older version of backup, and it failed to restore, too. The organisation ended up manually undoing the SQL script statement by statement, resulting in 3 days of motor-registry closure and significant financial losses. I did not see any test backup restorations across multiple organisations I dealt with over the last 20 years.

Secondly, there is a need for offline backup and off-site backup storage, as in case of cyber-attack one of the first things that an attacker does is poisoning online backups. It is getting expensive with tens, sometimes hundreds, of terabytes to be backed up, but it is necessary. During the days I was managing that software development, I used to keep an onsite copy of the last six months' full backups and another two copies of off-site backups for

12 months, yearly full, and monthly full backups. Some organisations treat Cloud replication as a form of backup. Wrong! Moreover, numerous organisations just back up data, not servers themselves. Wrong too!

Vagueness in backup requirements specified in Essential 8 for each of the maturity levels (Appendix A, B, and C in https://www.cyber.gov.au/resources-business-and-government/essential-cyber-security/essential-eight/essential-eight-maturity-model) opens the door for multiple interpretations. For example, does "Restoration of data, applications and settings from backups to a common point in time is tested as part of disaster recovery exercises" mean that this needs to happen monthly, or every quarter, or once a year, when disaster recovery is typically exercised?

Nobody is going to question the importance of multi-factor authentication (MFA). Of all the access security recommendations, MFA is arguably the most consistent. And there is a good reason why many best practice recommendations and frameworks now place MFA at the top of the list of security configurations needed to help protect against compromise. MFA can be the crucial layer preventing a breach, as passwords alone are often easy work for hackers. However, MFA isn't infallible. As much as MFA is important, it is not as bulletproof as many think, and there are multiple ways MFA can be compromised.

Let's explore the achievability of various maturity levels of Essential 8. The very **first thing that one should consider is whether achieving a certain level of maturity is a sustainable state or if it is just measured at a certain point in time. The hypothesis I have is that using a sustainable state approach is unachievable without some exceptions for any organisation**, especially for larger organisations. How risky are these exceptions? It is not clear from the approach taken by Essential 8, but if one takes a "black and white" approach, exceptions mean failure to achieve a certain level of maturity.

Now, let's look at some of the examples supporting this hypothesis.

Let's take, for example, Maturity Level 1. It requires, for example, disabling or removing MS Internet Explorer, but every organisation I dealt with over the last several years had at least one, sometimes more, legacy system(s) that will not work with any other browser. As such, MS Internet Explorer must stay operational, at least for certain group(s) of employees. Another requirement stipulated for Maturity Level 1 is that MS Office macros in files originating from the Internet are blocked. As always, the devil is in the details - shall a file that came from another organisation be classified as "originating from the Internet"? Blocking MS Office macros files received from service providers or other government agencies is a pretty unworkable arrangement. It is a typical example of a clash between usability and security.

Now, let's extend our example to Maturity Level 2. It requires that an automated method of asset discovery be used at least fortnightly. At first glance, it is not very difficult to achieve. However, to achieve the intent of this requirement, the organisation must have in place a solid IT asset management (ITAM), which is the process of ensuring an organisation's assets are accounted for, deployed, maintained, upgraded, and disposed of when the time comes. I am yet to see a large multi-site organisation that has an up-to-date asset management database that accounts for all IT assets. Patching is always on a collision course with business needs, especially when it must be done within 48 hours, which, by the way, doesn't give enough time for testing. Again, pretty much all organisations I dealt with since 2010 had periods of significant duration when no patching was allowed - be it the go-live of a new system, financial year end, construction activities on rail tracks or elections.

Now, let's look at Maturity Level 3, which, for example, requires the removal of applications that are no longer supported by vendors. Easier said than done, as migration can take years and can be very expensive...

The reality is that organisations cannot and do not comply despite their best efforts, and major expenditure is required. The dynamic of a continuously evolving threat landscape means that organisations are in a perpetual loop of maintaining and updating software, mitigating risks, and addressing vulnerabilities like a dog chasing its tail but never succeeding in doing so.

Essential 8 is meant to mitigate 85 percent of common types of cyberattacks or threats. Don't believe it. The number of threats has increased greatly and keeps increasing on a daily basis. Not only is it difficult or almost impossible to quantify or accurately measure the effectiveness of cyber security controls, but it is also disingenuous to make such a statement. Because Essential 8 controls are targeted only at a basic level of types of threats. Six, to be precise.

Essential 8 is by no means a "silver bullet." Because of many reasons. But mainly because it does not address any of the underlying insecurities - be it the insecurity of von Neumann computer architecture or the insecurities of TCP/IP, DNS, and BGP. It is not addressing growing complexities. It stays silent on new system deployment and pitfalls of the "agile" approach that is widely used now to build these new systems.

So, the question is: will washing one's hands before and after one goes into an infectious disease ward without any other protection prevent them from catching an infectious disease? No, there is no guarantee that it will. But it will decrease the chances of getting one. Decrease by how much? This is a very good question.

We must also remember that compliance is backwards-looking. The best analogy is - think about how one would drive one's car by only looking in the rear-view mirror. The result would be a major crash. One wouldn't get far.

In a dynamic world where information can travel around the world in a fraction of a second, where technological advancement cycles are measured in months or even weeks, compliance constitutes the minimum and is always behind what's happening in the world. Sometimes quite far behind. Years behind. At least by 1-2 years.

QUESTIONS

These questions are important, as they prompt thinking and allow the target audience to understand the organisation's potential exposure and what they personally can do to improve the organisation's cyber security posture. To get answers to some of these questions, the target audience may need to go to their CIOs and CISOs.

1. Does the organisation use any of the frameworks mentioned in this chapter?
2. If yes, when did the organisation embark on this journey, and what is the current organisation's maturity level in this space?
3. What is the cost of this? Is this cost and Return on Investment (ROI) actively managed?
4. Does this help improve the organisation's cyber security posture? What makes you believe so?

DESSERT

NIST CSF is linked to NIST SP 800-53, but they are not the same. NIST CSF focuses more on a risk-based approach, while the NIST SP 800-53 provides detailed technical security controls. NIST CSF is designed to be more flexible and adaptive to changing threats, while the SP 800-53 is more comprehensive and provides specific security controls for each system. Ultimately, both frameworks are essential for organisations to protect their IT infrastructure and data from cyber threats. There is some confusion about NIST SP 800-53, whether it is a standard or a framework. Many publications call it either a framework or a standard, while some publications call it simultaneously a framework and a standard.[6] To make it even more confusing, some treat NIST 800-53 as a set of guidelines.[7] The latest version of NIST SP 800-53 (Revision 5) contains over 1,000 security controls (see Chapter 4). These controls are organised into 20 control families. How many controls can an organisation implement and meaningfully and cost-effectively manage?

The NIST CSF guides organisations in building a powerful information security program, while ISO/IEC 27001 ensures that the organisation is keeping up with the latest best practices and helps the organisation to artic-ulate its cyber security posture to prospects and partners.

The NIST CSF and the ISO/IEC 27000 series have some similarities that bring multiple benefits to cyber security. Both frameworks and standards are based on risk management principles, are aligned with other international standards and best practices, and can be tailored to any organisation regard-less of size, sector, or geography. Moreover, they are meant to be used as a **continuous improvement cycle**, rather than a one-time compliance exercise, as they encourage organisations to review and update their security policies, procedures, and practices regularly. This commitment to security is recognised and respected by regulators, customers, partners, and stakeholders.

The main differences between[8] them are shown below:

	NIST	ISO/IEC 27001
Purpose	Designed as a guide	Designed as a compliance standard
Compliance process	No certification, serves as a guide	Requires a formal audit that results in certification
Maturity	Used in early stages	Used by more mature organisations
Cost	Free download	Requires buying a standard and hiring an auditor

This chapter will mainly focus on ISO/IEC 27001, which has its origins in British Standard BS7799.

In the early 1990s, the UK government's Department of Trade and Industry (DTI) asked the Commercial Computer Security Centre (CCSC) to create a set of evaluation criteria for determining the security of IT products (this led to the creation of ITSEC.) The CCSC was also asked to create a code of best practices for information security. The result was a document known as DISC PD003. Work on DISC PD003 continued and was split into two major directions: BS 7799-1 and BS 7799-2. In 1995, the British Standards Institution (BSI) published BS 7799, which consisted of several parts. The standard was significantly based on three principles of confidentiality, integrity and availability (CIA), which was a major step forward:

- **Confidentiality**: all information is confidential and should be available only to authorised personnel.
- **Integrity**: ensuring that data is securely stored and protected.
- **Availability**: data is always available for authorised users.

The first part of BS 7799 contained the best practices for information security management and was revised in 1998. In the late 1990s, the BS 7799-1 document was organised into ten sections, each one outlining a series of controls and control objectives. This document laid the groundwork for the ISO/IEC 27002 standard. After a lengthy discussion with the worldwide standards bodies, it was eventually adopted by ISO as ISO/IEC 17799, "Information Technology - Code of practice for information security management," in 2000. ISO/IEC 17799 was then revised in June 2005 and finally incorporated in the ISO 27000 series of standards as ISO/IEC 27002 in July 2007.

The second part of BS 7799 was first published by BSI in 1998, known as BS 7799 Part 2, titled "Information Security Management Systems - Specification with guidance for use." It has created a **formal standard for the development of Information Security Management Systems (ISMS)** and eventually evolved into ISO/IEC 27001. BS 7799-2 focused on how to implement ISMS, referring to the information security management structure and controls identified in BS 7799-2. In 2000, this standard was adopted in Australia and New Zealand as AS/NZS 7799.2:2000. This later became ISO/IEC 27001:2005. In November 2005, Part 2 of BS 7799 was adopted by ISO and IEC as ISO/IEC 27001 in November 2005.

Part 3 of BS 7799 was published in 2005, covering risk analysis and management. It is aligned with ISO/IEC 27001:2005.

In December 2000, ISO adopted BS7799-1 as the basis for creating its ISO/IEC 17799 standard.

ISO/IEC held a meeting in Oslo in April 2001 to discuss major revisions to ISO/IEC 17799, and work on a new version of the standard continued from 2001 to 2004. The new version of ISO 17799 was voted on and confirmed in April 2005 in Vienna and published in June 2005. Meanwhile, in October 2005, BS7799-2 was formally adopted as ISO/IEC 27001.

Fast forward to 2024, and we can talk now about the ISO/IEC 27000 family of standards as broad in scope and applicable to organisations of all types and sizes and in all sectors, including public and private companies, government entities, and not-for-profit organisations. The common thread, regardless of organisation size, type, geography, or sector, is that the organisation is aiming to demonstrate the best practice in its approach to information security management. Best practice can be interpreted differently, of course. As technology continually evolves, new standards are being developed to address the changing requirements of information security in different industries and environments. The ISO/IEC 27000 family of standards, also known as the ISMS family of standards or, more simply, ISO/IEC 27K, covers a broad range of information security standards. **The ISO/IEC 27000 family of standards consists of 97 individual standards.**[9]

ISO/IEC 27001 is an Information Security Management System standard and supports effective Information Security Management that helps organisations meet requirements for confidentiality, integrity, and availability of information. It is a globally recognised standard.

Organisations should rely on security guidance and suggestions when appropriate. As information security and risk management are dynamic disciplines, the ISMS concept incorporates continuous feedback and improvements to respond to the changes in threats or vulnerabilities that occur because of incidents. Information security experts suggest that **compliance with the ISO/IEC 27000 series is the first step towards an information security** program that will properly protect your organisation. The standards, however, are not specific to any industry, and this makes them able to be applied in any business, regardless of size and industry.

There is no question about the benefits of ISMS implementation. Having policies, processes, and procedures documented and followed enables their repeatable implementation, hopefully following the best practices in each of the areas covered. Regular checks that these policies, processes, and procedures are followed provide assurance that this is the case indeed. Continuous improvement and regular reviews/updates (typically - annual) enable ongoing refinement, identification and closure of any gaps and enable the organisation to rely on best practices as they keep evolving.

Implementation of ISMS helps organisations meet regulatory compliance and contractual requirements and provides a better grasp of the legalities surrounding information systems. Since violation of legal regulations comes with hefty fines, having an ISMS can be especially beneficial for highly regulated industries with critical infrastructures, such as finance or healthcare.

Essential 8 was initially published in February 2017 and mandated by the Australian Federal Government for federal departments, with additional requirements set by the Attorney-General's Department's Protective Security Policy Framework (PSPF). Since the introduction of Essential 8, there have been several updates and modifications to the strategies. The latest update was published on 27 November 2023.[10] It's important to note that Essential 8 is not a static set of mitigation strategies and is likely to continue to evolve over time as the cyber security landscape changes.

As much as MFA is important, it is not as bulletproof as many think, and there are multiple ways MFA can be compromised:

- **MFA fatigue attack (also known as MFA bombing or MFA spamming)**: it is a social engineering attack where attackers repeatedly push second-factor authentication requests to the target victim's email, phone, or registered devices. The goal is to coerce the victim into confirming their identity via notification, thus authenticating the attacker's attempt at entering their account or device. It is based on a feature of modern authentication apps, as they provide a push notification that prompts the user to either accept or deny the login request. While this is convenient for the end user, attackers can use it to their advantage. If they've already compromised a password, they can attempt to log in and generate an MFA prompt to the legitimate user's device. Then attackers hope that the user either thinks it's a legitimate prompt and accepts it, or gets tired of the continuous prompts and accepts it to stop their phone notifications.
- **Service desk social engineering**: attackers can use social engineering to trick helpdesks into bypassing MFA altogether by pretending they've forgotten their password and gaining access via a phone call. If service desk agents don't enforce verification at this stage (which more often than not they don't, especially in larger organisations with thousands of employees, or in the case of outsourced call centres with high levels of personnel turnover), they might unwittingly give a hacker an initial foothold in their organisation's environment. This exact scenario played out in the attack on MGM Resorts in September 2023. After gaining initial access by fraudulently calling the service desk for

a password reset, the attack group (Scattered Spider) was able to use their foothold in the environment to launch a ransomware attack.

- **Adversary-in-the-middle (AITM) attack:** an AITM attack essentially tricks a user into thinking they're logging into a legitimate network, application, or website, when in fact they're putting their details into a fraudulent lookalike. This means hackers can intercept passwords and manipulate MFA prompts and other types of security. For example, a spear phishing email might land in an employee's inbox impersonating a known source. The link they click on will take them to a fake site where hackers will harvest their credentials for reuse. In theory, MFA would stop this by requiring a second form of authentication. However, attackers will use a tactic called a "2FA pass-on," where as soon as the victim has entered their credentials into the fake site, the attacker enters those same details into the legitimate site. This will trigger an MFA request, which the victim is expecting and will likely accept, giving the attacker full access.

- **Session hijacking:** session hijacking is an MFA breach attack, like an AITM attack, as it involves an attacker positioning themselves in the middle of a legitimate process and exploiting it. When a user authenticates using their password and MFA, many applications use a cookie or session token to remember that the user is authenticated and grant access to protected resources. The cookie or token prevents the user from having to authenticate multiple times. But if an attacker uses a tool such as Evilginx to steal the session token or cookie, they can masquerade as an authenticated user, effectively bypassing the multi-factor authentication configured on the account.

- **SIM swap:** attackers know MFA often relies on cell phones as the "thing you possess" to complete an authentication process. A SIM swap attack is where cybercriminals trick service providers into switching services to a SIM card they control, effectively hijacking the victim's cell service and phone number. This allows attackers to receive MFA prompts from the hijacked service and grant themselves access. In Australia, this technique was used extensively, and a few people lost their money because of it.

- **Exporting generated tokens:** another tactic attackers can use is to compromise the back-end system that generates and validates multi-factor authentication. In a bold attack in 2011, attackers were able to steal the "seeds" possessed by Rivest–Shamir–Adleman (RSA) public-key cryptosystem for generating SecurID tokens (code-generating key fobs used for multi-factor authentication). Once the seed values were compromised, attackers were able to clone the SecurID tokens and even create their own. Sometimes, attackers will seek the help of malicious insiders, who are paid to provide session tokens for MFA approval. Threat group LAPSUS$'s Telegram channel has confirmed that in the past, they have indeed bought access from a company's employee - and are actively looking for other insiders to work as providers. Microsoft has also reported that LAPSUS$ was able to obtain passwords and session tokens with the use of RedLine stealer. These credentials and session tokens are then sold on underground forums.

- **Endpoint compromise:** one way to avoid MFA completely is to compromise an endpoint with malware. Installing malware on a device lets hackers create shadow sessions following successful logins, steal and use session cookies, or access additional resources. If the system allows users to remain logged on after an initial authentication (by generating a cookie or session token), hackers could keep their access for a significant period. Hackers may also look to exploit recovery settings and backup procedures that could be less safe than MFA processes. People often forget passwords and regularly need new or modified access. For example, a common recovery method is sending an email link to a secondary email address (or an SMS with a link). If this backup address or phone is compromised, hackers gain full access to their target.
- **Exploiting Single Sign-on (SSO):** SSO is a double-edged sword. It is convenient for users as they only need to authenticate once. However, it can be exploited by hackers who use it to log in, requiring just one compromised password, and then use SSO to gain access to other sites and applications that would normally require MFA. A sophisticated form of this technique was used in the 2020 SolarWinds hack, where hackers exploited Security Assertion Markup Language (SAML) - a method for exchanging authentication between multiple parties in SSO. The hackers gained an initial foothold, then got access to the certificates used to sign SAML objects. With these, they were able to impersonate any user they wanted to, with full access to all SSO resources.
- **Finding technical deficiencies:** like any software, MFA technology has bugs and weaknesses that can be exploited. Most MFA solutions have had exploits published, which temporarily exposed opportunities for hacking. For example, 0ktapus leveraged CVE-2021-35464 to exploit a ForgeRock OpenAM application server, which front-ends web applications and remote access solutions in many organisations.

While Essential 8 provides pragmatic recommendations for cyber security, there are challenges and considerations that organisations must be aware of during implementation. These include:

- **Resource Constraints:** implementing Essential 8 requires resources, including skilled personnel, technology, and time. Organisations with limited resources may struggle to achieve higher maturity levels without external support.
- **Rapidly Evolving Threats:** cyber threats are constantly evolving, and Essential 8 must be continuously updated and adapted to address new

risks. Organisations need to stay informed about the latest threats and adjust their cyber security strategies accordingly.

- **Compliance and Regulations:** in some industries, compliance with specific regulations or standards may be required in addition to implementing Essential 8. Organisations must ensure that their cyber security practices align with both the Essential 8 and any applicable regulatory requirements.
- **Cultural and Organisational Change:** effective cyber security requires more than just technical solutions - it also involves cultural and organisational change. Employees need to be educated about cyber security best practices, and leadership must prioritise and support cyber security initiatives.

NOTES

1 https://en.wikipedia.org/wiki/ISO/IEC_27000_family.
2 https://www.scribd.com/document/631573670/ISO-27001-controls-2022.
3 https://www.digital.nsw.gov.au/delivery/cyber-security/policies/essential-eight#:~:text=The%20Essential%20Eight%20are%20embedded,set%20in%20the%20Mandatory%20Requirements.
4 https://www.cyber.gov.au/resources-business-and-government/essential-cyber-security/essential-eight.
5 https://cybertheory.io/essential-eight-is-this-really-an-answer/.
6 https://www.6clicks.com/resources/comparisons/nist-cybersecurity-framework-csf-vs-nist-sp-800-53.
7 https://sprinto.com/blog/nist-800-53-guide/#:~:text=NIST%20SP%20800%2D53%20is%20a%20set%20of%20guidelines%20that,confidentiality%2C%20integrity%2C%20and%20availability.
8 https://www.vanta.com/collection/iso-27001/nist-csf-vs-iso-27001.
9 https://en.wikipedia.org/wiki/ISO/IEC_27000_family.
10 https://www.cyber.gov.au/resources-business-and-government/essential-cyber-security/essential-eight/essential-eight-maturity-model-changes.

Chapter 13

Tyranny of KPIs

"Well, in our country," said Alice, still panting a little, "you'd generally get to somewhere else - if you ran very fast for a long time, as we've been doing."

"A slow sort of country!" said the Queen, "Now, here, you see, it takes all the running you can do, to keep in the same place. If you want to get somewhere else, you must run at least twice as fast as that!"

Through the Looking Glass, and What Alice Found There by Lewis Carroll

---

APPETISER

- Peter Drucker said, "A strategy without metrics is just a wish. And metrics that are not aligned with strategic objectives are a waste of time."
- The aim of the balanced scorecard is "to align business activities to the vision and strategy of the business, improve internal and external communications, and monitor business performance against strategic goals."
- Where is cyber security on an organisation's balanced scorecard?
- But measurement became a religion in the business world.
- Dr William Edwards Deming: "If you can't measure it, you can't manage it." However, *this is just part of the quote* from his book "The New Economics" (1993), and this is not just a minor subversion of the actual quote; it is almost a total reversal of what Dr Deming actually said, which is: *"It is wrong to suppose that if you can't measure it, you can't manage it - a costly myth." But somehow the fallacy continues to thrive* in the marbled corridors of the corporate world and open offices of Silicon Valley. Because *it is easier to manage by numbers without diving deeply into the root causes.*
- Measuring and reporting is actually an inherently fear-based process.

DOI: 10.1201/9781003730514-14

- Goodhart's Law: "When a measure becomes a target, it ceases to be a good measure."
- Construction of the right KPIs is not as simple as it may look. It is a specific skill. It is critical because *it is about understanding how policy changes have both desired effects and undesired/unexpected effects.*

MAIN COURSE

No organisation today runs without measuring its performance using Key Performance Indicators (KPIs) that have become integral tools for gauging performance, tracking progress, and driving strategic decision-making.

KPIs are defined as quantifiable metrics used to evaluate the success or progress of an organisation in relation to its strategic objectives. They serve the role of measurable indicators of critical aspects such as performance, efficiency, and success. With the ability to provide clear insights into the performance and effectiveness of various functions within an organisation, today, KPIs play a pivotal role in guiding decision-making processes.

So, each key performance indicator is a measurement that evaluates how well a business is achieving its goals in activities and initiatives. KPIs may focus on the success of the overall business or indicate the success of an individual project, product, department, or strategy. A KPI must be measurable and is usually quantifiable, which helps organisations track and compare strategies against competitors and previous or similar initiatives.

Peter Drucker famously said, "What gets measured gets done." His other famous and frequently used quote is: "If you can't measure it, you can't improve it." As Peter Drucker said, **"A strategy without metrics is just a wish. And metrics that are not aligned with strategic objectives are a waste of time."** Key results should be measurable, either on a 0–100% scale or with any numerical value (e.g., count, dollar amount or percentage) that can be used by planners and decision-makers to determine whether those involved in working towards the key result have been successful. There should be **no opportunity for a "grey area" when defining a key result.**

KPIs saw a big change in their usage in the 1990s when the first true balanced scorecard was used. By this time, organisations started to use systems consisting of a mix of financial and non-financial measures to track, following an article published in early 1992 by Robert S. Kaplan and David P. Norton.

The balanced scorecard model is an attempt to help organisations measure business performance using both financial and non-financial data. The **aim of the balanced scorecard is "to align business activities to the vision** and strategy of the business, improve internal and external communications, and monitor business performance against strategic goals." The balanced scorecard provides a relevant range of financial and non-financial information that supports effective business management. It expanded the concept of KPIs beyond financial measures to include a balanced set of indicators across various perspectives, such as customer, internal processes, and learning and growth.

With this modified approach, the strategic objectives are distributed across the four measurement perspectives so as to "connect the dots" to form a visual presentation of strategy and measures. In this modified version of the balanced scorecard design, managers select a few strategic objectives within each of the perspectives and then define the cause-and-effect chain among these objectives by drawing links between them to create a "strategic linkage model." A balanced scorecard of strategic performance measures is then derived directly by selecting one or two measures for each strategic objective. This type of approach provides greater contextual justification for the measures chosen and is generally easier to work through. This style of balanced scorecard has been commonly used since 1996 or so. It is significantly different in approach to the methods originally proposed and so can be thought of as representing the "second generation" of design approach adopted for the balanced scorecard since its introduction.

As Robert S. Kaplan and David P. Norton said in their 1992 article:

> "**What you measure is what you get.** Senior executives understand that their organisation's measurement system strongly affects the behaviour of managers and employees. Executives also understand that traditional financial accounting measures like return-on-investment and earnings-per-share can give misleading signals for continuous improvement and innovation, activities that today's competitive environment demands. The traditional financial performance measures worked well for the industrial era, but they are out of step with the skills and competencies companies are trying to master today."

Is there any mention of cyber security or business continuity in the content of the balanced scorecard? The answer is "No." But the world has changed dramatically over the last 25 years, and now every organisation is heavily dependent on computers and the Internet. But balanced scorecard structure stayed frozen in time.

As much as it is of paramount importance to measure both achievement and continuous improvement, the **challenge is that measurement has become a religion in the business world.**

There is a frequently used quote attributed to the well-known American business theorist, composer, economist, industrial engineer, management consultant, statistician and writer Dr William Edwards Deming: "If you can't measure it, you can't manage it." However, **this is just part of the quote** from his book "The New Economics" (1993), and this is not just a minor subversion of the actual quote; it is **almost a total reversal of what Dr Deming actually said**, which is: "It is wrong to suppose that if you can't measure it, you can't manage it - a costly myth." But somehow the fallacy continues to thrive in the marbled corridors of the corporate world and open offices of Silicon Valley. This misquote has won its place in the big book of business dogma because this is what the bureaucratic edifice of the business world relies on, and it is all about measurement. **Measurement is now a religion in the business world!** If we can slap a metric on something, we're going to do it. But **measuring and reporting is an inherently fear-based process.**

So why is it that such a huge perversion of this statement has been seized upon and embraced by modern organisations, managers, and executives?

Unfortunately, the answer is quite simple - **it is easier to manage by numbers without diving deeply into the root causes.** If one believes that everything can be boiled down to measurement in dollars, feet, ounces, seconds, points/hour or some other absolute measurable unit, then life becomes much easier. **One knows when their decisions were good because the unit measure improved.** It makes so much sense, and the world becomes simple and "manageable." One can send reports upstairs where they can be reviewed, and people can **perpetuate the illusion** that things are understood and under control. This is so attractive, of course, because it disposes of all the difficult stuff. People want to look at business as a simple function with inputs and outputs and to have levers they can pull and see the results and tweak based on feedback, and yes, there is a lot within business that fits that model, and one should absolutely grab all the data one can and use it wisely in decision-making and course correction, but between all those highly measurable milestones is where the difficult stuff is. But people love to measure things because it makes them feel as though they're really doing something. Look at my report card, Mom! I got three As and two Bs. Am I a good kid? Am I smart?

Measurement has become a plague (or better to say HIV?) in the business world because people believe that by measuring everything and sending the good news upstairs to the C-suite, they can convince their boss that they are doing the right thing and doing it right.

When we are talking about measures, we should remember **Goodhart's law,** which is named after British economist Charles Goodhart, who is credited with expressing the core idea of the adage in his 1975 article on monetary policy in the UK: **"Any observed statistical regularity will tend to collapse once pressure is placed upon it for control purposes."** A more widely known formulation of this law reads like this: **"When a measure becomes a target, it ceases to be a good measure."** In other words, when we set one specific goal, people will tend to optimise for that objective regardless of the consequences. This leads to problems when people start neglecting other equally important aspects of a situation.

One real-life example of Goodhart's law in action happened at one (possibly more than one) call centre. The call centre manager thought that increasing the number of calls processed was a good objective, and his employees were dutifully focused on increasing their numbers. However, by choosing only one metric to measure success, this call centre manager motivated employees to sacrifice courtesy in the name of quantity. People respond to incentives, and people's natural inclination is to maximise the standards by which they are judged.

In the world of cyber security, Goodhart's law appears through an over-emphasis on certain metrics, for example, such as the number of daily security alerts resolved. This shifts the team's focus: they now focus on lowering the alert numbers and not on the larger goal of understanding underlying security threats. This is similar to a doctor treating symptoms without diagnosing the disease first.

Construction of the right KPIs is not as simple as it may look. **It is a specific skill.** It is critical because it is about **understanding how policy changes have both desired effects and undesired/unexpected effects**; some good examples can be found in "The Tyranny of Metrics" by Jerry Z. Muller.

It is also important to remember the specifics of human nature. As mentioned earlier, people want to be in "good books" or get their bonus or promotion. This human trait often results in a focus on defining KPIs using the lenses of their future "achievability" (especially around the language used for their definition) to ensure certain flexibility that may allow them to "tick off" their (KPIs) achievement in the future. Another aspect that needs to be remembered is that often the achievement of various KPIs is assessed by the people who are reporting on them and is done subjectively to present these people in the best possible light.

The balanced scorecard approach is not free of challenges.

Firstly, as mentioned earlier, **balanced scorecards do not have a sector for cyber security** or business continuity. Though it is not difficult to add another sector, it is not easy to add adequate measures to monitor success and improvements in this area.

Secondly, the balanced scorecard approach does not have any temporal aspects and thus does not offer any tools to balance long-term perspective with the current financial year objectives. This again reminds us of human nature and biases - both conscious and, more importantly, unconscious. I am yet to see a senior executive who will sacrifice the current financial year's bonus/STI by not meeting certain targets (written in their compensation criteria and plan) to ensure long-term success and sustainability (including cyber security) of the organisation.

Another challenge posed by the balanced scorecard approach is that, as Patrick Lencioni said in his "The Five Dysfunctions of a Team", "**If everything is important, then nothing is.**" One can possibly argue that the roots of this quote go back to a proclamation by the pigs who control the government in George Orwell's "Animal Farm": "All animals are equal, but some animals are more equal than others." This is where one should think about complexity (see Chapter 4) and human ability to prioritise in multidimensional (in this case, 4D) space, as in real life, people often need to select one of mutually exclusive options. Financial performance was (and still is) the main part of the balanced scorecard (whether it is linked with customer satisfaction or not), and with the latest significant shift of focus on Diversity, Equity and Inclusion (DEI), there is little hope that, despite multiple declarations, cyber security will feature strongly enough on CEOs' and Boards' agendas.

QUESTIONS

These questions are important, as they prompt thinking and allow the target audience to understand the organisation's potential exposure and what they personally can do to improve the organisation's cyber security posture. To get answers to some of these questions, the target audience may need to go to their CIOs and CISOs.

1. Does the organisation have any KPIs for cyber security and business continuity? Are they the right KPIs? Do they create undesirable, unintended consequences?
2. If yes, how does the organisation prioritise these KPIs against other KPIs on its balanced scorecard?
3. How frequently does the Board discuss cyber security KPIs, and when was the last time they were discussed by the Board?
4. Does the organisation measure continuous improvement in its cyber security posture?

DESSERT

Up until the early 1990s, business performance management was almost solely focused on financial performance and based on financial data. In the 1990s, individual performance management was reshaped by two key trends. The first was the increase in popularity of self-assessment of performance, sometimes followed by feedback sessions with line managers. The increase in performance self-assessment was natural as economies were dominated by knowledge workers, who were more independent in regard to decision-making and management of work processes. The second key trend was the integration between strategic performance management and individual performance management. Organisational goals became reflected in individual goals, and individual measures became aligned with organisational performance measures in an effort to increase the accountability of all employees to the execution of the organisational strategy.

KPIs saw a big change in their usage in the 1990s when the first true balanced scorecard was used. By this time, organisations started to use systems consisting of a mix of financial and non-financial measures to track, following an article published in early 1992 by Robert S. Kaplan and David P. Norton. This article gained fast popularity and success, and was quickly followed by a second article in 1993. In 1996, the two authors published their book "The Balanced Scorecard: Translating Strategy into Action." These articles and the first book spread knowledge of the concept of balanced scorecards, leading to Kaplan and Norton being seen as the creators of the concept. And their first book remains their most popular.

This period also saw businesses beginning to align individual employee performance objectives with organisational initiatives and goals. The first generation of balanced scorecard designs used a "four perspective" approach to identify what measures to use to track the implementation of strategy that included financial performance, customer satisfaction, efficiency, and innovation. Further development of this approach put on the map the vision and strategy.

In the late 1990s, the design approach to balanced scorecards had evolved yet again. One problem with the "second generation" design approach described earlier was that the plotting of causal links among twenty or so medium-term strategic goals was still a relatively abstract activity. In practice, it ignored the fact that opportunities to intervene to influence strategic goals are (and need to be) anchored in current and real management activity. Secondly, the need to "roll forward" and test the impact of these goals necessitated the reference to an additional design instrument: a statement of what "strategic success," or the "strategic end-state," looked like. This reference point was called a destination statement. It was quickly realised that if a destination statement was created at the beginning of the design process, then it became easier to select the appropriate strategic activity and outcome objectives, which, if achieved, would deliver it. Measures and targets could then be selected to track the achievement of these objectives. Design methods that incorporate a destination statement or its equivalent represent a tangibly different design approach to those that went before and so have been proposed as representing a "third generation" design method for balanced scorecards.

The KPI Institute was established in 2004 in Melbourne, Australia. At that time, it was called the eab group and was designed as a provider of organisational performance management services in Australia, supporting clients mainly through training and advisory services. Today, the KPI Institute is considered the global authority on KPI research and education.

Measuring and reporting is actually an inherently fear-based process because the reason people measure everything in business is to prove to someone who's not in the room that they did what they were told to do. The more numeric, visible, and reward-tied the metric is, the more likely it is to be gamed and turn toxic to its original purpose. At the end of the day, everyone wants to be in "good books" or get a bonus or promotion.

There are multiple examples when KPIs constructed without enough thought process (and, unfortunately, the vast majority of people do not or are simply not able to think about unintended consequences) lead to undesirable and not anticipated consequences:

- A leader in India said that too many people were dying from venomous snakes, so he offered money to anyone who brought him a dead one.
  - **Unintended Negative Result**: people started breeding venomous snakes in private so they could kill them and bring them to the government.
- Surgeons are sometimes judged by how often there are complications or deaths in their surgeries, which affects their marketability and insurance rates.
  - **Unintended Negative Result**: many surgeons stopped taking high-risk or complicated cases, which resulted in people who really need help getting inferior care.
- Some governments in the last couple of decades have focused on making sure more students can hit a minimum level of competency in subjects such as English and Math.
  - **Unintended Negative Result**: many schools have taken this to an extreme and basically spend all their classroom time teaching to the test, which results in no freedom, enthusiasm, and ultimately a loss of curiosity and creativity in the students.
- Some organisations use maintaining conformity or compliance (with ISO/IEC27001 or a certain maturity level of Essential 8) as one of the KPIs.
  - **Unintended Negative Result**: actual focus shifts from proactive management of cyber security to managing the evidence of conformity or evidence of compliance.

Some other examples of poorly constructed metrics and unintended consequences include:

- A number of governments of countries with air pollution problems have started alternating which cars can be on the roads each day by even and odd licence plate numbers, which, unfortunately, led many to buy an additional vehicle so they could drive every day.
- Chinese peasants used to be paid for finding dinosaur bones, but this actually led to them breaking every bone they found into multiple pieces so they could be paid multiple times.
- Salespeople being rewarded based purely on the number of leads, which often creates tons of poor, unqualified leads that take up quality time that should have been spent elsewhere.
- Salespeople being rewarded based purely on the number of deals signed, which often creates tons of poor deals that become unprofitable (or not profitable enough) contracts.

- Hospitals getting penalised for readmissions would treat returning people as outpatients instead of treating them as inpatients.
- Police departments labelling worse crimes as misdemeanours to show a decrease in the number of serious crimes.
- Glass plant workers were told to produce as many square feet of sheet glass as possible and soon started making it so thin that it wasn't usable for anything.
- Wells Fargo massively incentivised the metric of "new accounts," which caused the creation of thousands of fake accounts, ultimately resulting in major lawsuits and financial impact.

Chapter 14

Gone phishing

"No wise fish would go anywhere without a porpoise."

Alice's Adventures in Wonderland by Lewis Carroll

APPETISER

- People are often seen as the weakest link in cyber security.
- Phishing is a way cyber criminals trick an individual into giving them the individual's personal or the organisation's information.
- Spear phishing is when these emails and text messages are highly targeted to the recipient.
- Business email compromise (BEC) is a form of targeted phishing, or spear phishing.
- Malicious emails may originate either from individual cyber criminals, organised groups of cyber criminals, or nation-state actors.
- Vishing, which is short for voice phishing, uses fraudulent phone calls to trick victims into providing sensitive information.
- The main difference between these scams is that they have different audiences. Phishing attacks are more often directed at organisations (though individuals can be targeted too), and vishing attacks are more often directed at individuals (though organisations can be targeted too).
- Phishing may have different purposes: getting a foothold in the organisation's IT ecosystem or simply stealing money.
- Phishing email statistics suggest that nearly 1.2% of all emails sent are malicious, which translates to 3.4 billion phishing emails daily.
- In 2025, phishing remains a prevalent cyber threat, with an estimated 3.4 billion phishing emails sent daily and a significant percentage of data breaches attributed to it.
- Google blocks around 100 million phishing emails daily.

DOI: 10.1201/9781003730514-15

- Millennials and Gen-Z Internet users are most likely to fall victim to phishing attacks.
- The use of stolen credentials is the most common cause of data breaches.
- 30% of opened phishing emails increase the chances of malware.
- Since 2024, AI use has driven a surge in phishing attacks both in volume and sophistication.

MAIN COURSE

One can often hear that people are the weakest link in cyber security. People who make errors can be manipulated through social engineering, bribes, and threats. Indeed, weak passwords, messages sent to the wrong recipients, and human errors are often the cause of cyber insecurities. And then there is an insider threat (see Chapter 9), social engineering, and phishing.

Earlier in the book, we were talking about root causes and distribution mechanisms (see Introduction). One of the distribution mechanisms is phishing, which is a form of social engineering.

Phishing is a way cyber criminals trick an individual into giving them the individual's personal or the organisation's information. They send fraudulent emails or text messages, often pretending to be from either a service desk, a service provider, or a large organisation that the recipient knows or trusts. They may try to steal login credentials, online banking logins, credit card details or passwords, or lead the recipient to a fraudulent website that infects the recipient's device with malware, or use an attachment infected with malware. Phishing can result in the loss of information, money, or identity theft. Spear phishing is when these emails and text messages are highly targeted to the recipient.[1]

Business email compromise (BEC) is a form of targeted phishing, or spear phishing. Criminals target organisations and try to scam them out of money or goods. They also target employees and try to trick them into revealing important organisational information.[2] BEC attacks commonly involve convincing victims to make unauthorised payments, transfer funds, or share confidential data. Often, it exploits trust in internal or vendor/service provider communications.

About 8 years ago, the CFO of the company I worked for at that time received an email from the company's CEO (who was at that time on a business trip in the UK) requesting the transfer of £27,000 to somewhere. The transaction was almost completed when the CEO's executive assistant stopped it at the last moment, as she had picked up that the language in this email did not match the CEO's writing style. The lesson from this incident is very simple: one can't trust an email even if it looks like it is coming from a legitimate source, as the originating email address can be spoofed (forged for those who do not know this word) or hijacked. Especially when the recipient is tired and the email says something like "urgent" or "important."

Business email compromise can lead to significant financial damage. In FY23–24, the total self-reported BEC losses in Australia were almost $84 million, with over 1,400 reports averaging over $55,000 in losses per incident.[3]

These malicious emails may originate either from individual cyber criminals, organised groups of cyber criminals, or nation-state actors.

Smishing is a type of cyberattack where criminals use fraudulent text messages (SMS) to trick individuals into revealing sensitive information, like bank account details, passwords, or personal data. These messages often appear to be from legitimate sources like banks, delivery services, or government agencies. They may include malicious links that lead to fake websites designed to steal information or install malware on the recipient's device.

For completeness of the picture, we should also mention **vishing**. Vishing, which is short for voice phishing, uses fraudulent phone calls to trick victims into providing sensitive information, like login credentials, credit card numbers, or bank details. However, these attacks aren't limited to phone calls. Many vishing attacks start with a phishing email, urging the recipient to dial a number. Once in a call, scammers use social engineering tactics to convince the target to share their personal details. Lately, audio deepfakes have been used to commit fraud by fooling people into thinking they are receiving instructions from a trusted individual. These deepfakes are often composed with the help of AI (see Chapter 15).

The main difference between these scams is that they have different audiences. Phishing attacks are more often directed at organisations (though individuals can be targeted too), and vishing attacks are more often directed at individuals (though organisations can be targeted too). Phishing may have different purposes: getting a foothold in the organisation's IT ecosystem or simply stealing money. Sometimes, cyber criminals try to steal money not from individuals, but from organisations.

In 2018, it was estimated that by 2022, a ransomware or phishing attack would occur every 11 seconds. Phishing attacks are common and costly: in 2022, phishing was the second most common cause of data breaches, costing organisations an average of US$4.91 million in breach expenses.

Phishing email statistics suggest that in 2022, over 48% of all emails sent were malicious or spam.

In 2025, phishing remains a prevalent cyber threat, with an estimated 3.4 billion phishing emails sent daily and a significant percentage of data breaches attributed to it; for example, Google blocks around 100 million phishing emails daily, over a fifth of which originate in Russia.

Millennials and Gen-Z Internet users are most likely to fall victim to phishing attacks.

Phishing attacks are a major component of cybercrime, with estimates varying but generally placing them as a significant percentage of all attacks. 92% of Australian organisations and 83% of UK organisations suffered a successful phishing attack, showing a 53% increase from the year 2021. According to IBM's 2022 Data Breach Report, breaches caused by phishing took the third longest mean time to identify and contain at 295 days.

The use of credentials stolen through phishing is the most common cause of data breaches. However, it is difficult to pinpoint the exact numbers, as various sources quote wide-ranging (from 16% to 93%) statistics.

According to another source, 75% of cyberattacks start with a deceptive email - whether it's malware, credential theft, or impersonation scams - and **30% of opened phishing emails increase the chances of malware.**

In 2024, phishing attacks surged in volume and sophistication, driven by AI (see Chapter 15) and deepfakes. Security awareness training is now more critical than ever.

Here are the most infamous tactics cybercriminals use when it comes to phishing emails:

- Spear phishing: ultra-targeted and personally tailored to a creepy degree - employees are tricked into sharing sensitive information. Attackers research their targets to make emails look shockingly authentic.
- Malware-laced attachments: like contaminated meat that sends diners to the hospital and shuts down the whole restaurant, intentionally infected PDFs, Word docs, and Excel files unleash chaos with just one click. These files can install ransomware, spyware, or backdoors without the user ever realising it.
- Credential-stealing links: deployed by true masters of deception, employees believe a login page is legitimate and surrender their credentials with just a few keystrokes. Some of these fake sites are near-perfect replicas, making them incredibly easy to fall for - even for IT pros.

Phishing performed with the goal of getting a foothold in the organisation's IT ecosystems is another example of the **cumulative effect,** be it through malware implantation or theft of credentials.

QUESTIONS

These questions are important, as they prompt thinking and allow the target audience to understand the organisation's potential exposure and what they personally can do to improve the organisation's cyber security posture. To get answers to some of these questions, the target audience may need to go to their CIOs and CISOs.

1. Do you think the organisation is taking adequate measures to protect itself from phishing breaches?

2. What else can be done to protect the organisation against phishing breaches?
3. Do you think it is possible to fully protect the organisation against phishing breaches?

DESSERT

Indicators of phishing/BEC may include:

- Suspicious emails from your email address requesting payments, changes to bank details, or sensitive information.
- Unusual emails or notifications about suspicious login activity, such as alerts for sign-ins from unfamiliar locations or devices, or unexpected password reset requests. These may be signs that someone is attempting to gain unauthorised access to your account.
- Emails that have been unexpectedly deleted or moved to different folders without your knowledge. This may indicate that an attacker is trying to hide evidence of their activity or prevent you from noticing fraudulent communications.
- New email forwarding rules in your mailbox that were not created by you. Attackers often use this tactic to secretly redirect incoming emails to themselves, allowing them to monitor conversations and intercept sensitive information even after victims regain access to their compromised email accounts.

These indicators of compromise need to be promptly investigated and, if necessary, acted upon to minimise potential financial or data loss.

Indicators that someone else may be a victim of phishing/BEC:

- Vendor not following usual processes: sudden changes in a vendor's email address, approval steps, or communication methods may indicate a compromised email account.
- Requests to update or change bank details: be wary of unexpected messages requesting bank account updates, as attackers may provide fraudulent account information to redirect payments.
- Requests for payments outside of the schedule: payment requests that are urgent, confidential, or do not match the usual schedule could be signs of BEC, as fraudsters often pressure targets to act quickly.
- Communication from unfamiliar email addresses: emails from slightly altered or unfamiliar addresses may be attempts to impersonate trusted contacts. Verify by searching prior conversations and reporting suspicious emails.

- Changes in tone or language: unusual language, spelling, formatting, or missing signatures in emails from regular contacts may indicate a compromised account.
- Unexplained urgency or secrecy: requests emphasising secrecy, discouraging verification, or creating a sense of urgency should be treated with caution, as these are common BEC tactics.

The use of stolen credentials is the most common cause of data breaches, but it is difficult to pinpoint the exact numbers, as various sources quote wide-ranging statistics:

- A 2019 Threat Report by Symantec showed that 65% of cyberattacks are perpetrated through spear phishing.
- According to a report by UpGuard, phishing is involved in over 90% of all data breaches.
- According to Astra Security, phishing is involved in nearly 93% of all data breaches.
- Cofense's Q3 2021 phishing review shows that nearly 93% of modern breaches involve phishing attacks.
- According to the FBI's 2021 IC3 Report, phishing is involved in nearly 22% of all data breaches.
- According to IBM's 2022 Data Breach Report, phishing is involved in 16% of all data breaches.
- According to Verizon's 2022 report, 36% of all data breaches involved phishing.

According to another source, 75% of cyberattacks start with a deceptive email - whether it's malware, credential theft, or impersonation scams - and **30% of opened phishing emails increase the chances of malware.**

An Astra Security report[4] uncovered and explained how phishing kits, malware loaders, and ransomware operators continue to infiltrate systems (often through low- or medium-risk vulnerabilities that were left unpatched).

NOTES

1 https://www.cyber.gov.au/threats/types-threats/phishing.
2 https://www.cyber.gov.au/threats/types-threats/business-email-compromise.
3 https://www.cyber.gov.au/about-us/view-all-content/reports-and-statistics/annual-cyber-threat-report-2023-2024.
4 https://www.getastra.com/blog/security-audit/cyber-security-statistics/.

Chapter 15

Emerging threats

"It's no use going back to yesterday, because I was a different person then."

Alice's Adventures in Wonderland by Lewis Carroll

APPETISER

- No organisation has yet developed an incident response plan specifically for cyber security incidents affecting AI.
- Palo Alto Networks' study discovered that 61% of organisations fear that AI-powered attacks will compromise sensitive data.
- AI-powered attacks can learn and evolve over time. This means that AI-enabled attacks can adapt to avoid detection or create a pattern of attack that a security system can't detect.
- Fewer than a third of IT leaders say their companies are ready to withstand AI-powered cyber-attacks.
- Whatever has been fed into AI or asked AI immediately becomes part of the AI. As such, the *notion of Confidentiality* is *immediately violated. One can't sign a Confidentiality Deed or Non-Disclosure Agreement with AI.*
- Agentic automation is likely to have a side effect of further increasing complexity and thus vulnerability of organisations' IT ecosystems.
- Some results of a survey of 1,300 ethical hackers and security researchers were surveyed:
  - 93% agree that organisations using AI tools have created a new attack vector.
  - 82% believe that the AI threat landscape is evolving too rapidly to be effectively secured from cyber-attacks.
  - 86% believe that AI has fundamentally changed the approach to hacking.
  - 74% agree that AI has made hacking more accessible, opening the door for newcomers to join the fold.

DOI: 10.1201/9781003730514-16

- For contracts that were signed before AI became widely used, AI needs to be considered throughout the service lifecycle, where use of AI may not be present at signing or renewal but introduced as part of service improvement or optimisation.
- AI-enhanced malicious attacks were the top emerging risk for organisations in the third quarter of 2024. It's the third consecutive quarter with these attacks being the top emerging risk.
- The pace of improvement in AI-driven offensive security is rapidly accelerating.
- AI proliferation is greatly outpacing security and governance in favour of do-it-now adoption.
- 13% of organisations using AI reported breaches of AI models or applications.
- Quantum computing is an area of computer science that explores the possibility of developing computer technologies based on the principles of quantum mechanics and building computers that can perform certain types of calculations much faster than traditional classic computers.
- Quantum computers will be able to break commonly used encryption methods at an alarming speed, and as a result, encryption tools currently used to protect everything from banking and retail transactions to business data, documents, and digital signatures can be rendered ineffective.
- Have you heard of the RSA hack?
- Quantum computers may be able to break blockchain algorithms. What will happen to cryptocurrencies then?
- Harvest encrypted data now, and decrypt later at risk.
- Q-Day - a day when a quantum computer so powerful is built it could break the public encryption systems. Q-day can be 2 years away or 20 years away.
- As historically it has taken almost two decades to deploy modern cryptography infrastructure, regardless of the exact time of the arrival of Q-day, it is of paramount importance to begin to prepare information security systems to be able to resist quantum computing now.
- On August 13, 2024, NIST released the first three post-quantum cryptography (PQC) standards and encouraged organisations to begin transitioning to the new standards as soon as possible.

MAIN COURSE

The ever-growing pace of progress in the technology space means the frequent emergence of new technologies that often (if not always) bring with them new risks. This is becoming especially important in today's world, where all organisations are dependent upon computers and the Internet. Two of these new technologies have a profound impact on cyber security and will be discussed in this chapter.

As Accenture's head of Australia and New Zealand, Peter Burns, recently said, commenting on the acquisition of Cyber CX,[1] "The need for responsible governance is also rising as AI and quantum technologies advance."

Let's start with the Artificial Intelligence (AI) idea, which goes back thousands of years to ancient philosophers considering questions of life and death. Let's skip the long history and move straight to the current AI boom that started in 2017 and is leading to the new AI era that began around 2020-2023. This era resulted in the development and implementation of numerous AI systems, the use of which brought a new plethora of risks and problems for many organisations.

Expansion of AI introduces several security risks, primarily because it can be used to create deceitful and manipulative content. The potential for generating deepfakes, synthetic identities, and counterfeit documents can lead to fraud, misinformation, and other malicious activities. These capabilities pose a significant threat to personal, corporate, and national security, making the potential abuse of generative AI technologies a critical issue. Some of these other risks include generating factually incorrect or fabricated content (hallucinations), producing biased outputs, leaking sensitive information, creating inappropriate content, infringing on copyrights, and being vulnerable to security attacks.

Recently, OpenAI admitted that AI hallucinations are mathematically inevitable, not just engineering flaws, as large language models will always produce plausible but false outputs, even with perfect data, due to fundamental statistical and computational limits.[2] Experts believed the mathematical inevitability of AI errors demands new enterprise strategies. As a result, governance must shift from prevention to risk containment; this means stronger human-in-the-loop processes, domain-specific guardrails, and continuous monitoring.

The latest trend is the proliferation of shadow AI, as people sneak AI into work. And the vast majority (91%) of surveyed employees said they believe that shadow AI poses no risk, very little risk, or some risk that's outweighed by the reward.[3] Perhaps even more disturbing, over a third of employees admitted to sharing sensitive information with these unauthorised AI tools.

Results of the study of cyber security risks to AI[4] identified numerous risks and looked into the design phase (12 risks), development phase (8 risks), deployment phase (8 risks), and maintenance phase (4 risks) and provides a description of 22 associated with AI security incidents that have taken place between 2020 and 2023. This report also notes that **none of the users have yet developed an incident response plan specifically for cyber security incidents affecting AI.** In another study, Palo Alto Networks discovered that **61% of organisations fear that AI-powered attacks will compromise sensitive data.**

AI is subject to various types of security risks, such as, for example, when a bad actor attempts to abuse the AI application for financial gain or to cause harm.

Some of the already known cyber-attacks that use AI include:

- **Phishing campaigns:** hackers use AI to write emails that target employees based on their job profiles and needs. AI can craft more personalised and convincing emails, which makes it difficult for the receiver to identify as a phishing email.
- **Phone phishing (vishing):** hackers use voice synthesis over the phone and pretend to be reputable individuals and organisations. Victims can reveal sensitive information or transfer money to the attacker since these AI-generated calls seem real and resemble their known individual's voice and speech pattern.
- **Doxing:** AI can scrape social media profiles, publicly available records and other public databases to compile detailed dossiers that hackers can use for blackmail, intimidation, or other malicious activities. This whole process can be easily automated with AI.

As some security researchers suggest, agentic AI web browsers that can act autonomously on users' behalf appear to be extremely gullible and unsafe to use, falling for hoary old scams as well as newer attacks.[5]

Some organisations, like, for example, Microsoft, are already using AI for software development. This creates another risk, as some of the security researchers say that the use of artificial intelligence for software development is threatening to make a specific type of web application flaw, insecure direct object references (IDORs), far more common.[6]

Like all AI algorithms, the ones used for AI-powered attacks can learn and evolve over time. This means that AI-enabled attacks can adapt to avoid detection or create a pattern of attack that a security system can't detect. For example, the recently introduced Google Gemini CLI agent, which provides a text-based command interface to the company's artificial intelligence large language model, could be tricked into silently executing malicious commands, a security researcher has discovered.[7]

The pace of improvement in AI-driven offensive security is rapidly accelerating. Recently, XBOW experimented with GPT-5, building a model as the exploit crafting engine within XBOW's autonomous agent framework. XBOW measured the number of iterations required for an agent to craft an exploit, and the median for the agent using GPT-5 was 17 iterations, a significant improvement over the 24 required by the agent when using Sonnet/ Gemini, the best-performing engine to date. This indicates that the new model can arrive at a successful exploit path more directly. Furthermore, the quality of the findings has improved; the GPT-5 agent found more elaborate exploits. The number of successful exploits found in the wild, using GPT-5, the agent hacked nearly twice as many unique targets in the same time.

As mentioned earlier, AI can leak or inadvertently disclose PII or other sensitive or confidential details. This can occur when sensitive or confidential information is included as part of AI's original training dataset or entered by the user when they are asking a question or prompting AI. One should **remember that whatever has been fed into AI or asked AI immediately becomes part of the AI.** As such, the **notion of Confidentiality is being immediately violated.** One can't sign a Confidentiality Deed or Non-Disclosure Agreement with AI. This actually means that using AI potentially immediately deprives any competitive advantage organisation that uses it (as information used in this process becomes potentially available to all competitors by them, for example, asking a question, "What do my competitors do to achieve XYZ?"). It is also plausible to imagine that if AI is used to deploy or store certificates, they can potentially be leaked to an interested third party.

Recently, Slovakia-based cyber security vendor ESET discovered "the first known" artificial intelligence-powered ransomware that generates malicious scripts on the fly on infected machines.[8] This later turned out to be an academic research prototype and not an actual attempt at creating the first AI-powered criminal malware.[9] PromptLocker, an experiment called "Ransomware 3.0" conducted by researchers at NYU's Tandon School of Engineering, clearly demonstrated the danger and potential of AI-generated ransomware.[10] ESET said that the malware "leverages Lua scripts generated from hard-coded prompts to **enumerate the local filesystem, inspect target files, exfiltrate selected data,** and **perform encryption**" and noted that the sample hadn't implemented destructive capabilities, which makes sense for a controlled experiment but could be implemented by malicious actor(s).

A lot of organisations are already using AI as a productivity tool to summarise documents and/or meeting minutes. Even such an innocuous use of AI comes with a huge risk. Security researchers from Singapore security vendor CloudSEK have developed a sophisticated prompt injection attack that abuses trusted AI summarisation tools and potentially turns these into ClickFix-style step-by-step instructions to compromise user systems.[11] This approach exploits the gap between what humans can see on a webpage and what artificial intelligence models process when generating summaries.

Some organisations are starting to realise this. For example, the Office of the Victorian Information Commissioner (OVIC) has drawn a clear line when it comes to the insertion of generative AI into meetings between its staff and external parties.[12] In recently issued guidance, the state's privacy regulator said it prefers that external participants refrain from using Generative AI (GenAI) services to record, transcribe, summarise, or draft minutes of meetings, especially when discussions involve sensitive issues. More firmly, OVIC has explicitly banned the use of publicly available GenAI tools during meetings involving its staff, both online and in person. The issue of trust is starting to be recognised already,[13] as in the public sector, especially, trust must be earned through a combination of legal compliance, transparency, ethical behaviour, and clear accountability.

AI can be and is being used to boost organisations' cyber security capability. And there is a lot of marketing happening in this space. However, incorporating AI technology into cyber security can be expensive and requires a lot of resources, including limited human expertise to set up, deploy, and manage AI systems.

Like any double-edged tool, AI tools designed to improve an organisation's cyber security can open up another attack surface. For example, a recently released AI-powered framework for fast automated testing has quickly become abused by threat actors to develop and execute attacks, including current ones on Citrix Netscaler appliances.[14]

Additionally, AI-powered solutions may need specialised hardware, supporting infrastructure, and significant processing capacity and power to run complex computations. Although the benefits of utilising AI in cyber security are undeniable, **organisations must have a comprehensive understanding of the expenses involved** to avoid unpleasant surprises. Also, one should remember that **over-reliance on AI can create a cyber security skills gap** as people depend more on technology than on their intelligence and skills. **This can lead to security teams becoming complacent,** as they assume that AI systems will detect any potential threats.

The latest AI-related buzzword is agentic automation. It is the latest step in automation's evolution, which enables software "agents," powered by AI, to take autonomous actions. Without going into details of the pros and cons of this approach from a business point of view (as Robodebt is fresh in my memory[15]), it is important to understand that this approach[16] is likely to further increase the number of APIs (and thus - attack surface) and the complexity of the IT ecosystem (see Chapters 4 and 5).

Use of AI in cyber security raises additional ethical questions. When considering risk factors related to ethical concerns, AI bias, and the lack of transparency are the two that often come up, as they can lead to unfair targeting and discrimination of specific users or groups. This can result in the misidentification of an individual or group as an insider threat, causing irreparable harm.

In 2024, approximately 1,300 ethical hackers and security researchers were surveyed on their views across the broad range of activities generally referred to as "hacking." Some of the key (and scary) findings from the survey include the following:

- **93% agree that organisations using AI tools have created a new attack vector.**
- **82% believe that the AI threat landscape is evolving too rapidly to be effectively secured from cyber-attacks.**
- **86% believe that AI has fundamentally changed the approach to hacking.**
- **74% agree that AI has made hacking more accessible, opening the door for newcomers to join the fold.**

According to Gartner, **AI-enhanced malicious attacks were the top emerging risk for organisations** in the third quarter of 2024. It's the **third consecutive quarter with these attacks being the top emerging risk.**

Fewer than a third of IT leaders say their companies are ready to withstand AI-powered cyber-attacks, a global survey has found, as security teams battle to contain escalating risks from both hackers and rogue AI agents. Although 61% of surveyed enterprise IT leaders reported a "significant" or "moderate" increase in cybersecurity risk from AI-using cybercriminals, just 31% said they were confident they could manage the risks that AI presents.[17]

New global research from IBM and the Ponemon Institute reveals how AI is greatly outpacing security and governance in favour of do-it-now adoption. The findings show that ungoverned AI systems are more likely to be breached and more costly when they are breached. In its 2025 report, IBM points out that 13% of organisations using AI reported breaches of AI models or applications.[18]

Another risk that needs to be considered throughout the service lifecycle is where use of AI may not be present at signing but is introduced as part of service improvement or optimisation.[19]

Finally, for those interested in the subject, it may be worthwhile to read about some of the warnings expressed by "Godfather of AI" Yoshua Bengio in his recent article[20] and what former Cloudflare executive John Graham-Cumming is doing with pre-AI, human-created content.[21]

Let's move to the topic of quantum computing. A quantum computer is a device that employs properties described by quantum mechanics to enhance computations. **Quantum computing is an area of computer science** that explores the possibility of developing computer technologies based on the principles of quantum mechanics and seeks to harness these principles to build **computers that can perform certain types of calculations much faster than traditional classic computers.** It is a technological innovation that offers unprecedented computing power.

A quantum computer is a computer that exploits quantum mechanical phenomena. On small scales, physical matter exhibits properties of both particles and waves, and quantum computing leverages this behaviour using specialised hardware. In the context of quantum computing, the superposition principle is represented by qubits (quantum bits), which can be both 0 and 1 at the same time, unlike classical bits that are either 0 or 1. This allows quantum computers to process vast amounts of data in parallel, exponentially increasing their computational power.

This makes quantum computers potentially millions of times faster than classic computers and is one reason they are excellent at solving complex mathematical problems, such as breaking encryption.

In the early 1990s, researchers Peter Shor and Lov Grover developed **algorithms that showed how quantum computers could perform certain tasks,** such as factoring large numbers and searching databases, **exponentially**

faster than classical computers. These algorithms showed that a quantum computer could factor large numbers exponentially faster than the best-known classical algorithms, posing a potential **threat to widely used public-key cryptographic systems.** In 1996, Lov Grover introduced an **algorithm for database searching** that delivered a **quadratic speedup over classical algorithms.** These discoveries highlighted the transformative potential of quantum computing.

Since the beginning of the Internet, cryptography has been protecting online data and conversations by hiding or coding information that only the person receiving the message can read on traditional computers.

There are two main types of encryption: symmetric, in which the same key is used to encrypt and decrypt the data; and asymmetric, or public-key, which involves a pair of mathematically linked keys, one shared publicly to let people encrypt messages for the key pair's owner, and the other stored privately by the owner to decrypt messages.

Symmetric cryptography is significantly faster than public-key cryptography. For this reason, it is used to encrypt all communications and stored data. Public-key cryptography is used for securely exchanging symmetric keys and for digitally authenticating or signing messages, documents, and certificates that pair public keys with their owners' identities. When one visits a secure website that uses the HTTPS protocol, one's browser uses public-key cryptography to authenticate the site's certificate and set up a symmetric key for encrypting communications to and from the site. The math for these two types of cryptography is quite different, which affects their security. Because virtually all Internet applications use both symmetric and public-key cryptography, both forms need to be secure.

In the 1970s, mathematicians developed encryption methods that consisted of numbers hundreds of digits long. The **difficulty of mathematical problems was such that it could take hundreds of years to solve** if using the right parameter size and numbers. To break the encryption, the numbers need to be split into their prime factors, but this could take hundreds, if not thousands, of years with traditional algorithms and traditional computers. The threat of codes being cracked was therefore not a big worry. **That was true up until 1994,** when Peter Shor showed how it could be done with an algorithm using a then-hypothetical quantum computer that could split large numbers into their factors much quicker than a classic computer, and then in 1996, Lov Grover's algorithm showed its ability to crack symmetrical encryption.

However, like a lot of new discoveries and technologies, quantum computing is a double-edged sword and poses a significant threat to existing cryptographic schemes, such as the Ron Rivest - Adi Shamir - Leonard Adleman (RSA) encryption algorithm, which relies on the difficulty of factoring large numbers. The earlier-mentioned Shor's algorithm, for example, has the potential to break RSA encryption.

Quantum computers will be able to break commonly used encryption methods at an alarming speed, and as a result, encryption tools currently used to protect everything from banking and retail transactions to business data, documents, and digital signatures can be rendered ineffective.

What does this mean in practice? To understand this, one may look at how in 2011 Chinese spies stole the crown jewel of cyber security and stripped protection from organisations, including government agencies.[22]

Adding more qubits to this quantum computer scales up its power exponentially. Further to this, Chinese researchers have been able to factor a 48-bit key on a 10-qubit quantum computer. And they calculated that it's possible to scale their algorithm for use with 2048-bit keys using a quantum computer with only 372 qubits. But such a computer already exists today at IBM, for example, so the need to replace cryptography throughout the Internet suddenly stopped being something so far in the future that it wasn't really thought about seriously. Moreover, in 2023, California-based start-up Atom Computing created the first quantum computer to surpass 1,000 qubits (1,180 qubits, to be precise). The number of qubits is significant because each additional qubit exponentially increases the processor's potential computing power, which has implications for code breaking. Although it is uncertain when commercial-scale quantum computers will be developed, **cryptographers are worried about the immediate data harvesting risks** ("steal now, decrypt later") to modern computers. In the meantime, for comparison, China's most advanced programmable and deliverable superconducting quantum computer is Origin Wukong, a third-generation 72-qubit quantum computer.

In 2015, intelligence agencies determined that advancements in quantum computing are happening at such a speed that this poses a threat to cyber security. At the moment, qubits, the processing units of quantum computers, are still not stable for long enough to decrypt large amounts of data. They called it **Q-Day - a day when a quantum computer so powerful is built that it could break the public encryption systems.** When will humanity face Q-Day? Who knows - it may be 2 years, or it may be 20 years. If it takes 20 years to arrive at Q-Day, there will be no (or almost no) panic. However, if Q-Day is just 2 years away, then this is a totally different situation. And it may not be as far away as some may hope.[23]

While in the past there were a lot of question marks around the physical possibility of building large enough quantum computers, today many scientists believe that it is just a significant engineering challenge. Some engineers even predict that within the next 20 or so years, sufficiently large quantum computers will be built to break essentially all public key schemes currently in use.

Notwithstanding that historically it has taken almost two decades to deploy modern public key cryptography infrastructure, regardless of whether the exact time of the arrival of the quantum computing era can be accurately

estimated, it is of paramount importance to begin to prepare information security systems to be able to resist quantum computing now.

This situation served as a catalyst for research into both **quantum cryptography, which leverages the principles of quantum mechanics to secure communication,** and **post-quantum cryptography, which aims to develop new cryptographic schemes that can resist attacks from both classical and quantum computers.**

Governments are not standing by for that to happen, and the cryptographic community is building encryption methods that can withstand the quantum threat, known as post-quantum cryptography (PQC), also known as Quantum-Resistant Cryptography (QRC). On August 13, 2024, **NIST released final versions of the first three PQC Standards and encouraged organisations to begin transitioning to the new standards as soon as possible.**[24] The US legislation has mandated that the timeline to change to PQC will be from 2025 to 2033, by which time the cyber security supply chain will have to be transitioned to using PQC by default. NIST also continues to evaluate two other sets of algorithms that could one day serve as backup standards.

Now, can we trust PQC and NIST? In light of statements made by Daniel Bernstein (University of Illinois, Chicago), the answer is not so clear. In 2023, he said that the NIST is deliberately obscuring the level of involvement the US National Security Agency (NSA) has in developing new encryption standards for PQC.[25] He also believes that NIST has made errors - either accidental or deliberate - in calculations describing the security of the new standards. NIST denied these claims. Though this is a big claim, it seems plausible, considering that "spooks" always wanted (and still want) to have a backdoor for any encryption system.

Organisations need to move today's public key cryptographic systems from where they are today to new quantum-safe algorithms. While moving today's public key cryptographic systems might seem simple on the surface, it's a big job entailing complete cryptographic inventories of assets and technology, mapping this to sensitive data, and developing and executing a post-quantum cryptography migration strategy. It's a very large and very expensive project that will touch every piece of IT infrastructure and span over several years, especially if the Internet of Things (IoT) is involved. How difficult and expensive will it be to integrate PQC with legacy systems? How many organisations that are deeply immersed in (never-ending) digital transformations (see Chapter 5) are thinking about this, incorporating such a project into their forward planning and budgeting for it?

Dr Michele Mosca stresses the **need for organisations to begin due diligence in the post-quantum space immediately.**[26] Once organisations are aware of their risk, they should be in a position to prioritise activity and mitigate or eliminate risks. However, this may not be a quick or simple process and may take years for each organisation.

Microsoft already issued a warning[27] that scalable quantum computing could "break public-key cryptography methods currently in use and undermine digital signatures, resulting in compromised authentication systems and identity verification."

Microsoft has outlined a timeline to protect its services and customers from future quantum computing threats that could render current encryption methods obsolete. Microsoft plans to "enable early adoption of quantum-safe capabilities by 2029, gradually making them default in subsequent years, or sooner where possible." It aims to complete the transition of all Microsoft services and products to quantum-resistant cryptography by 2033. But what if Q-Day arrives earlier than that?

In Australia, to address this quantum threat, the Australian Signals Directorate (ASD) is encouraging organisations to understand and make plans to transition to the use of PQC algorithms within their own environments.

The rapidly growing power of quantum computing comes with numerous risks.[28] Among many forecasts about the future of quantum computing is the one made recently by BeyondTrust. According to their forecast, quantum computing threats loom large and will challenge existing cryptographic defences, especially for large organisations. While NIST's post-quantum encryption standards were released in 2024, the transition to these new standards will be gradual. Larger enterprises, particularly in finance, must begin planning for this quantum shift to protect sensitive data.

QUESTIONS

These questions are important, as they prompt thinking and allow the target audience to understand the organisation's potential exposure and what they personally can do to improve the organisation's cyber security posture. To get answers to some of these questions, the target audience may need to go to their CIOs and CISOs.

1. Does the organisation use AI?
2. Does the organisation have an AI use policy?
3. Did the organisation formally assess AI-related risks?
4. How does the organisation ensure that confidential information and PII are not being fed into AI?
5. Is the organisation aware of cryptography risks associated with quantum computing?
6. Does the organisation have a plan to transition to quantum-safe cryptography? What is the priority the organisation puts on this initiative? When does the organisation plan to finalise the transition to quantum-safe cryptography?

DESSERT

As the proliferation of AI and its use continues, researchers and developers face a unique challenge, as AI is fundamentally different from traditional software in one key way: non-determinism. Conventional programs are predictable. Given the same input, they produce consistent output. Not so with AI. AI can generate varied responses to identical prompts, introducing an element of unpredictability. This both challenges and fascinates the AI community. Controlling this non-determinism is a nuanced task. Developers can influence AI's output through various means. Temperature settings adjust the randomness of responses. Sampling methods can balance creativity and coherence. Even the choice between greedy decoding and more exploratory approaches impacts determinism. But when is this variability valuable? In creative tasks, it's good. It allows AI to generate diverse ideas, mimicking human creativity. For open-ended problem-solving, it can lead to novel solutions. However, in scenarios demanding consistency, like factual recall or precise calculations, this variability becomes a liability.

AI is a large and complex piece of software that is coupled with and relies strongly on training data. Opacity around AI testing (both software and training data) raises a lot of question marks. Is it just "black box" testing only? Is "white box" testing used? What constitutes "wrong data" in the case of AI? One should ask a very simple question: "Would flight control software have been approved, if it was tested using the same methods and same rigor as AI?" In the absence of a solid and firm "Yes" answer to this question, how can one trust AI?

While AI technologies have advanced and enhanced efficiency and productivity in a number of areas, they remain susceptible to an ever-growing number of security threats and vulnerabilities. AI is highly vulnerable to various types of attacks, including adversarial attacks, evasion attacks, and poisoning attacks. These attacks exploit weaknesses in AI models and training data, making it crucial to implement robust security measures to protect against AI hacking.

AI can be manipulated or "hacked" by users to generate specific content. This is known as prompt hacking and can be used to trick the AI into generating inappropriate or harmful content. Prompt hacking is a term used to describe attacks that exploit vulnerabilities of AI by manipulating their inputs or prompts. Unlike traditional hacking, which typically exploits software vulnerabilities, prompt hacking relies on carefully crafting prompts to deceive the AI into performing unintended actions. There are three known types of prompt hacking: prompt injection, prompt leaking, and jailbreaking. Each relates to slightly different vulnerabilities and attack vectors, but all are based on the same principle of manipulating AI prompts to generate some unintended output. It's important to be aware of this potential issue when using AI, especially in public-facing applications.

Let's have a look at some of the AI risks:

- **Cyber-attacks:** AI can be trained to identify and exploit vulnerabilities in software and systems, potentially leading to major breaches. The concept of Adversarial AI is a growing concern in the cyber security community. According to one of the definitions, this involves **attackers using AI algorithms to automatically discover vulnerabilities in systems and networks, enabling them to launch better-targeted and more effective attacks.** For instance, an attacker could use AI to analyse network traffic and determine patterns indicative of weak spots in the system, like unfixed bugs or misconfigured firewalls. Another definition is focused on situations when an attacker aims to disrupt the performance or decrease the accuracy of AI systems through manipulation or deliberate misinformation. Attackers use several adversarial techniques that target different areas of model development and operation. These include:
  - Poisoning attacks: poisoning attacks target the AI model training data, which is the information that the model uses to train the algorithm. In a poisoning attack, the adversary may inject fake or misleading information into the training dataset to compromise the model's accuracy or objectivity.
  - Evasion attacks: evasion attacks target an AI model's input data. These attacks apply subtle changes to the data that is shared with the model, causing it to be misclassified and negatively impacting the model's predictive capabilities.
  - Model tampering: model tampering targets the parameters or structure of a pre-trained AI/ML model. In these attacks, an adversary makes unauthorised alterations to the model to compromise its ability to create accurate outputs.
- **Cyber-attack optimisation:** attackers can **use AI to scale attacks at an unseen level of speed and complexity.** They may use AI to find fresh ways to exploit cloud complexity and take advantage of geopolitical tensions for advanced attacks. They can also optimise ransomware and phishing attack techniques by polishing them with generative AI.
- **Malicious GPTs:** a generative pre-trained transformer (GPT) is a type of AI model that can produce intelligent text in response to user prompts. A malicious GPT is an altered version of GPT that produces harmful or deliberately misinformed outputs. **In the context of cyber-attacks, a malicious GPT can generate attack vectors (such as malware) or supporting attack materials (such as fraudulent emails or fake online content) to advance an attack.**
- **Ransomware attacks:** AI-enabled ransomware is a type of ransomware that leverages AI to improve its performance or automate some aspects of the attack path. For example, **AI can be leveraged to research targets, identify system vulnerabilities, or encrypt data. AI can also be used to**

adapt and modify the ransomware files over time, making them more difficult to detect with cyber security tools.

- Internet of Things (IoT)/critical infrastructure operations: malicious actors can leverage AI to disrupt critical infrastructure operations, such as power grids, transportation systems, and water and sewage treatment infrastructure. As more and more systems, such as autonomous vehicles, manufacturing and construction equipment, and medical systems, use AI, the risks of AI to physical safety can increase. For example, an AI-based true self-driving car that suffers a cyber security breach could result in risks to the physical safety of its passengers or other road users and pedestrians. Similarly, the dataset for maintenance tools at a construction site could be manipulated by an attacker into creating hazardous conditions.
- Deepfakes, impersonation, reputational damage: the ease with which AI produces hyper-realistic fake images, videos, or audio recordings has made deepfakes a critical instrument for misinformation. The ability to create realistic audio, photo and video forgeries through AI, or deepfakes, threatens not only biometric-based systems but also public trust. It is already impossible to use biometrics (be it voice recognition or face recognition) remotely; it can be used only in a face-to-face situation. Jennifer DeStefano experienced a parent's worst nightmare when her daughter called her, yelling and sobbing. Her voice was replaced by a man who threatened to drug her and abuse her unless she paid a $1 million ransom. Experts speculate that the voice was generated by AI. Law enforcement believes that, in addition to virtual kidnapping schemes, AI may help criminals with other types of impersonation fraud in the future, including grandparent scams. One plausible explanation of the Qantas overseas call centre hack on 30 June 2025 is that cyber criminals used an AI deepfake voice.[29]
- Fraud/scam/manipulation: AI can generate synthetic data to perpetuate financial scams, manipulate online interactions, and negatively impact individuals and groups. These manipulations are potent tools for creating false narratives, impersonating public figures, or misleading viewers, with ramifications on politics, media, and personal reputations.
- Coordinated inauthentic behaviour (CIB): AI can be used to create and manipulate online accounts, spread misinformation and influence public opinion (on a very large scale) through bots and other automated methods.
- Training data leakage: training data leakage in AI refers to the unintended exposure of sensitive training data. This can occur if AI inadvertently memorises and regenerates private information, like personal identities or intellectual property, which can lead to breaches of privacy and confidentiality. The risk increases with the complexity of the data and the generality of the AI model.

- **Data privacy of user inputs:** when users interact with AI, they often provide personal or sensitive information that can be exploited if not properly protected. This risk is heightened in environments where AI is used for processing large amounts of user-generated data, such as in customer service chatbots or personalised content recommendations. In what was an embarrassing bug for OpenAI CEO Sam Altman, ChatGPT leaked bits of chat history of other users. Although the bug was fixed, there are other possible privacy risks due to the vast amount of data that AI crunches. For example, a hacker who breaches an AI system could access different kinds of sensitive information. An AI system designed for marketing, advertising, profiling, or surveillance could also threaten privacy in ways George Orwell couldn't even imagine. In some countries, AI-profiling technology is already helping states invade user privacy. The use of personal data by AI and algorithms can be complex, so it can be difficult for individuals to understand how their data is being used to make decisions that affect them. For example, the Department of Veterans' Affairs (DVA) is preparing to pilot AI to help manage a growing caseload of 82,645 ex-service personnel seeking financial support.[30] The agency has developed a proof-of-concept tool called MyClaims, which uses AI to extract specific medical details from the extensive documentation that accompanies veterans' claims for compensation or benefits. DVA was among the first agencies to trial a secure Azure-hosted environment established by the Department of Finance aimed at supporting AI development and testing under the Federal GovAI strategy. But what is the risk of PII leakage here?
- **AI model and data poisoning:** AI model poisoning occurs when attackers insert malicious data into the training set of an AI model, aiming to compromise its integrity. This can cause the AI model to fail or behave unpredictably once deployed. Such attacks could be especially damaging in applications like autonomous driving or automated financial decision-making, where errors or unexpected behaviour could lead to serious consequences. If the data is modified or poisoned, an AI-powered tool can produce unexpected or even malicious outcomes. In theory, an attacker could poison a training dataset with malicious data that would change the AI's results. An attacker could also initiate a more subtle form of manipulation called bias injection. Such attacks can be especially harmful in industries such as healthcare, automotive, and transportation.
- **Exploitation of bias:** AI systems can inadvertently perpetuate or exacerbate biases if their training data contains these biases (and, unfortunately, it always does). This exploitation can lead to discriminatory outcomes, such as racial or gender bias in facial recognition technology or gender bias in job recommendation algorithms. AI trained on biased data can lead to discriminatory outcomes, jeopardising fairness,

and justice and further marginalising already disempowered groups. Such biases not only harm individuals but can also have broader implications on social justice and equity.

- **Phishing attacks:** phishing attacks utilising AI are becoming increasingly sophisticated. **AI systems can now generate context-aware phishing content, mimic writing styles, and automate social engineering attacks at scale. These emails or messages are often indistinguishable from legitimate communications,** significantly increasing the risk of scams being successful.

- **Malware attacks: AI can be used as a tool in creating sophisticated malware,** including the **generation of polymorphic or metamorphic viruses that continually change their identifiable features to evade detection.** This presents significant challenges for cyber security defences, which traditionally rely on recognising patterns of known malware. While AI systems have some protections to prevent users from creating malicious code, experts can use clever techniques to bypass them and create malware. For example, in 2023, Forcepoint security researcher Aaron Mulgrew was able to find a loophole and create a nearly undetectable complex data-theft executable, **showing how ChatGPT can be used as a cyber weapon.** The executable had the sophistication of malware created by a state-sponsored threat actor.[31] And this can be only the tip of the iceberg. Suspected cases of AI-created malware have been spotted in real attacks. For example, cyber security company Proofpoint discovered a malicious PowerShell script that was likely created using AI. After brute-forcing the password, the HP security researchers analysed the code and found that the attacker had neatly commented on the entire code, something that rarely happens with human-developed code, because threat actors want to hide how the malware works. As per the HP security report: "These comments describe exactly what the code does, much in the same way that generative AI services can create exemplar code with explanations." As less technical malicious actors are increasingly relying on AI to develop malware, in early June 2024, HP security researchers found a malicious campaign that used code commented in the same way a generative AI system would create. **Future AI-powered tools may allow developers with entry-level programming skills to create automated malware,** like an advanced malicious bot, that can steal data, infect networks, and attack systems with little to no human intervention.

- **Stealing AI models:** there is a risk of AI model theft through network attacks, social engineering techniques and vulnerability exploitation by threat actors such as state-sponsored agents, insider threats like corporate spies and regular hackers. **Stolen models can be manipulated and modified to assist attackers with different malicious activities, compounding AI risks to society.**

- **Model inversion attacks:** model inversion attacks **reverse-engineer AI models to steal sensitive data.** Attackers use model outputs to infer sensitive training data, posing privacy risks, and potential breaches.
- **Membership inference attacks:** in membership inference attacks, adversaries attempt to determine whether a specific data point was part of the AI model's training dataset. This can expose private data about individuals or organisations.
- **Exploratory attacks:** exploratory assaults **probe AI systems to learn their underlying workings.** Attackers can employ searches or inputs to find vulnerabilities, model behaviour, or proprietary information for subsequent assaults.
- **Supply chain attacks:** AI system **development and deployment are targeted by supply chain threats.** Attackers hack software or hardware to insert malicious code into or access AI resources, including third-party libraries or Cloud services.
- **Resource exhaustion attacks:** resource exhaustion attacks **overload AI systems with requests or inputs, degrading performance or creating downtime.** These assaults might decrease AI service availability and are a form of Denial of Service (DoS) attack.
- **Model drift and decay:** data distributions, threats, and technology obsolescence can render AI models less effective over time. This **threatens AI system accuracy and dependability, especially in dynamic contexts.**

One of the most controversial uses of AI technology is in the area of surveillance. AI-based surveillance systems have the potential to revolutionise law enforcement and security, but they also pose significant risks to privacy and civil liberties. While the use of AI-based surveillance systems may seem like a valuable tool in the fight against crime and terrorism, it raises numerous concerns about privacy and civil liberties. Critics argue that these systems can be used to monitor and control individuals, potentially resulting in individuals losing freedom and civil liberties. To make matters worse, the use of AI-based surveillance systems is not always transparent. It can be difficult for individuals to know when they are being monitored or for what purpose. Another example of the use of AI in law enforcement is facial recognition technology. This technology uses algorithms to match images of people's faces to a database of known individuals, allowing law enforcement to identify and track individuals in real time. While facial recognition technology has the potential to help law enforcement solve crimes, it also raises concerns about privacy and civil liberties. In some cases, **facial recognition systems have been found to misidentify individuals, leading to false accusations and wrongful arrests.**

Among many forecasts about the future of AI is the one made recently by BeyondTrust. According to their forecast, AI2 ("Artificial Inflation" of Artificial Intelligence) is set to see its hype deflating across industries. While

AI will remain a useful productivity tool for basic automation and work-flows, many of the over-promised capabilities, particularly in cyber security, will fall short in 2025.

In October 2024, the Australian Digital Transformation Agency (DTA) published an evaluation report that illustrates this trend. The DTA report provided a detailed view of how some 5,765 MS 365 Copilot licences were used in the first 6 months of 2024. According to this report, **two-thirds of participants in a 6-month trial of MS 365 Copilot across the federal government used the tool "a few times a week" or less, with high expectations largely going "unmet."**

The Economist Intelligence Unit (EIU), the research and analysis division of global media organisation the Economist Group, has released its Technology and Telecoms Outlook 2025 report, which may dash hopes of organisations looking to make a quick buck off AI. EIU forecasts that 2025 will be the year when the vast sums of money already invested in AI will run up against the wall of hard, cold reality rather than the year of AI monetisation: "EIU does not expect these investments to start creating returns on investment as hoped." According to the report, in 2025, users will struggle to deliver returns on their investment, and most companies will still be at the proof-of-concept stage for implementation: "Next year will be the year of realism for artificial intelligence (AI), because we expect companies to struggle to deliver a return on their investment."

So far, the track record of AI projects is not great, as 80% of them end up failing, twice the rate of traditional IT projects.[32] Only one in four executives in a global survey report meaningful returns on their AI investments, as the shift to AI hurts customer service, forcing the organisations to rehire humans: some 55% of UK executives who replaced workers with AI later regretted it. In the rush to automate, workers are often seen as expendable. This approach to AI leads to what US economists Daron Acemoglu and Pascual Restrepro call "so-so automation," where technology displaces workers without delivering meaningful productivity gains.

Martin Eftimoski, an AI researcher at the University of New South Wales and former economist at the RBA, is worried that the more than $150 billion that big tech spent on Artificial Intelligence this year won't yield the promised results. And he warns Australians might be overexposed, as funds like AustralianSuper invest heavily in tech giants. Mr Eftimoski is so concerned about a potential crash that earlier this year, he took a drastic step with his own superannuation.[33]

And lawyers should pay attention to this, too. Recently, an Australian lawyer has been penalised for the first time for submitting fake AI-generated cases to court.[34] The Victoria-based lawyer - known only as "Mr Dayal" - has been stripped of his ability to practise as a principal lawyer and can no longer operate his own law practice after submitting documents to the Federal Circuit and Family Court of Australia last year containing AI-generated false citations.

Despite being perceived as something related to the 21st century, quantum computing has a long history. The origins of quantum computing can be traced back to the early 20th century, when several groundbreaking discoveries in the field of quantum mechanics laid the foundation for this novel approach to computation. Some of the fundamentals of quantum theory include superposition (particles can exist in multiple states simultaneously), entanglement (a phenomenon where the state of one particle becomes dependent on the state of another, even when separated by large distances) and wave-particle duality (particles exhibit both wave-like and particle-like properties).

Classical physics cannot explain the operation of these quantum devices, and a scalable quantum computer could perform some calculations exponentially faster than any modern "classic" computer. In particular, a large-scale quantum computer could break widely used encryption schemes and aid physicists in performing physical simulations. However, the current state of the art is still largely experimental.

Currently, there are three types of quantum computers:

- **Quantum Annealers:** these are available today. They are the least powerful with the narrowest use cases. However, attackers can use them to factor large numbers using quantum algorithms, which is how to break asymmetric encryption.
- **Analog Quantum Simulators:** these solve physics problems that are beyond the ability of classical computers, such as quantum chemistry, materials sciences, optimisation problems, factoring large numbers, sampling, and quantum dynamics.
- **Universal Quantum Computers:** these are the hardest to build because they require many physical qubits. They solve the broadest range of use cases, and several companies are targeting the end of this decade for commercialising them.

Quantum computers create a multi-dimensional space comprised of many entangled qubits in which to solve complex problems. For example, classical computers take each element of a database, process it, and then combine it with other elements after processing all the elements. Quantum computers use an algorithm that solves the problem for every state and outcome one is looking for. They pass the entire database through the algorithm simultaneously, analysing the data for every outcome.

The basic unit of information in quantum computing, the qubit, serves the same function as the bit in classic computing. However, unlike a classic bit, which can be in one of two states, a qubit can exist in a superposition of its two "basis" states, which kind of means that it is in both states simultaneously. When measuring a qubit, the result is a probabilistic output of a classic bit. If a quantum computer manipulates the qubit in a particular way, wave interference effects can amplify the desired measurement results. The design of quantum algorithms involves creating procedures that allow a quantum computer to perform calculations efficiently and quickly.

Over the years, experimentalists have constructed small-scale quantum computers using trapped ions and superconductors. In 1998, a two-qubit quantum computer demonstrated the feasibility of the technology, and subsequent experiments have increased the number of qubits and reduced error rates. In 1999, physicists at Japanese technology company NEC hit upon an approach that would go on to become the most popular approach to quantum computing today. In a paper in Nature, they showed that they could use superconducting circuits to create qubits and that they could control these qubits electronically. Superconducting qubits are now used by many of the leading quantum computing companies, including Google and IBM. In 2001, a team led by computer scientist John Martinis at the University of California, Santa Barbara, built the first quantum computer using superconducting qubits. In the same year, IBM and Stanford University published the first implementation of Shor's algorithm on a 7-qubit processor.

The real launch of the first commercially available quantum computer happened in May 2011, when Canadian company D-Wave Systems heralded the start of the quantum computing industry. D-Wave One featured 128 superconducting qubits and cost roughly $10 million. However, the device wasn't a universal quantum computer. It used the earlier-mentioned approach known as quantum annealing to solve a specific kind of optimisation problem, and there was little evidence that it provided any speed boost compared to classic approaches for other types of problems.

In 2016, IBM made quantum computing available on the IBM Cloud. In 2019, Google AI and NASA announced that they had achieved quantum supremacy with a 54-qubit quantum computer, performing computations that are impossible for any classic computer. However, Google's claim of quantum supremacy was met with scepticism from some corners, in particular from arch-rival IBM, which claimed the speedup was overstated. A group from the Chinese Academy of Sciences and other institutions eventually showed that this was the case by devising a classic algorithm that could simulate Google's quantum operations in just 15 hours on 512 GPU chips. They claimed that with access to one of the world's largest supercomputers, they could have done it in seconds. This was a reminder that classic computing still has a lot to offer, so quantum advantage is likely to remain a moving target.

One of the biggest barriers for today's quantum computers is that the underlying hardware is highly error-prone. Due to the quirks of quantum mechanics, fixing those errors is tricky, and it has long been known that it will take many physical qubits to create so-called "logical qubits" that are immune to errors and able to carry out operations reliably. In December 2023, Harvard researchers working with start-up QuEra smashed records by generating 48 logical qubits at once - 10 times more than anyone had previously achieved. The team was able to run algorithms on these logical qubits, marking a major milestone on the road to fault-tolerant quantum computing.

Quantum computing has gone from an academic curiosity to a multi-billion-dollar industry in less than half a century and shows no signs of stopping. It holds promise in various fields, including AI, drug discovery, and optimisation. Quantum computers can potentially solve certain optimisation problems much faster than classic computers, leading to improvements in areas such as logistics, finance, and supply chain management. In AI, quantum computing can potentially enhance machine learning algorithms, enabling faster training and more accurate models. In drug discovery, quantum computers may be able to simulate complex molecular interactions, leading to the development of new pharmaceuticals and a deeper understanding of biological processes. Since 2021, new achievements in quantum computing have demonstrated rapid progress in this area. As researchers continue to address challenges related to scalability, error correction and fault tolerance, and continue exploring new algorithms and applications, the potential impact of quantum computing across various domains becomes increasingly apparent. With sustained investment and research, quantum computing is likely to revolutionise multiple industries and drive significant advancements in technology and science.

To put things into perspective, it is important to note that, as it was estimated in 2018, future code-breaking quantum computers would need 100,000 times more processing power and an error rate 100 times better than today's best quantum computers have achieved. So far, all experts agree that a quantum computer large enough to crack RSA would probably be built no sooner than in around a few decades. To factorise an integer 2048 bits long, which is usually used as an RSA key, the Shor algorithm needs to be run on a quantum computer with millions of qubits. That is, it's not a matter of the near future, since the best quantum computers today use 300-400 qubits, and this is after decades of research. But already in 2024, the new 56-qubit H2-1 quantum computer developed by Quantinuum broke the previous record in the "quantum supremacy" benchmark first set by Google in 2019 and smashed it by a factor of 100.[35]

In 2023, California-based start-up Atom Computing created the first quantum computer to surpass 1,000 qubits (1,180 qubits, to be precise). While the largest quantum computers, such as those from IBM and Google, use superconducting wires cooled to extremely low temperatures for their qubits, Atom Computing uses neutral atoms trapped by lasers in a 2-dimensional grid. IBM is currently developing a 1,386-qubit quantum computer, dubbed "Kookaburra," which may be released in 2026.

Dr Michele Mosca has developed a theorem that suggests a pathway to consider in order to protect data and keep it quantum-safe.[36] This theorem stresses the **need for organisations to begin due diligence in the post-quantum space immediately.** It states that the amount of time that data must remain secure (X), plus the time it takes to upgrade cryptographic systems

(Y), is greater than the time at which quantum computers have enough power to break cryptography (Z). Once organisations are aware of their risk, they should be in a position to prioritise activity and mitigate or eliminate risks. However, this may not be a quick or simple process and may take years for each organisation.

There are numerous risks that come from the growing power of quantum computing[37]:

- **Modern encryption methods become useless:** as Pavlo Sidelov, CTO of UK-based SDK. Finance said,

  "Financial technologies are completely dependent on modern encryption methods. Any password or key can be cracked by a brute-force attack, but currently, computing power does not allow attackers to succeed in a reasonable time. With the release of quantum computing into the public sector, all encryption becomes useless, and currently, the industry has no answer on how to deal with it."

- **Web interactions will be at risk:** according to Atul Tulshibagwale from identity management company SGNL.ai,

  "The breakdown of prevalent cryptographic technology is an infrastructural risk. Most security technology is based on our current inability to quickly find the prime number factors of a key. Quantum computers can crack current cryptographic keys quickly, so every existing Web interaction is at risk. Motivated attackers can leverage a small number of quantum computers to cause widespread damage." Everything from web browsing to remote access to digital signatures will be impacted.

- **Harvest now, decrypt later:** as Peter Gregory from GCI Communications rightly noted:

  "A new threat, known as 'harvest now, decrypt later,' is a technique in which an attacker will attempt to steal encrypted data and hold on to it, potentially for years, with hopes that advances in quantum computing will eventually make decryption possible. Even years later, some encrypted content may still have value for the attacker."

- **What about undiscovered yet vulnerabilities:** this concern has been raised by Roland Polzin from Wing Assistant:

  "With enormous computing power, quantum computing has the potential to unhinge technology as we know it today. The biggest risk is that the consequences are not foreseeable today because bad actors will have an opportunity to leverage new capabilities to exploit previously undiscovered vulnerabilities. This is concerning, since even traditional cyber security is still neglected."

The threat of quantum attacks will rise. The quantum revolution has the potential to give rise to a new, difficult-to-prevent series of threats and exploits called quantum attacks.

- **Blockchain algorithms could be broken**: according to Vishwas Manral from Skyhigh Security,

> "The rise of quantum computing can cause risk to the fledgling blockchain and crypto economy. Blockchains rely on asymmetric key cryptography. These algorithms can be cracked via quantum computing, resulting in malicious manipulations of the blockchain. This is one big potential risk that companies and consumers investing in blockchain technology could face."

In recent years, numerous organisations started to rely on the blockchain (not to mention cryptocurrencies) to keep sensitive information secure. While many advocates previously regarded blockchain as all-powerful, it is increasingly clear that this was never the case and that blockchain has always been rife with risk. Moving forward, organisations that are committed to blockchain will need to acknowledge the strong potential of quantum computing to disrupt even the most advanced blockchain technologies. This includes consensus mechanisms like proof-of-work (PoW) and proof-of-stake (PoS), which have thus far proven fundamental to the integrity of the entire blockchain. This presents especially significant concerns.

- **It will be even more difficult to evaluate deep neural networks**: Somdip Dey from Nosh Technologies made this observation:

> "If quantum computing is used for machine learning - quantum machine learning - then it could present the ultimate black box problem. Deep neural networks (DNNs) are notoriously opaque. Though there are tools to unravel how hidden layers in a DNN work, with quantum machine learning, it will be more difficult to evaluate DNNs and judge the decision-making process across data."

An interesting event happened in early February 2024. NASA's quantum computer project has been put on hold after a startling turn of events, sending shockwaves across the scientific community.[38] Following a series of developments that have left experts wondering about the future of quantum computing and AI, this unexpected decision came as a shock. The abrupt shutdown of NASA's quantum computing project was triggered by an unforeseen incident during a routine test. During the analysis of a complex simulation, the quantum computer demonstrated unprecedented computational power, solving a previously unsolvable problem. However, this remarkable achievement had an equally alarming consequence: quantum computers began generating outputs that made no sense, challenged conventional thinking, and were inconsistent with known physical laws. Researchers and government officials were concerned that NASA's quantum computer might have connected with an extraterrestrial intelligence or even entered an unknown realm of computation. Potential risks associated with such an unpredictable and powerful machine prompted NASA and the US government to take swift action, halting operations and initiating a thorough investigation. The shutdown of NASA's quantum computing project is like a big alarm bell ringing about how amazing yet risky this new technology can be.

NOTES

1 https://ia.acs.org.au/article/2025/australian-cyber-firm-cybercx-acquired-by-accenture.html?ref=newsletter&deliveryName=DM28329.
2 https://www.computerworld.com/article/4059383/openai-admits-ai-hallucinations-are-mathematically-inevitable-not-just-engineering-flaws.html.
3 https://www.cio.com/article/4053086/shadow-ai-is-on-the-rise-heres-how-to-turn-it-into-a-strategic-advantage.html?utm_date=20250910234125&utm_campaign=CIO%20Australia%20First%20Look&utm_content=slotno-1-title-Shadow%20AI%20is%20on%20the%20rise.%20Here%E2%80%99s%20how%20to%20turn%20it%20into%20a%20strategic%20advantage&utm_term=ANZ&utm_medium=email&utm_source=Adestra&aid=16578935&huid=40eef72f-d3d6-4c7b-971a-f71e96817901.
4 https://www.gov.uk/government/publications/research-on-the-cyber-security-of-ai/cyber-security-risks-to-artificial-intelligence#:~:text=While%20AI%20technologies%20have%20advanced,of%20security%20threats%20and%20vulnerabilities.
5 https://www.itnews.com.au/news/ai-browsers-fall-for-scams-and-phishing-security-researchers-say-619746?eid=1&edate=20250822&utm_source=20250822_AM&utm_medium=newsletter&utm_campaign=daily_newsletter.
6 https://www.itnews.com.au/news/ai-coding-threatens-to-make-common-security-flaw-more-prevalent-619135?eid=1&edate=20250806&utm_source=20250806_AM&utm_medium=newsletter&utm_campaign=daily_newsletter.
7 https://www.itnews.com.au/news/googles-gemini-cli-agent-could-run-malicious-code-silently-619086?eid=1&edate=20250730&utm_source=20250730_AM&utm_medium=newsletter&utm_campaign=daily_newsletter.
8 https://www.itnews.com.au/news/eset-spots-promptlock-ai-powered-ransomware-619869?eid=1&edate=20250828&utm_source=20250828_AM&utm_medium=newsletter&utm_campaign=daily_newsletter.
9 https://www.itnews.com.au/news/academic-researchers-created-ai-powered-promptlock-ransomware-620104?eid=1&edate=20250908&utm_source=20250908_AM&utm_medium=newsletter&utm_campaign=daily_newsletter.
10 https://www.tomshardware.com/tech-industry/cyber-security/ai-powered-promptlocker-ransomware-is-just-an-nyu-research-project-the-code-worked-as-a-typical-ransomware-selecting-targets-exfiltrating-selected-data-and-encrypting-volumes.

11 https://www.itnews.com.au/news/ai-summarisers-open-to-clickfix-social-engineering-attacks-619841?eid=1&edate=20250827&utm_source=20250827_AM&utm_medium=newsletter&utm_campaign=daily_newsletter.

12 https://www.itnews.com.au/news/ovic-sets-limits-on-genai-tool-use-in-external-meetings-619363?eid=1&edate=20250807&utm_source=20250807_AM&utm_medium=newsletter&utm_campaign=daily_newsletter.

13 https://www.themandarin.com.au/298938-ai-and-trust-the-next-grand-challenge-for-the-aps-is-already-underway/?utm_campaign=TheJuice&utm_medium=email&utm_source=newsletter.

14 https://www.itnews.com.au/news/agentic-cyber-security-ai-abused-for-citrix-netscaler-attacks-620083?eid=1&edate=20250905&utm_source=20250905_AM&utm_medium=newsletter&utm_campaign=daily_newsletter.

15 https://en.wikipedia.org/wiki/Robodebt_scheme and https://robodebt.royalcommission.gov.au/publications/report.

16 https://www.theaustralian.com.au/sponsored/Pfv3aNFIu9bKigoypLNO/the-new-era-of-ai-has-arrived-is-your-business-ready/?dicbo=v4-cfRdTC7-1086836272-1.

17 https://ia.acs.org.au/article/2025/businesses-not-ready-for-ai-powered-security-threats.html?ref=newsletter&deliveryName=DM28608.

18 https://newsroom.ibm.com/2025-07-30-ibm-report-13-of-organizations-reported-breaches-of-ai-models-or-applications,-97-of-which-reported-lacking-proper-ai-access-controls.

19 https://www.itnews.com.au/feature/cyber-accountability-common-pain-point-says-slipstream-cyber-security-director-619564?eid=1&edate=20250908&utm_source=20250908_AM&utm_medium=newsletter&utm_campaign=daily_newsletter.

20 https://www.livescience.com/technology/artificial-intelligence/people-always-say-these-risks-are-science-fiction-but-they-re-not-godfather-of-ai-yoshua-bengio-on-the-risks-of-machine-intelligence-to-humanity?utm_source=facebook.com&utm_medium=social&utm_content=livescience&utm_campaign=socialflow.

21 https://arstechnica.com/ai/2025/06/why-one-man-is-archiving-human-made-content-from-before-the-ai-explosion/?utm_source=facebook&utm_medium=social&utm_campaign=dhfacebook&utm_content=null.

22 https://www.wired.com/story/the-full-story-of-the-stunning-rsa-hack-can-finally-be-told/.

23 https://www.ft.com/content/0a16281f-6bb4-4e60-a6f0-3a9d6f8d764a.

24 https://utimaco.com/news/blog-posts/nists-final-pqc-standards-are-here-what-you-need-know and https://www.entrust.com/blog/2024/08/nist-pqc-standards-are-available-what-comes-next.

25 https://www.newscientist.com/article/2396510-mathematician-warns-us-spies-may-be-weakening-next-gen-encryption/.

26 https://eprint.iacr.org/2015/1075.pdf.

27 https://www.itnews.com.au/news/microsoft-plans-full-quantum-resistant-cryptography-transition-by-2033-619779?eid=1&edate=20250825&utm_source=20250825_AM&utm_medium=newsletter&utm_campaign=daily_newsletter.

28 https://www.forbes.com/councils/forbestechcouncil/2022/11/08/13-risks-that-come-with-the-growing-power-of-quantum-computing/.

29 https://ia.acs.org.au/article/2025/did-the-qantas-hackers-use-ai-voice-deepfakes-.html?ref=newsletter&deliveryName=DM26762.

30 https://www.itnews.com.au/news/veterans-affairs-tests-using-ai-to-tackle-82645-unprocessed-claims-619224?eid=1&edate=20250801&utm_source=20250801_AM&utm_medium=newsletter&utm_campaign=daily_newsletter.

31 https://www.foxnews.com/tech/ai-created-malware-sends-shockwaves-cybersecurity-world.

32 https://theconversation.com/companies-are-betting-on-ai-to-help-lift-productivity-workers-need-to-be-part-of-the-process-258396.

33 https://www.news.com.au/finance/superannuation/my-super-is-in-cash-exrba-economists-ai-warning/news-story/6d8655a9812173cced6cf8c76c02f9ba.

34 https://ia.acs.org.au/article/2025/first-australian-lawyer-penalised-for-ai-blunder.html?ref=newsletter&deliveryName=DM28521.

35 https://www.livescience.com/technology/computing/new-quantum-computer-smashes-quantum-supremacy-record-by-a-factor-of-100-and-it-consumes-30000-times-less-power.

36 https://eprint.iacr.org/2015/1075.pdf.

37 https://www.forbes.com/councils/forbestechcouncil/2022/11/08/13-risks-that-come-with-the-growing-power-of-quantum-computing/.

38 https://content.techgig.com/technology/nasas-quantum-computing-project-hits-pause-button-reason-is-shocking/articleshow/107532517.cms.

Conclusion

"I don't think…"

"Then you shouldn't talk," said the Hatter.

Alice's Adventures in Wonderland by Lewis Carroll

So, you have just turned over the last page of the last chapter of this book. And maybe you feel disappointed - the book did not give you any explicit recipes for improving your organisation's cyber security posture. And in a sense, this is true, as the purpose of the book is not to provide any recipes (as a recipe that is great for one organisation may be useless for another, as each organisation has its own combination of financial, competitive, stakeholder, political, customer, legal/regulatory, etc. circumstances), but to prompt the thinking process.

If the book prompted you to start thinking, asking questions, and seeking answers to these questions, then I have achieved my goal.

One can throw their hands in the air and ask, "what can I do in this dire and so multifaceted situation?" One can't move away from von Neumann architecture; one can't replace Internet protocols. Yes, this is true, but there are many things one can do to improve the cyber security of their organisation. It takes time, and it is a long journey, but there is no other way, unless one wants to resign oneself to the situation of "a disaster waiting to happen."

The reason this book is addressed to Board Members and CEOs is that unless the scale of the current cyber security exposure of organisations is recognised at this level, nothing will change and organisations will continue walking (or better to say flying on autopilot) into a disaster.

So, what can Board Members and CEOs do to improve the organisation's cyber security posture? They can do a lot of things!

To start with, they need to recognise and acknowledge the inherent insecurities of the Internet, on which organisations' business is built today. By doing this, they will start thinking in the right direction (e.g., "we live and operate in a high-crime area"). They may start focusing on the strength of the domain/subdomain and certificate management processes and ensure that they are bulletproof.

Secondly, they can look at expanding the organisation's KPI to include cyber security with carefully and correctly selected KPIs (like, year-on-year decrease in the complexity of the organisation's IT ecosystem). They can also consider their approach to the use of devices unmanaged by the organisation (like BYOD devices and home computers).

Thirdly, they can have an additional lens to look at the business cases by introducing "cyber security risk-reward" analysis (oh, isn't this just another KPI?). This will help with the way they look at the digital revolution. It will also enable looking at the agile approach from a different angle and, possibly, reconsider its use. It will also help with the containment of the SaaS sprawl and shadow IT.

Then, they can ensure that the organisation has a full understanding of the shared security responsibility concept and ensure its correct implementation and management.

Another area they can impact is understanding (and management!) of the supply chain cyber security risks (and dependencies!) across all (not only IT!) vendors and service providers. They may pay more attention to who (and how) is managing the organisation's DNS and what cyber risks this poses to the organisation. This may also push them to start thinking about the organisation's commitment to the use of the "digital monopolies" (like, Microsoft or CrowdStrike).

They may at last recognise that Compliance ≠ Security and that as much as a proper implementation of the chosen standard(s) and framework(s) may (or may not) improve an organisation's cyber security posture, it does not offer any guarantees about the actual cyber security posture of the organisation.

Finally, they may get out of the fear of missing out (FOMO) trap and start looking at AI adoption through a cyber security risks lens and start thinking about and planning the implementation of post-quantum cryptography.

Historically, cyber security was always a "poor relation" in the eyes of the majority of Boards and CEOs, considered inferior, less important, or not as well-regarded as other issues or compared to them, and treated as an annoying cost centre requiring more and more money that could potentially have been spent "better" elsewhere. This is a result of inertia, a **cumulative effect** of multiple factors and, more importantly, a lack of understanding of how the landscape has changed in the last 25 or so years.

But it can't continue like this, as today's operation of all organisations has become so heavily dependent on the Internet. And as such, cyber security is rapidly becoming an issue of business continuity and survivability for all organisations. Just think for a second what happens to the organisation (both financially and reputationally) if the Internet (or any of the systems accessed via the Internet) goes down, say for 2 or 3 days. There are plenty of examples in this book that can make one shiver.

This book is an attempt to be a "wake-up call" and a call to action that will prevent organisations from "sleepwalking" into a disaster…

And if this is not enough, the fresh reminders keep coming every week. The latest examples (at the time of writing these lines) include the latest hack at UnitedHealth's technology unit that exposed PII of 192.7 million people[1], iiNet Internet service provider breach that exposed PII of 280,000 of its customers[2], breach including 2.5 billion Gmail accounts[3] and recent cyber-attack on major European airports[4].

NOTES

1 https://www.itnews.com.au/news/hack-at-unitedhealths-tech-unit-impacted-1927-million-people-619598?eid=1&edate=20250815&utm_source=20250815_AM&utm_medium=newsletter&utm_campaign=daily_newsletter.

2 https://www.news.com.au/national/internet-provider-iinet-hit-in-cyberattack-280k-customers-data-exposed/news-story/15063c1d4c84dc5403fa83f66b0a8924.

3 https://www.news.com.au/technology/online/hacking/25-billion-gmail-accounts-exposed-as-massive-hack-uncovered/news-story/dcbeecf4779b436ad9d7dd732968f457.

4 https://www.news.com.au/travel/travel-advice/airports/cyberattack-brings-major-airports-to-a-grinding-halt-causes-delays-and-cancellations/news-story/d90e97b307fb08b703e48eb73d4554d6 and https://ia.acs.org.au/article/2025/ransomware-causes-mayhem-at-european-airports.html?ref=newsletter&deliveryName=DM28608.

For Product Safety Concerns and Information please contact our EU
representative GPSR@taylorandfrancis.com
Taylor & Francis Verlag GmbH, Kaufingerstraße 24, 80331 München, Germany

www.ingramcontent.com/pod-product-compliance
Lightning Source LLC
Chambersburg PA
CBHW070229180526
45158CB00001BA/220